T0355453

Asia after Europe

Asia after Europe

Imagining a Continent in the Long Twentieth Century

SUGATA BOSE

THE BELKNAP PRESS OF HARVARD UNIVERSITY PRESS

Cambridge, Massachusetts & London, England

2024

First printing

Library of Congress Cataloging-in-Publication Data

Names: Bose, Sugata, 1956– author.
Title: Asia after Europe : imagining a continent in the long
  twentieth century / Sugata Bose.
Other titles: Imagining a continent in the long twentieth century
Description: Cambridge, Massachusetts ; London, England : The Belknap
  Press of Harvard University Press, 2024. | Includes bibliographical
  references and index.
Identifiers: LCCN 2023028125 | ISBN 9780674423497 (cloth)
Subjects: LCSH: East and West. | Asians—Attitudes. | Asia—History—
  20th century. | Asia—History—21st century.
Classification: LCC DS35 .B68 2024 | DDC 950.4/2—dc23/eng/20230719
LC record available at https://lccn.loc.gov/2023028125

For Ayesha

Contents

Preface

Asia stands today at the end of an era as alternative futures beckon. This book offers my interpretation of the changing balance of global power during the long twentieth century between Asia and Euro-America by painting a portrait of an age. I made a deliberate decision to opt for an expansive spatial and temporal scope—the landscapes and time frames—for my history of the Asian continent as a connected zone. This is a history of intellectual, cultural, and political conversations across Asia to imagine a pluralized continentalism against the backdrop of phases of material poverty and prosperity. It provides a fresh perspective on Asianism through its choice of a fresh cast of characters—some well-known, others rescued from undeserved oblivion. Without compromising on the basic tenets of scholarly rigor, I have written the book in an accessible literary style for a broad readership. I see it as a tribute to those who a century ago challenged European colonial domination to dream of the futurism of young Asia.

Asia after Europe is a deeply personal book, and not just because of the long years of my scholarly engagement with the subject. The sections where I have drawn on my earlier formulations, for example, on different universalisms and colorful cosmopolitanisms are duly indicated in the notes. While delving into the past, the passion and sense of urgency in the writing stem from my concern about the present crossroads and the paths to be forged for the future. I have taken the liberty of switching from a more academic prose to a tone of personal reflection in the later chapters. What should we choose among inheritances from the past to take with us on the uncertain journey ahead?

This book has been long in the making. My only regret is that I was not able to complete it before my mother, Krishna Bose, passed away on February 22, 2020. She would sometimes lament in her final years that my Asia book had been delayed by my foray into Indian parliamentary politics between 2014 and 2019—a decision that she had encouraged and wholeheartedly endorsed. She had herself bridged the distance between academia and India's Lok Sabha (House of the People) with rare grace and eloquence. In 2014, I felt I had to do my bit in defense of Indian federalism and democracy by taking a stand against the rising tide of religious majoritarianism and centralized authoritarianism. It was a true privilege to represent the people of the Jadavpur parliamentary constituency in the Sixteenth Lok Sabha—a role that my mother had played with such distinction in the Eleventh, Twelfth, and Thirteenth Lok Sabhas. While placing the writing of my book on the back burner, my years as a member of parliament gave me fresh insights into Asian and global politics that have enriched what readers will find in these pages. I enjoyed and learned a great deal from my service in the Parliamentary Standing Committee on External Affairs during these years.

I have tried out the ideas presented in this book over the years in my graduate seminar at Harvard on "Asia in the Modern World." On one occasion, Amartya Sen joined me in teaching this seminar, making it an altogether more enjoyable experience. The searching questions of my students helped in sharpening my arguments. I have also shared some of the material in this book in the "Approaches to Global History" seminar I have taught alternately with my wonderful colleagues Sven Beckert and Charles Maier. My ambition of presenting the big picture on Asia in the long twentieth century would not have been possible without the pathbreaking research in the early twenty-first century by many historians, especially of the younger generation, on different facets of Asian connections. Their contributions are acknowledged in the notes to my text. I have especially benefited from the work of and conversations with Nicole Aboitiz, Seema Alavi, Sunil Amrith, Cemil Aydin, Prasenjit Duara, Selcuk Esenbel, Jayati Ghosh, Sarvani Gooptu, Tim Harper, Engseng Ho, David Ludden, Tansen Sen, Gayatri Chakravorty Spivak, and Eric Tagliacozzo. Research on Asian and transnational themes by several of my former students including Sana

Aiyar, Tariq Omar Ali, Mou Banerjee, Antara Datta, Hardeep Dhillon, Semanti Ghosh, Kris Manjapra, Neeti Nair, Julia Stephens, Gitanjali Surendran, and Chitralekha Zutshi—all distinguished colleagues by now—has illuminated different aspects of my book. My current graduate students—Aniket De, Sudarshana Chanda, Mahdi Chowdhury, and Mahia Bashir—have kept me alert to new trends in historical writing. A recent Tufts graduate, Yiyun (Tom) Guan provided competent research assistance in the final stages of preparing this manuscript and corresponded on my behalf in Chinese with the Xu Beihong Museum in Beijing. A sparkling Harvard undergraduate, Eleanor Villafranca Wikstrom has shared poignant insights into America's and Harvard's historical relationship with the Philippines and its long aftermath.

Aniket De read the manuscript of this book in its penultimate version with great care. He gave more incisive critical commentary than I have been able to provide on the pages of his excellent doctoral dissertation on the imperial and anti-colonial lineages of federalism in Asia. He kept up a steady supply of new sources for me to read and absorb for this project. In particular, I enjoyed discussing with him the local roots and global itineraries of that formidable early twentieth-century Asian intellectual Benoy Kumar Sarkar.

I have presented portions of this work at several venues in North America, Europe, and Asia. It was a real pleasure to deliver the GRIPS Forum Lecture in Tokyo in January 2018 and to spend two weeks as honorary visiting professor at Peking University in May 2018. Audiences in India stretching from Kashmir to Kerala and Gujarat to Manipur have contributed to refinements in my argument.

I have missed the deft editorial hand of Joyce Seltzer, with whom I had the privilege of working while writing *A Hundred Horizons* and *His Majesty's Opponent*. Sam Stark carefully read the manuscript and made astute suggestions on how to make it more appealing to the nonspecialist reader. Sharmila Sen kept a kind eye on the proceedings. Two anonymous readers for Harvard University Press wrote detailed and constructive reports that were very helpful in carrying out the final revisions. Jillian Quigley helped to prepare the manuscript for production, and Stephanie Vyce's expert advice was invaluable in securing permissions for rights to reproduce images. I am grateful to the Netaji Research Bureau, Calcutta, the National Gallery of Modern Art, New Delhi, the Xu Beihong Museum, Beijing, the University of Massachusetts, Amherst, the Yale Art Gallery, New Haven, and the Fine Arts Library at Harvard for the photographs and works of art that embellish this book. For names of Asian places, I have generally used English spellings current at the time—for example, Peking for the earlier period but Beijing from the late twentieth century onward. I have used pinyin rather than Wade-Giles for the names of Chinese persons, excepting Sun Yat-sen, Chiang Kai-shek, and Hu Shih.

The final version of this book being brought before the public eye was crafted during the pandemic from March 2020 onward. During lengthy spells of home confinement during lockdowns, Ayesha Jalal and I joyfully inflicted on each other in the evenings our daily spells of writing—a ritual we had turned into a habit more than four decades ago. Listening to and reading her manuscript of *Light upon Light: Muslim Enlightened Thought beyond Western Liberalism* lit up the process of my own writing of *Asia after Europe*. Our twenty-first-century travels together from Konya in the west to Kyoto in the east have subtly influenced the ideas I articulate in this book. Our visits to Myanmar and Indonesia in 2015 and to Japan, China, Hong Kong, and Singapore in 2016 have informed my perspective on Asian connections. I am dedicating this book to her with love for sharing life's journey.

The undying legacy of my parents, Sisir Kumar Bose and Krishna Bose, and the values they had instilled will be evident in the pages of this book. My younger brother Sumantra Bose has been a pillar of support in sharing the public responsibilities we have inherited in India. Sumantra and I have in part coped with the loss of our mother in February 2020 by cultivating her fine art of writing. My mother's face has been my inspiration for all my creative work. I am relieved to be able to tell her that my Asia book is finally done.

Introduction

The Idea of Asia in Modern History

THE JAPANESE ART critic Okakura Tenshin first came to India in December 1901. He was accompanied by a Buddhist monk, Prince Oda, as well as Sarah Ole Bull and Josephine MacLeod, two American devotees of Swami Vivekananda. The Indian sage went with Okakura and Oda to the Buddhist pilgrimage sites of Bodhgaya and Sarnath in north India. It was Vivekananda's favorite Irish disciple, Margaret Noble, renamed Nivedita (The Devoted One), who introduced Okakura to the Tagore family in Calcutta. During his eleven-month stay, lively conversations animated the Tagores' mansions in the Jorasanko neighborhood of north Calcutta. A cultural and political bridge between East and South Asia was forged.

The book that Okakura published in 1903, *The Ideals of the East,* had a memorable first sentence: "Asia is one." The history of Japanese art was for Okakura "the history of Asiatic ideals—the beach where each successive wave of Eastern thought has left its sand-ripple." Sister Nivedita added a further embellishment in her introduction to the book. "Asia, the Great Mother," she wrote, "is forever One."[1] She lauded Okakura for having shown Asia "not as the congeries of geographical fragments that we imagine, but as a united living organism, each part dependent on all the others, the whole breathing a single complex life."[2] *The Ideals of the East* was substantially a collaboration between two art critics, both interested in variants of Asian spirituality.

From his Indian sojourn, Okakura took back with him another manuscript that remained unpublished at the time, titled "The Awakening of Asia." "Brothers and Sisters of Asia!" it declaimed. "A vast suffering is on the land of our ancestors. The oriental has become a symbol of the effeminate, the native is an epithet for the slave." He also conveyed the spirit of Asian universalism back to India, dispatching the talented Japanese artists Taikan Yokoyama and Shunso Hishida to Calcutta. Taikan taught the Japanese wash technique to Abaninindranath Tagore, Rabindranath's nephew, who painted the iconic image *Bharatmata* (Mother India, 1905) in that style. A Japanese rendering of that image on a giant silk scroll was paraded around in procession in the streets of Calcutta to the accompaniment of Rabindranath Tagore's freshly composed patriotic songs. Indian nationalism had come to be fused with Asian universalism.

Rabindranath Tagore was a universalist with a difference.[3] It is sometimes mistakenly assumed that the colonized peoples of Asia tended toward a cultural defensiveness and wished to erect guardrails around their imagined nations. Quite the contrary, they were active contributors of creative ideas that circulated across cosmopolitan thought zones. Their ambition included retaking the idea of Asia from European hegemony as a step toward influencing a global future. Their cosmopolitanism did not emanate from the stratosphere of abstract reason. It sprang from knowledge and learning in a variety of Asian languages. Asian universalism became one strand of looking beyond the nation in an age of anti-colonial nationalism, alongside Islamic and Buddhist universalism as well as Leninist and Wilsonian internationalism. It was an expression of a cosmopolitan aspiration that leavened patriotic zeal.

Champions of cosmopolitanism who see detached reason as its only source display a visceral distaste for patriotism, confusing it with the narrowest forms of particularism. Colorless cosmopolitanism is assigned a high moral ground; colorful patriotism is deemed to be seductive but devoid of any ethical content.[4] A figure like Rabindranath Tagore can be annexed to this version of cosmopolitanism only by denuding him of much of his poetry and music and all his passion and moral philosophy. In his conception, there were various forms of patriotism perfectly compatible with a cosmopolitan attitude that transcended the lines of cultural differences.

Within the terms of the Anglophone philosophical debate, the opposition to cosmopolitanism based on abstract universal reason is articulated by proponents of reason embedded in inherited traditions.[5] A useful enough corrective to the excesses of colorless cosmopolitanism, this intellectual position falters because of its insistence on the bounded and implicitly unchanging nature of inheritances from the past. It fails to bring to light the dynamic process of creating and re-creating traditions as well as the flows between cultures over time and the fluidity of cultural boundaries across space. The history of what I call colorful cosmopolitanism rather than the legacy of the deadweight of traditions might be a better antidote to the philosophical hubris of the votaries of colorless cosmopolitanism.[6] Asia was one expansive venue for the play of this colorful cosmopolitanism for Asian patriots.

The form of colorful cosmopolitanism and the spirit of different universalism that appealed to Asian anti-colonial nationalists were often carried by them in their travels across the Indian Ocean. The connections across the oceanic interregional arena facilitated new imaginations of Asia. How, then, were these conceptions of Asia different from the "myth of continents" that has been critiqued by Martin Lewis and Karen Wigen as "a meta-geographical concept" hopelessly tainted by the hubris of European imperialism? It is important to note that their "critical metageography" is aimed against "a cartographic celebration of European power." "After centuries of imperialism," they write, "the presumptuous worldview of a once-dominant metropole has become part of the intellectual furniture of the world."[7] Although it is true that some historians of Asia are still ensnared by the European mapmaking project, a process of intellectual rediscovery is in progress to elucidate the ways in which Asians reimagined Asia in the age of Western imperialism.

In his insightful essay "Asia Redux," Prasenjit Duara notes "that regions and regionalizations tend to follow the dominant or hegemonic modes of spatial production during a period."[8] Yet, as Ranajit Guha has taught us, European imperialism in Asia typically achieved dominance without hegemony.[9] Asia as conceptualized by Asians was certainly at variance with the concrete expression of Asia invented by nineteenth-century European geographers and cartographers. To ask simplistically whether Asia is one or many—as has been done by a historian better at reading European maps than interpreting Asian writings—is quite the wrong way to pose the question, which in turn yields a banal answer.[10] Asia as a space and a concept in the writings of Asian thinkers—many variations on the theme notwithstanding—contained a creative spark absent in the European cartographic depictions. Asians contested both European constructions of the myth of continents and European imports of notions of monolithic sovereignty and rigid linear borders. Their visions of Asian federation articulated in the early twentieth century drew on precolonial conceptions of layered and shared sovereignty over territory and were fundamentally different from contemporaneous ideas of European federation based on white racial superiority and Christian religious exclusivity. The affective space conjured in the Asian imagination had room for multiple identities and was less state driven even as it crafted a basis for solidarity in anti-colonial politics.

This is not to deny that there were strands within Asian thought worlds that merely inverted and did not undermine the Europe-Asia dichotomy, being content to invest the latter with a higher order of value and virtue. That forms a less interesting dimension of the modern tug-of-war between Europe and Asia. The propaganda about Asian communitarian values orchestrated by Lee Kuan Yew of Singapore and Mahathir Mohammad of Malaysia in the late twentieth century has served as a soft target for critics who wish to trivialize the idea of Asia. The early twentieth-century intellectual challenge mounted from colonized Asia was by comparison far more sophisticated. Asian thinkers imagined Asia as an abstract entity transcending the imperial and national frontiers being etched by colonial powers onto the physical and mental maps of the colonized and thereby serving as a prism to refract the light of universal humanity. "Asia knows, it is true," Okakura had written, "nothing of the fierce joys of a time-devouring locomotive, but she has still the far deeper travel-culture of the pilgrimage and the wandering monk."[11] The idea of Asia was articulated in global destinations well beyond the geographical borders of the continent.

Okakura would catalog Ernest Francisco Fenollosa's magnificent collection of Japanese and Chinese paintings for the Boston Museum of Fine Arts. It was Okakura who was instrumental in getting Tagore invited to Harvard in 1913 to deliver the lectures in philosophy that were published in a book titled *Sadhana (Quest)*. When Tagore won the Nobel later that year for *Gitanjali (Song Offerings),* the *Harvard Crimson* reported awkwardly, "The Nobel prize for literature has recently been awarded to the British Indian poet, Mr. Rabindranath Tagore. This is the first time that the award has been made to other than a member of the white race. Last spring Mr. Tagore gave a series of lectures in English at Emerson Hall, dealing with subjects of far-eastern philosophy."[12]

"Neither the colorless vagueness of cosmopolitanism," Tagore wrote in his 1917 book on *Nationalism,* "nor the fierce self-idolatry of nation-worship is the goal of human history."[13] Tagore undoubtedly was a powerful critic of worshipping the nation as god and was horrified by the crimes committed by modern nation-states. Yet he loved the land that had nurtured him and never abandoned a basic anti-colonial stance. He simply wanted India to avoid the dangerous trap into which Japan had fallen. Japan's folly was "not the imitation of the outer features of the West, but the acceptance of the motive force of western nationalism as her own."[14] In Tagore's conception, there were various forms of patriotism perfectly compatible with a cosmopolitan attitude that transcended the lines of cultural differences.

Addressing the faculty and students at Tokyo Imperial University in 1924, Tagore made a moving reference to Okakura, "one of your idealists who had a large heart and a great originality of mind." "From him," Tagore declared, "we first came to learn that there was such a thing as an Asiatic mind."[15] On the eve of his departure from Japan, Tagore noted the patience and time the people of that country took "to give beauty to everything that is for daily use." "This," he said, "is the genuine spirit of hospitality. For things that are beautiful are hospitable."[16] His voyage had been undertaken in search of "a better understanding between China, Japan and India" and "to preach the fundamental unity of the Asiatic mind." Tagore was quick to explain that he did not consider any quality to be "exclusively oriental." "All great human ideals are universal," he asserted, "only in their grouping, emphasis, and expression they differ from one another."[17]

THE NEWS FROM ASIA in the early 2020s presents a picture of a fractured continent riven by nationalist rivalries. Yet underlying developments reveal a closer economic and cultural intertwining than ever before.

If the idea of Europe could survive the carnage of two world wars as well as current economic and cultural tensions, the idea of Asia needs to be evaluated in terms of its ability to withstand similar stresses and strains. The post–World War II political and bureaucratic process toward European integration ended up buttressing the structure of nation-states, belying the promise to transcend it.[18] Recent European historiography has turned to rediscovering "lost Europes" envisioned by intellectuals concerned about the dangers embedded in the nation-state model of the interwar period.[19] There were many imaginative and generous conceptions of Asia that deserve to be rescued from historical oblivion.

Asia after Europe narrates and interprets the creative process of imagining Asia by tracking the intersecting journeys of Asian intellectuals and subalterns alike. It addresses the major debates around the concept of Asia and the circulation of ideas across the colonial borders of Asia against the backdrop of the existential realities of different phases of poverty and prosperity in the continent. The book also explores the conditions under which Asian solidarity was forged and fractured.

The articulation of competing and overlapping visions of Asian universalism was intertwined in complex ways with the arc of the economic and political decline and rise of Asia. To bring these elements together on a canvas as vast as Asia requires the deployment of an innovative method. *Asia after Europe* focuses more on connections than comparisons and pays close attention to the themes of circulation and competition. A work of interpretation, it weaves together stories, many of whose characters reappear in successive chapters. Creatively trespassing across arbitrarily drawn intellectual and political boundaries, this approach pursues intra-Asian connections in a global context. Circular migration of Asian elites and subalterns breached supposed civilizational borders as well as frontiers of colonies and nation-states, turning Asia into a dynamic space of connection, circulation, and competition.

The phrase "after Europe" in this history of Asia is interpreted not just temporally but also conceptually. To do so, it is necessary to sternly refuse to operate on European categories and theories. My approach to provincializing Europe does not require canonical European theorists as pegs on which to hang a history of Asian negotiations with global capitalism and the nation-state as key signs of modernity.[20] *Asia after Europe* presents a historical narrative that shows how a continental identity of, by, and for Asians was and can still be fashioned in myriad ways based on exchanges among people belonging to multiple races and religions. These interactions span a whole spectrum of intimacies, affective bonds, solidarities, and alliances transcending boundaries of the nation. I am offering here an interpretation of the history of Asia not only after the European colonial presence but also a conceptual history of universalism and cosmopolitanism that struggles to leave behind and move beyond European definitions of reason, national identity, and federation.

A delineation of the decline and fall of Asia during the nineteenth century sets the stage for the study and lays out its spatial and temporal context. Contrary to popular misconceptions, there was nothing ancient about Asia's poverty. In a pathbreaking book titled *Asia before Europe*, K. N. Chaudhuri documented and analyzed the economic dynamism of Asia and the Indian Ocean world in the millennium until 1750.[21] Economic historians probing why Europe grew rich and Asia became poor broadly agree that the second decade of the nineteenth century marked the moment of the global economic divergence.[22] The decade of the 1810s was a watershed during which Indian artisanal products lost their ability to compete in the global marketplace. China tea replaced Indian textiles as the most valuable commodity in the English East India Company's trade, increasingly paid for by Indian opium rather than New World silver.

A connected history of capital, labor, and colonial conquest across the continent reveals the transformation of space and sovereignty in Asia. This new colonial spatiality was founded on the power of Western capital that chose its spheres of operation in new mines and plantations, the interplay of settled peasant labor and migrant coolie labor across agrarian Asia, and Western imperial dominance based on principles of unitary sovereignty and maps marking linear borders. While fundamentally transformative and destructive of the precolonial space of Asia based on layered and shared sovereignty as well as fuzzy boundaries, this re-drawn colonial space paradoxically created material conditions for forging anti-colonial connections by Asians on the move. By the late nineteenth century, the abjection of colonial rule stoked powerful critiques of

Western imperialism in Asia, not least directed at the pernicious trade in opium.

An array of visual and literary sources display vividly that the early intimations of Asian universalism preceded the famous Japanese military victory over Russia in 1905. Taking on an impressive variety of forms, these universalist aspirations transcended incipient economic and political conflicts such as those between China and Japan. Chinese intellectual figures including Kang Youwei, Liang Qichao, and Sun Yat-sen found refuge in Japan after the failed reforms of 1898. Not limited to Japan, China, and India, the authorship of late-nineteenth-century universalisms emanated equally from West Asia and Southeast Asia as the contributions of Jamaluddin al-Afghani and José Rizal exemplified. The events of 1905 quickened the pace of the eastward movement of scholars and students toward Japan from countries as varied as Vietnam, Turkey, and India. The cultural milieu of the Indian swadeshi ("own country") movement that began in 1905—despite its interest in rejuvenating indigenous traditions and industries—was not wholly inward looking. Its protagonists were curious about innovations in different parts of the globe and felt comfortable within ever-widening concentric circles of Bengali patriotism, Indian nationalism, and Asian universalism. Aspiring to reconcile a sense of nationality with a common humanity, they were not prepared to let colonial borders constrict their imagination. The affective space of Asia imagined in the domains of literature, the fine arts, and culture in this Asian universalist moment formed the basis for a shared anti-colonial politics that gathered momentum in subsequent decades.

The decade of the 1910s, especially the years of the Great War, witnessed a qualitative change in Asian connections. If the links crafted in the 1905 moment were primarily cultural infused with an inchoate spirit of anti-colonialism, the era of World War I was characterized by a more determined move toward interdependent political and revolutionary action. On his eastward voyage in 1916, Rabindranath Tagore had journeyed from Calcutta to Rangoon, Penang, Singapore, and Hong Kong. In Hong Kong, Tagore made an uncannily accurate prophecy about the future balance of power in the world. "The nations which now own the world's resources," he contended, "fear the rise of China, and wish to postpone the day of that rise."[23] Tagore's three-month sojourn in Japan represented the fulfill-ment not just of a personal quest but the search for an Asian universalism that had begun at the turn of the twentieth century. Japanese art im-pressed Tagore; the Japanese penchant for imitating European national-istic imperialism less so. It was only after rebuking Japan on that count that Tagore undertook the long Pacific crossing to the United States on September 7, 1916 to deliver his critical lectures on nationalism. The Asianism expressed during Benoy Kumar Sarkar's visits to Japan and China during 1915–1916, including his view of Islam as a thread tying together the entire continent, was premised on the imperative to build political solidarities. His exhortations to "young Asia" constituted a remarkable exercise in politically engaged scholarship.

In 1919, most Asian anti-imperialists were not inward looking. They harbored universalist aspirations and were keen to establish connections that transcended the boundaries of their own nations. Woodrow Wilson had a formidable rival in Vladimir Ilyich Lenin for anti-colonial hearts and minds in Asia. The limited reach of Wilsonian benevolence—limited as it was to Europe—came as a huge disappointment to Asians, and Lenin won that particular contest hands down. Yet godless Bolshevik internationalism had to contend with preexisting bonds of Asian solidarity and a range of religiously tinged universalisms. Far from being "the Wilsonian moment,"[24] 1919 to 1922 constituted the quintessential Islamic universalist moment in global history casting even the 1905 spirit of Asian universalism into the shade. The mass noncooperation and Khilafat movement orchestrated by Mohandas Karamchand Gandhi and his compatriot Muhammad Ali tied Indian nationalism to Islamic universalism. "Let Hindus not be fright-ened by Pan-Islamism," Gandhi declared in *Young India.* "It is not—it need not be—anti-Indian or anti-Hindu."[25] For Mahatma Gandhi, a territorial conception of nationalism was perfectly compatible with an extraterritorial anti-colonial sentiment.

During the 1920s, the scope of political action in Asia was expanded to include a wide range of mass movements drawing on varieties of Asian spatial imaginations. The multiple universalisms not only competed and contended with one another for popular allegiance but overlapped to a significant degree in different places and at different times. Universalisms of the Asian, Islamic, and Bolshevik assortments mingled in central Asia, Indonesia, and China. Li Dazhao and Sun Yat-sen advanced sophisticated variants of Asianism as nationalists and communists in China searched for common ground in the early 1920s. These universalisms resolutely refused to acknowledge the nation-state as the normative political unit undergirding the post-1919 international system even as their votaries argued for a healthy dose of federalism for regions that constituted overarching nations.

The abolition of the institution of the caliphate by Mustafa Kemal Ataturk in 1924 led many Indian patriots to rekindle the lamp of Asian universalism. That year, Rabindranath Tagore set off for East Asia again. One of his hosts in China was none other than Liang Qichao who in welcoming Tagore evoked the age-old brotherly affection between India and China. The radical Chinese youth who had their baptism of fire in the May Fourth Movement of 1919 mistook the modern Indian poet to be a traditionalist and derided the messenger of spirituality from a defeated nation. Tagore's advocacy of a shared Asian cultural universe had a mixed reception. Hurt by the passage of what was widely referred to as the Orientals Exclusion Act in the United States, Tagore's friends and admirers set up an Asiatic Association in Shanghai to further the cause of Asian unity. In Japan, the Asian universalist turn in the domain of art was alive and well. The artist Nandalal Bose, who accompanied Tagore, had the privilege of being hosted by Tagore's friend, Yokoyama Taikan, and he was introduced to masterpieces of Japanese art.

During the 1920s, elite networks had coalesced and the masses had come into anti-colonial politics across Asia. The tensions and affinities between the elite and subaltern domains of politics in the name of Asia came to a head in 1927. In Tim Harper's telling of the drama of "underground Asia," the crushing of the communist uprising in Indonesia by early 1927 followed by the internal conflicts between nationalists and communists in Wuhan dealt severe blows to the cause of Asian revolutions.[26] Yet 1927 did not represent a definitive end of the search for a shared Asian future.

The onset of the Great Depression ruptured many of the economic ties binding Asia. The flows of intermediary capital and migrant labor were either arrested or reversed. Economic disjunctions, despite their severity, did not in this period derail the quest for Asian solidarity. If anything, the depression decade saw new societal engagements with the idea of Asia leading to a plethora of women's conferences and labor congresses being organized under its sign. The second World Islamic Conference held in Jerusalem in 1931 showed a creative accommodation between Muslim and Asian universalisms might still be possible. Muhammad Iqbal, who starred at that meeting, pointedly called for dropping the pejorative prefix "pan" before Islamism—a recommendation that applied equally to Asianism. This did not mean that Asian solidarity as an ideal was not acutely vulnerable to the shifting political and economic contexts of the later 1930s.

During the 1910s, the South Asian poet-philosophers Rabindranath Tagore and Muhammad Iqbal had been shocked by the carnage triggered by rival European nationalisms. The decade of the 1930s showed that Asia was by no means immune from that virus. Japan's invasion of China in 1937 undermined the idea of Asia as never before. Tagore was dismayed. His correspondence in 1937 with the Japanese poet Yone Noguchi, who had visited him in 1935, revealed the chasm in their interpretations of the Sino-Japanese conflict. Writing in the *Modern Review,* Subhas Chandra Bose, soon to be president of the Indian National Congress, recalled that Japan had "done great things for herself and for Asia." But, he lamented, could not Japan's aims be achieved "without Imperialism, without dismembering the Chinese Republic, without humiliating another proud, cultured and ancient race?" "No," he replied, "with all our admiration for Japan, where such admiration is due, our whole heart goes out to China in her hour of trial." China, he prophesied, would once again rise phoenix-like from the ashes. India had to draw some lessons in political ethics from the conflict in East Asia. "Standing at the threshold of a new era," he wrote, "let India resolve to aspire after national self-fulfillment in every direction— but not at the expense of other nations and not through the bloody path of self-aggrandizement and imperialism."[27] A medical mission was sent from India to China as a gesture of Asian solidarity in the face of Asian aggression.

The crisis of World War II both hastened the process of Asian freedom and intensified the contradictions in the project of building Asian solidarity. Three gigantic wartime famines in China, India, and Vietnam followed in the wake of ruptures in social and economic relations occasioned by the connected experience of the worldwide depression. The high levels of mortality and morbidity were a measure of the depths of poverty to which colonized and semicolonized Asia had sunk since the early nineteenth century. Large-scale starvation destroyed the last vestiges of legitimacy of the colonial and nationalist regimes that presided over these colossal human tragedies. The experience of the famines recorded in literature and art supply fascinating insights into processes of historical memory and forgetting that marked the advent of Asian independence.

The Japanese promise of "Asia for the Asiatics" during World War II was self-serving in the extreme but not merely an empty slogan. The undermining of British, French, Dutch, and American colonial rule quickened the pace of anti-colonial nationalisms across South and Southeast Asia and brought Asian freedom movements in closer contact with one another. The sense of Asian solidarity evinced by the colonized as they battled for freedom was real and keenly felt. At the same time, the ferocity of the Japanese aggression against the Chinese exposed the hollowness of the rhetoric proclaiming Asian brotherhood. The defeat of Japan in 1945 did not negate the advances made by colonized Asian subjects on the road to freedom from Western rule.

At the end of World War II, the idea of Asia was still alive. Welcoming Sarat Chandra Bose to Burma in July 1946, the Burmese leader Aung San evoked the vision of "a pan-Asiatic federation" in the foreseeable future.[28] An Asian Relations Conference was convened in India before independence in the spring of 1947 hosted by Jawaharlal Nehru and attended by Mahatma Gandhi. The 1950s witnessed a spurt in "civil society" initiatives to forge closer ties among the peoples of the newly independent countries of Asia. Of particular significance were the efforts to build fraternal relations between India and China after 1949. There were state-led initiatives as well to build Asian and African solidarity that found eloquent expression at the Bandung Conference in April 1955. The statist bias within this official strand of Afro-Asian engagement entailed denial of representation to anti-colonial movements that were still striving for independence.

It was the consolidation of independent nation-states with unitary concepts of sovereignty imported from modern Europe and inherited from their erstwhile colonial masters that fractured the idea of Asia in its political dimension. The borders between postcolonial nation-states proved to be more rigid than even the frontiers drawn by colonial powers. The early euphoria surrounding Asian solidarity evaporated into a cloud of animosity. One of the most dramatic manifestations of this trend was the dissolution of the bonds of the much-trumpeted brotherhood between India and China that culminated in a brief but bitter border war between the two countries in the autumn of 1962.

Yet even at that moment of rivalry and conflict between Asian nation-states, an intellectual quest began to discover what a Japanese scholar of modern Chinese literature, Takeuchi Yoshimi, evocatively called in a 1960 lecture "Asia as method." He added a caveat to say it was "impossible to definitely state what this might mean." Takeuchi believed all cultural values to be universal while noting "values do not float in the air." The values of freedom and equality propagated by the West had been "sustained by colonial invasion," thereby weakening them. Poets like Tagore and Lu Xun had "grasped this point intuitively" and felt it was their duty to achieve global equality. Takeuchi called on Asia to re-embrace and change the West since only "such a rollback of culture or values would create universality." He wanted all Asians, including the Japanese who had emulated the West, to understand this vital political and cultural issue.[29] It is significant that in the 1960s, Japanese art in the domain of culture enabled the spirit of an Asian universalism to survive the wartime depredations of Japanese nationalistic imperialism. One example was Nandalal Bose's celebration of the Indian countryside in his art creatively drawing on the Japanese *sumie* style (figure I.1).

There is sometimes a tendency to exaggerate the element of anti-westernism in Asian thought. All that the best Asian thinkers were questioning was the European claim to monopoly on universalism. They were quite skillful in negotiating and even accepting knowledge from the West while taking a strong stand against Western imperialist power. Tagore's vision of "creative unity" certainly had a global scope, as did his travels. Yet "Asia" became "a privileged geography of relations" for Tagore.[30] Most Asian intellectuals in the age of European empire were not the forebears of political activists who today propagate a visceral hatred toward the West.

"As the West retreats into parochial neuroses," a recent study of Asian intellectuals proclaims, "Asian countries appear more outward-looking,

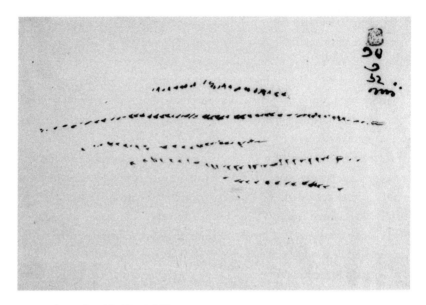

1.1 Landscape (1962) by Nandalal Bose (Courtesy of National Gallery of Modern Art, New Delhi)

confident and optimistic." Yet "no alternative intellectual universalism," is seen to have "successfully challenged the prestige and authority of Western modernity."[31] This view misrecognizes political failure as intellectual failure in crafting alternative Asian versions of modernity. The four decades since the end of World War II represented the heyday of the territorial model of the European nation-state in Asia. In the early twenty-first century, universalist aspirations swept aside at the moment of formal political decolonization received a new breath of life.

Asian scholars and intellectuals have been of late looking beyond the nation in efforts to invest supranational, interregional arenas such as Asia and the Indian Ocean with new meaning. They have been generally attentive to the power as well as the ambiguities underpinning the idea of Asia and have not been oblivious to the imperative of conversing with rather than posturing against the rest of the globe.[32] The innovative forms of spatial imagination emanating from the world of Asian scholarship are of critical importance in determining the future of heightened intra-Asian economic and cultural connections. Asian economic interdependence increased rapidly between 1979 and 2019 with East, Southeast, and South Asia conducting more than half of their international trade among themselves in the 2010s as compared to one-third in the 1980s. Cultural flows have been enhanced contributing to fresh synergies in the domains of Asian arts and humanities. The pace of intra-Asian migration quickened with people on the move across the vast continent in numbers unimaginable between the 1940s and the 1980s.

The world of contemporary Asian thought has been grappling to make sense of and give direction to these trends. Precolonial networks of overland and maritime trade and finance as well as anti-colonial visions of political solidarity have been invoked in attempts to soften the hard borders of postcolonial nation-states. Asian intellectuals have generally run ahead of managers of Asian states in creatively trespassing across national boundaries. It may be just as well that Asian connectivity is less state driven than European integration with its white and Christian identity and more generous in accommodating a multiplicity of races and religions. The more farsighted among the statesmen and diplomats of Asia have not been far behind intellectuals and scholars in this project of reconceptualizing the contours of their continent and its relations with the West. The discourse has moved well beyond trumpeting the superiority of Asian values—associated with the Singaporean leader Lee Kuan Yew—to a more nuanced articulation of an interconnected and interreferential Asia seeking to shape a global future. "The potential of Asia as method," a Taiwanese Chinese scholar, Chen Kuan-hsing, writes in 2010 harking back to Takeuchi Yoshimi's essay fifty years ago, "is this: using the idea of Asia as an imaginary anchoring point, societies can become each other's points of reference, so that the understanding of the self can be transformed, and subjectivity rebuilt."[33] An Asia without borders may not be on the near horizon, but an Asian free trade area and a shared Asian cultural ecumene are already in the process of formation.

The challenge of imagining Asia in the age of contemporary globalization and anti-globalization must wrestle with the dual tension between economy and culture as well as respecting the distinctive qualities of the parts while constructing the whole. The sharpest critical insight into the dilemma of searching for an "inclusive cultural matrix" comes from Gayatri Chakravorty Spivak. She sternly reminds us that "regional economic initiatives, that may seem unifying, do not provide a specifically cultural cement, but rather produce a global managerial culture." Located at the vortex of US multiculturalism in New York, she warns us, "Asian-America is not Asia." Yet she argues a persuasive Asian case for "a pluralized continentalism" dependent on "a responsible pedagogy in the humanities," much the same way as W. E. B. Du Bois "pluralizes Africa." As a scholar and a teacher, she advocates for "a pluralized Asian Comparative Literature." "Let the Asian universities also become utopias," goes out her call, "but not on the US model," that has been corroded by crass corporatization.[34]

What might "pluralized continentalism" look like beyond the ivory tower of the university? The interreferential mode of learning need not be restricted to the precincts of the university and may easily encompass social and political movements in a variety of Asian settings. The notion of pluralized continentalism can accommodate the articulation of Asian universalism alongside "alternative horizons and perspectives."[35]

Navigating the tricky terrain between economy and culture has fewer pitfalls than probing the politics of imagining Asia. This intellectual exploration has been attempted in the twenty-first century by the Chinese theorist Wang Hui in a systematic, if somewhat didactic, vein. His "genealogical analysis" leads him to conclude that "any attempt to characterize Asia as a unitary culture is not plausible." Based on a study of history and contemporary policies, it seems clear that "Asia lacks the conditions for creating a European Union-style superstate." In a sense, respect for difference was the basis for Asian unity. "A high degree of cultural heterogeneity," Wang contends, "does not mean that Asia cannot form definite regional structures—it merely reminds us that any such structure must have a high degree of flexibility and pluralism." While recognizing that "the category of an Asian totality was established in contradistinction to Europe," he begins with a nod to the politics of imagining Europe by invoking Jürgen Habermas's 2001 essay titled "Why Europe Needs a Constitution." In excavating the idea of Asia as a problem in world history, Wang comes up with its "ambiguity and contradictions":

The idea is at once colonialist and anti-colonialist, conservative and revolutionary, nationalist and internationalist, originating in Europe and, alternatively, shaping Europe's image of itself. It is closely linked

to issues relating to both nation-state and empire, a notion of civilization seen as the opposite of the European, and a geographic category
established via geopolitics. . . . As we examine the political, economic,
and cultural autonomy of Asia we must take seriously the derivative-
ness, ambiguity, and inconsistency that were intertwined with the history of its advent—these are products of specific historical relationships
and it is only from these relationships that they can be transcended or
overcome.

The substance of the essay makes clear the author's normative preference
for the anti-colonialist, revolutionary, and internationalist versions of the
idea of Asia.[36]

The chief frailty in the politics of imagining Asia is traced to a European
legacy. Wang notes that "the dominance of the nation-state in Asian imaginaries arose from the empire/nation-state binary created in modern
Europe." The nation-state remained "the main force behind advancing
regional relations within Asia." Added to this inability to shed Europe is
a second weakness in failing to include subaltern visions in imagining
Asia in the twenty-first century unlike what had been achieved in the
early twentieth century during the heady wave of national liberation movements. Wang laments that the question of Asia today is the preserve of "intellectual elites" or "state actors," leaving out the voices of workers, students,
peasants, and women. The pessimism is leavened by an exhortation. "If it
can be said that the socialist and national liberation movements of the
twentieth century have drawn to a close," Wang says on reflection, "their
fragmentary remains can still be a vital source for stimulating new ways
of imagining Asia."[37]

The dream of Asian universalism had been shattered in the twentieth
century by the conflict between Japan and China. Its fate in the twenty-first
century will depend to a significant extent on the ability of China and India
to peacefully manage their simultaneous "rise." Both Asian giants are beset
with internal problems of inequity, and the ability to address those may
be just as important as the state of their mutual relations, which in any
case face challenges from nationalist posturing. The politics of Hindu
majoritarianism in India may undercut the vision of a broad Asian solidarity.

The future of Muslim Asia will be shaped by efforts in working out a symbiosis between Islam and democracy. The experiments with democracy in Pakistan, Turkey, and Indonesia seem to have fallen prey to the global march of majoritarianism rampant, excepting that the Indonesian center has conceded autonomy and applied the healing touch in regions like Aceh. Muslim cosmopolitanism with its deep history is being challenged by Muslim exclusivism across Asia. Buddhist universalism had once served as a connective thread binding an Asian imagination transcending colonial borders. Trapped within the constraining logic of the modern postcolonial nation-state, Buddhist majoritarianism has made a mockery of Gautama Buddha's philosophy of nonviolence in Myanmar and Sri Lanka.

Asia after Europe does not view the continent as composed of discrete nation-states but rather as an arena of circulation and connection. It is more interested in the idea of Asia in its many iterations than in the map of Asia. "To promote an adjective to a noun," Engseng Ho notes, "Inter-Asia, thought of not as a unitary continent but an old world crisscrossed by interactions between parts that have known and recognized one another for centuries, provides an unmatched depth and breadth of mobile experience and material."[38] Flows of culture and commerce may yet prevail over interstate competition and conflict in a postimperialist and potentially postnationalist Asia. In reenvisioning the idea of Asia for what many anticipate will be an Asian century, it is necessary to take a normative and ethical position on the side of a generous universalism against the hubris of an arrogant imperialism and narrow nationalism. The most sophisticated Asian intellectuals of the last two centuries aspired to keep that lofty goal in their sights, even if not everyone managed to climb up the slippery slope and reach the peak.

No one said it better than Tagore as early as 1932, during a visit to Iran. He wrote, "We are the people of Asia, grievances against Europe are in our blood. Ever since their pirates and marauders came to suck the blood of this weak continent in the eighteenth century, they have disgraced themselves before us. If a new age has dawned in Asia, let Asia give it utterance in a new authentic voice. If instead Asia merely imitates Europe's beastly cry, were it even to be the lion's roar, it will be a loss."[39]

CHAPTER 1

The Decline and Fall
of a Continent

J AMSHETJEE JEEJEEBHOY, A Parsi trader from Bombay, was on
his fourth voyage to China aboard the *Brunswick* in 1805 when the ship
was captured by the French at the height of the Napoleonic Wars. His
immediate misfortunes and losses would be more than made up by the
lasting relationship he forged with the *Brunswick*'s assistant surgeon,
William Jardine, a Scotsman who had first traveled to China in 1802.
Another Scotsman, James Matheson, arrived in Calcutta in 1815 and after
several trips to Canton, settled there in 1825. Once Jardine partnered with
Matheson to set up Jardine Matheson and Company in 1832, Jeejeebhoy
worked hand in glove with the British duo as their chief supplier of Indian
opium for the Chinese market. Jeejeebhoy was simply the king of opium
in Bombay; the Wadias and Cowasjees, Motichund Aminchund and
Khemchund Motichund, and several others were the merchant princes of
the China trade.

Fictional narrative reinforces the historical narrative of the connections
forged between India and China during the 1830s. "One thing Zachary did
know about the *Ibis*," Amitav Ghosh writes in his novel *Sea of Poppies*, "was
that she had been built to serve as a 'blackbirder,' for transporting slaves. . . .
As with many another slave-ship, the schooner's new owner had acquired
her with an eye to fitting her for a different trade: the export of opium." It
was not until the *Ibis* reached the river Hooghly near Calcutta that Zachary
Reid, the son of a Maryland freedwoman, encountered Ben Burnham, the

ship's new owner. Burnham informed young Zachary that the *Ibis* would not carry opium on its first voyage as the Chinese were having difficulty understanding the benefits of free trade. Instead, the vessel would do just the kind of work she was intended for. "D'ya mean to use her as a slaver, sir? But have not your English laws outlawed that trade?" a startled Zachary asked. Burnham replied that those who would stop at nothing to halt the march of human freedom had indeed outlawed the trade. "Well sir," Zachary demurred, "if slavery is freedom then I'm glad I don't have to make a meal of it. Whips and chains are not much to my taste." But Burnham was reassuring. The *Ibis* would carry not slaves but coolies. "Have you not heard it said that when God closes one door he opens another? When the doors of freedom were closed to the African, the Lord opened them to a tribe that was yet more needful of it—the Asiatick."[1]

This imagined scene captures the stark historical reality of the catastrophic decline and fall of Asia as a connected space in the course of the nineteenth century. Amitav Ghosh's second novel in his *Ibis* trilogy, *River of Smoke,* features a new character, Bahram Mody, a Parsi opium trader.[2] Fact was stranger and perhaps more fascinating than fiction. The company found quite willing Indian collaborators, especially but not exclusively among Parsi traders, who helped transport opium from the hinterlands of northern and central India to the ports of Bombay and Karachi and from there by sea to China through Southeast Asia. Jamshetjee Jeejeebhoy emerged as the most prominent among the Parsi opium dealers. The opium trail from India to China went through Southeast Asia. There, Indian capitalists from Madras presidency had started their business in the 1820s by selling cotton piece goods from the Coromandel coast before finding a niche for themselves in the opium trade.[3]

From one angle of vision, the long nineteenth century is seen to have witnessed the rise of global uniformities in social and religious behavior.[4] A clearer and more dramatic trend was the emergence of global economic disparities between Europe, which grew rich, and Asia, which fell into poverty. In 1820, China and India contributed to approximately 50 percent of the world's gross domestic product (GDP). By 1913, that share had fallen to about 18 percent.[5] Yet the trajectory of this economic divergence, whose pace quickened after 1870, was less salient than the collective sense of humiliation accompanying the decline and fall that went far beyond what was captured in imprecise statistical trends.

Economic historians have tended to compare Asia's descent into poverty with Europe's acquisition of wealth. What this approach has tended to obscure is the ability of European imperialism to manipulate intra-Asian connections in bringing about this divergence. The acquiescence of China to unequal treaties imposed by European powers, for example, cannot be explained without reference to the British colonial conquest of India and the use of Indian opium to pay for China tea. The trajectory of economic decline was accompanied from the mid-nineteenth century by a drastic transformation of imaginative precolonial concepts of layered sovereignty and overlapping political space to be replaced by imported ideas of unitary sovereignty and rigid borders into Europe's Asian colonies. At the same time, colonial states monitored the movements of indentured and semi-indentured Asian labor across these borders to be set to work in mines and plantations after the formal end of slavery. Asian intermediary capital flowed into economic sectors that lay beyond the direct interest of Western colonial capitalists. The new colonial spatiality undermined earlier forms of political accommodation of differences while enabling conditions for closer interactions among the colonized. By the 1880s, the shared sense of abjection elicited anguished intellectual critiques against Europe's domination of an interconnected Asia from figures as diverse as the Bengali poet Rabindranath Tagore, the Muslim anti-imperialist ideologue Jamaluddin Al-Afghani, and the Filipino patriot José Rizal.

"Eur-America had been challenging Asia for about a century," wrote Benoy Kumar Sarkar in the preface to his 1922 book *The Futurism of Young Asia*. "It was not possible for Asia to accept that challenge for a long time. It is only so late as 1905 in the event at Port Arthur that Eur-America has learned how at last Asia intends to retaliate."[6] In pinpointing the date marking the beginning of the Asian fightback, Sarkar considered not so much the fact of Japan's spectacular victory over Russia as the enthusiastic celebration of this reversal of fortunes between east and west across the length and breadth of the vast continent. The intellectual fightback had preceded the politico-military one. Sarkar was on the mark, however, in calculating the European challenge to have lasted just about a hundred years. Fully aware of the historical significance of the defeat inflicted by Robert Clive on Nawab Siraj-ud-Daula of Bengal at the Battle of Plassey way back in 1757, Sarkar was intuitively correct in seeing the decline and fall of Asia as primarily a nineteenth-century phenomenon.

The Great Divergence between Europe and Asia

The general prosperity of Asia prior to the European colonial conquest has been well documented by historians of the premodern and early modern eras.[7] Before 1800, in Kenneth Pomeranz's view, there was "a polycentric world with no dominant center." In agriculture, commerce, and nonmechanized industry, the advanced regions of China and Japan compared favorably with their counterparts in England and France. Average life expectancy in the low to mid-thirties was similar in Asia and Europe around 1800, with Japan probably performing slightly better than others. Pomeranz stresses the proximity of fossil fuel energy and the contingent availability of New World resources in explaining the European breakthrough. Prasannan Parthasarathi notes "profound similarities in political and economic institutions between the advanced regions of Europe and Asia" until the late eighteenth century. In his analysis, two pressures—the competitive challenge of Indian textiles and shortages of wood—generated the process of the British industrial leap forward. In the early nineteenth century, Latin America, especially Mexico, served as the source of silver. The dislocations caused by the Latin American independence movements resulted in a reduction in silver and also gold production after 1811. Taking account of this global context, Man-houng Lin has claimed that "the British could not find enough silver to pay for tea and silk and ended up using opium as the medium of exchange for them." Barring a few exceptions, economic historians have typically reached consensus in identifying the decade of the 1810s as the beginning of the global economic divergence.[8]

The great divergence cannot be explained merely by reference to proximity of fossil fuel energy resources or the New World windfall for Europe. A connective history reveals the critical importance of the colonial conquest of India and the opium trail that led from India to China.

A close study of the deliberations in the British Parliament leading up to the revision of the East India Company's charter in 1813 reveals that the decision not to pay in silver for Asian commodities was very much part of "the calculations, strategies, forms and practices of imperial rule." Lisa Lowe has brilliantly brought to light the intimacies of four continents—America, Europe, Asia, and Africa—by showing the connections between African slave labor in the cotton fields of the US South, textile production and design in Asia, and the tea and opium trades of India and China in the making of British "free trade imperialism."[9]

Without political dominion over Indian territories, the English East India Company would not have been able to survive for half a century after the loss of its Indian trading monopoly in 1813. It had access to India's land revenue, a process that had begun with its acquisition of the diwani of Bengal in 1765. Control over the land revenue of Bengal had obviated the need to bring in silver to pay for Indian textiles. From the second decade of the nineteenth century, Indian textiles lost out in world markets to the manufactures of England's Industrial Revolution. The era dominated by opium grays and indigo blues lasted in an interconnected Asia from the 1810s to the 1850s. The "indigo system" based on peasant cultivation of the blue dye under the aegis of mostly European planters provided the mechanism through which the colonial state funneled its remittances to the metropolitan center. The lucrative China tea trade was now funded by seeking to assert a government monopoly over opium cultivation in India. Despite attempts by the Qing state to restrict the influx of the deadly drug, huge illegal sales of Indian opium smuggled into China made it unnecessary for the company to bring in silver to finance their purchase of tea.[10]

The number of chests of opium imported from India into China rose from about 4,570 in 1800–1801 to more than 40,000 chests in 1838–1839 on the eve of the outbreak of the First Opium War.[11] The East India Company had the dubious reputation of being by far the largest corporate drug dealer in the world during the first half of the nineteenth century. Its ruthless resort to cruelty and coercion was tempered by a search for complicity among the colonized. The company's effective monopoly on opium cultivation did not extend beyond the Gangetic plain where the Patna and Benares varieties were processed in a factory at Ghazipur. Private traders sourced the drug from Malwa in central India and initially exported the commodity from the Portuguese port of Daman. Not to be cut out of the profits from drug trafficking, the British allowed Malwa opium into Bombay, which soon acquired the appellation of "opium city."[12]

The formal abolition of slavery coincided with the extinguishing of the company's monopoly to trade with China through the revision of the Charter Act in 1833. Several ships that transported slaves were now redeployed to carry opium. The schooner *Psyche* and the brigs *Ann* and *Kelpie* had been slavers but were in the late 1830s engaged in the opium trade. The connection stretched from the Atlantic to the Indian Ocean. The Boston merchant Bennet Forbes sent the *Lintin* out on opium runs from 1830 and then commissioned the clipper *Rose* to work on the China coast with Russell and Company. The Qing Empire observed these developments with increasing disquiet. Once the local Chinese authorities led by the special high commissioner in Canton, Lin Zexu, took the drastic step in June 1839 of dumping more than 20,000 chests of illegal opium into the sea, war became inevitable. With some $6 million or 2.5 million pounds sterling worth of contraband sunk in saltwater, London decided to send an expeditionary force, which arrived in June 1840. By the time this war ended two years later, the British took possession of Hong Kong and won concessions in five more treaty ports on the east coast—the first major step in what they reckoned was the opening up of China.

Between 1808 and 1856, as much as $384 million worth of silver flowed out of China as opium paid for Chinese tea that accounted for 85 percent of the world's exports of the commodity until 1871. The colonial state was directly embroiled in the production and trade in opium. Throughout the nineteenth century, peasant producers were not just enmeshed in relations of debt peonage but faced extra-economic coercion as well at the hands of a state-landlord nexus.[13] The state's involvement with indigo was indirect—but quite as significant—through the setting up of financing mechanisms and bolstering of the power of European indigo planters. The blue dye drawn from the indigo plant grown in Bengal and Bihar had a buoyant market in the West. There was an intra-Asian dimension to the indigo trade as well with significant markets in West Asia, especially Iran, and Central Asia. A mere 4 percent of the indigo production was locally consumed. The average annual value of indigo exports from Calcutta rose from Rs. 4 million in the decade 1796–1805 to Rs. 21 million during 1836–1845. The "blue mutiny" by peasants in 1859–1860 brought the indigo system to an end in Bengal, but an alliance between planters and landlords ensured its continuation in Bihar until World War I.[14]

Opium and indigo were commodities of critical importance in the global economy of the first half of the nineteenth century and had key connections with the forms of servile labor that rose to prominence from the 1830s onward. Indentured Asian labor—both Indian and Chinese—and to a lesser degree convict or penal labor filled the breach in the plantation sector left by formal abolitions of slave trades and slavery. A great majority of these migrant laborers went to destinations across the Indian Ocean while some traveled to Atlantic and Pacific islands as well. Yet there was something else of immense significance for the nineteenth-century world economy going on in the agrarian hinterlands of Asia. What was fashioned in the first half of the nineteenth century was a settled and sedentarized peasantry, which during its latter half produced primary products for a capitalist world market.[15] The colonial state held wandering peoples without fixed addresses in deep suspicion.

PRODUCTION RELATIONS BASED ON settled peasant labor and migrant-indentured or quasi-indentured labor on plantations were bound in a dialectical relationship. New sets of intra-Asian connections were forged in the latter half of the nineteenth century based on the specialized flows of capital, labor, skills, and services. In East Asia, intraregional trade flourished in this period, especially between Japan and China. There was also "relatively free technological transfer from Japan to China."[16] Not all of the intra-Asian connections in the context of labor-intensive industrialization was benign. It was Japan's colonial conquest of Taiwan in 1895 and Korea in 1910 that enabled it to receive labor-intensive imports of rice and sugar from these colonies. Close attention to Asian consumer taste spurred along a wide array of Japanese exports to other Asian countries at the turn of the twentieth century, including "cotton yarn, silk spun yarn, cotton cloth, silk cloth, undershirts and drawers of cotton knot, socks and stockings, European-style umbrellas, and parasols of cotton knit, matches, paper and paper manufacture, pottery, glass bottles and flasks, lamps, ropes, bags, mats of straw, toilet soap, drugs and medicines."[17]

Southeast Asia developed new interregional connections with both South and East Asia from the mid-nineteenth century onward. European capital was invested in plantations and mines, which drew migrant labor from India and China. These laborers came from old-settled thickly populated agrarian regions facing severe demographic and market pressures. Tamil laborers went to work in large numbers to the tea plantations of Ceylon and the rubber plantations of Malaya. Chinese laborers became the mainstay of the tin mines in the Malayan peninsula. These new concentrations of population had to be provisioned with food. The traditional rice-producing regions of which Bengal, Tamil Nadu, Java, and Tonkin could barely supply domestic markets. Chinese and Indian intermediary capitalists financed the reclamation of the new rice-producing and -exporting frontiers of the Mekong delta in Cochin-China, the Chao Phraya delta in Thailand, and the Irrawaddy delta in Lower Burma. A finely balanced interregional specialization based on flows of Chinese and Indian capital and labor connected the old agrarian zones, new plantations and mines, and newer rice-exporting zones. Forged from the middle decades of the nineteenth century onward, the interregional connections formed the intermediate layer of the structure of modern global capitalism.[18]

During the late nineteenth century, much of colonized Asia served as a vast market for Western manufactured products, especially British textiles, and the source for a wide array of agricultural raw materials. Raw cotton, raw jute, tea, coffee, oil seeds, wheat, and hides and skins were the chief exports of colonial India. Kaoru Sugihara has depicted the period after the Meiji Restoration of 1868 as one of labor-intensive industrialization in East Asia, especially Japan.[19] South Asia, by contrast, witnessed a process of labor-intensive commercialization of agriculture in this era. Peasants in the cotton and jute tracts switched to higher-value and more labor-intensive cash crops. Unlike Japan, cottage industries did not flourish in the rural sector, and there was no effort to improve the quality of labor through formal schooling or otherwise.

The labor-intensive commercialization of agriculture in India did not create conditions for sustained prosperity. Cotton and jute by now had far surpassed opium and indigo in terms of relative value on the export list of colonial India.[20] However, the volume and value of the drug and the dye had continued to grow throughout the long nineteenth century. The average annual value of indigo exported from Calcutta rose from Rs 21 million in 1836–1845 to Rs 38 million in 1886–1895.[21] Opium cast a "long shadow" on the connected destiny of Asia.[22] On the eve of the First Opium War, just over 40,000 chests of opium were being smuggled into China; the volume more than doubled to 90,000 chests by 1875. The trade in opium was "the most long-continued and systematic international crime." "The image of the Raj," in Carl Trocki's words, "was itself a delusion created by opium." Portrayed as "a great and glorious enterprise," it was "also a global drug cartel which enslaved and destroyed millions and enriched only a few."[23] In that imperial project of enslavement and destruction of millions, Indian traders and soldiers had played an ignoble, collaborative role with their colonial masters.

Perhaps the first and certainly one of the most powerfully articulated Indian expressions of empathy with the Chinese in their predicament came from a twenty-year-old Rabindranath Tagore in May 1881. In the Bengali journal *Bharati*, Tagore excoriated the British drug trade as an unprecedented form of "cruel thuggery." This "dacoity" in the name of "commerce" entailed forcing an entire people to ingest poison. The infection was pouring an incessant deluge of death into the body and mind of "a great and ancient civilized country of Asia." This was nothing but a case of a strong nation in search of profit selling death and destruction to a weak nation.[24]

Written as a sympathetic review essay on the German theologian Theodore Gottlieb's book *The Indo-British Opium Trade*, Tagore was nevertheless unsparing in his diatribe against the unholy alliance between Christianity and commerce. Gottlieb had done his best to draw an analogy between the evils of slavery and the opium menace in his appeal to the Christian conscience. Tagore had come across an English translation of Gottlieb's German book during a visit to England in 1879. He was well aware of the participation in the opium trade by his Anglophile grandfather, Dwarkanath Tagore, who had died in 1846 and lay buried in Kensal Green

Cemetery in London. Rabindranath revered his Brahmo father, Deben-dranath, but typically maintained a stony silence about his grandfather Dwarkanath throughout his life. The "lowly selfishness and unbridled greed" of a foreign nation, he argued, had hurled tens of millions of Chinese on the rapid path of "physical, political and social decline." Religion, duty, or empathy held no appeal for the English; only the lure of wealth was powerful. "This," Tagore declared, "was their nineteenth-century, Christian civilization."[25]

Having brought ruin to China, opium threatened degradation in India as well. Tagore held poppy cultivation responsible for the famine in Bengal in 1878–1879 and social malaise in Rajputana and Assam. The politics of empathy, if not solidarity, with an Asian neighbor gathered momentum in the late 1880s and 1890s. Anti-opium protest demonstrations were held across western and northern India. A woman social reformer from Maharashtra, Soonderbai Powar, took the campaign to the heart of metropolitan Britain through speaking tours. Her pamphlet titled *An Indian Woman's Impeachment of the Opium Crime of the British Government* remains one of the most trenchant indictments of the global opium policy of imperial Britain.[26]

The economic downturns of the 1870s and the 1890s exposed the vulnerabilities of the Indian agrarian economy. A series of terrible famines occurred in the late 1890s and the turn of the twentieth century that devastated the peasantry in the cotton-growing regions of western India. A premier British medical journal, the *Lancet,* estimated famine mortality in India during the 1890s at 19 million, which was about half the population of Britain. The death toll for the 1897 famine ranged from the official figure of 4.5 million to unofficial claims of up to 16 million. These were the severest of the many "late Victorian holocausts."[27]

Historians of the "new imperialism" after 1870 often regarded the early Victorian era beginning in 1837 as one that displayed a relative lack of imperialist aggression. Although partially true of other Western powers, this view was something of an optical illusion that missed the significance of the British advance in Asia as a continuous phenomenon. Even as it fought the First Opium War with the help of Indian troops, the British completed the colonial conquest of Sind and Punjab between 1839 and 1849. The Second

Anglo-Burmese War of the early 1850s consolidated the gains that had been made during the first war of 1824–1826. In 1856 came the final annexation of Awadh, the northern Indian kingdom with its capital in Lucknow, and the grasping of its sizable land revenues. Awadh became a storm center of the great rebellion of 1857—a series of regional patriotic revolts that engulfed much of northern and central India under the symbolic leadership of the last Mughal emperor, Bahadur Shah Zafar. The 1857 rebellion and its aftermath coincided with the Second Opium War in China fought between 1856 and 1860.

If the reverses in the First Opium War inaugurated in 1842 what came to be remembered as China's "century of humiliation," the savagery that accompanied the repression of the 1857 rebellion in India left equally deep psychological scars. The before and after portraits of Delhi left by the Urdu and Persian poet Mirza Asadullah Khan Ghalib in his letters and literature offer insights into the cataclysmic changes occasioned by this watershed event. For the company, it was a Pyrrhic victory as its Indian territories were taken over by the British Crown in 1858. The Mughal emperor, whose legitimacy had far outlasted his power, was tried in the historic Red Fort built by Shah Jahan and deported to Rangoon. The Mughal *shah-en-shah* had occupied the apex of a structure of layered and shared sovereignty. The British now sought to replace it with the imposition of unitary sovereignty—a territorial form imported from modern Europe that broke with time-honored Asian norms of accommodative relations between states and space.

Following the end of the Franco-Prussian War in 1870, western Europe saw relative internal peace during the last three decades of the nineteenth century. This was the same period when European balance of power rivalries played themselves out in the sordid scramble for Africa and the grasping of vast territories in Southeast Asia. Formal proclamations of annexation were typically followed by brutal wars of "pacification" against dogged guerrilla resisters, whether in Burma, Vietnam, or the Philippines. The rule of colonial difference contradicted the principles of international law enunciated from the 1870s onward. State-supported geographical societies based in Western capitals sponsored exploitation in the name of exploration in Asia, which became more than ever before the obverse of Europe.

Lamenting the Loss of Asia

The desacralization accompanying the deportation of the Mughal emperor set the stage for looking west among the colonized toward another locus of temporal sovereignty. The Ottoman Empire straddled large portions of western Asia, eastern Europe, and northern Africa as it extended its umbrella of layered sovereignty. A theme in Ottoman historiography of decline since the age of Süleyman obscures the longevity and resilience of the empire through the long nineteenth century. Derided in this period as "the sick man of Europe," the empire centered in western Asia strove through the Tanzimat reforms of the 1830s and 1840s as well as the efforts under Sultan Abdul Hamid in the late nineteenth century to come to terms with the myriad challenges of modernity. This is not to say that it did not suffer structural weakness as a result of deep indebtedness to European banking institutions. Yet it provided a haven of relative safety to those seeking refuge from the repression of Western empires in South and Southeast Asia. The interstices of the Ottoman and British Empires provided the venue for the articulation of a Muslim cosmopolitanism by men of religion who had fled westward in the aftermath of the 1857 rebellion. Those who remained in India, including Sayyid Ahmad Khan and Shibli Nomani, discovered intimacies of Muslim universalism in their travels and scholarly quests in Ottoman domains.[28]

Perhaps the most fascinating intellectual figure "who remade Asia" in the late nineteenth century was Jamaluddin al-Afghani.[29] Born in Asadabad near Hamdan in Iran, al-Afghani embarked on an anti-imperialist odyssey that took him across the western expanse of the Asian continent to India, Afghanistan, Iran, Egypt, and Turkey. Al-Afghani was an eloquent proponent of an Islamic fraternity rather than Asian solidarity, even though these affinities shared a significant overlap. During his years in Calcutta and Hyderabad in the 1870s and 1880s, he was canny enough to stress Hindu-Muslim unity in the face of the British imperialist threat. In common with many Indian Muslims who had turned toward the Ottoman sultan-caliph after Queen Victoria was proclaimed empress of India in 1877, al-Afghani also looked the Istanbul way once the British crushed Arabi Pasha's resistance and turned Egypt into a protectorate in 1882. Al-Afghani was in crucial ways a modern thinker refusing to differentiate between Muslim science and European science. His international itinerary took him to London and Paris where he engaged with European intellectuals and had a famous debate on Islam with the French savant Ernest Renan. As a political strategist, al-Afghani lived ahead of his times and his peripatetic endeavors brought him little success during his lifetime. In 1897, al-Afghani died a painful death from cancer as a virtual prisoner in Istanbul.[30]

At the other end of the Asian continent, Japan's response to the challenge of the West had a distinctive quality. When Commodore Matthew C. Perry's fleet had sailed into Edo Bay guns blazing in 1853, Japan had been forced much like its Asian neighbors to acquiesce in unequal treaties. By striking the death knell of a wobbly Tokugawa shogunate, the West's gunboat diplomacy jolted Japan to embark on its tryst with modernity following the Meiji Restoration of 1868. The quest to be rid of the unequal treaties would trap Japan into an ambivalence between seeking the European tag of civilization and rediscovering its bonds with the rest of Asia. This oscillation would create a disjunction between the imperatives of the Japanese state and the aspirations of sociopolitical movements animating Japanese society.

An editorial titled "Datsu-A Ron" (On leaving Asia) in the *Jiji shinpō* newspaper on March 16, 1885, attributed to Fukuzawa Yukichi—the most renowned public intellectual of the Meiji era—has been generally heard as a clarion call for Japan to bid goodbye to Asia and gain admittance to the club of "civilized" nations of the West. A few months before the appearance of this essay, Hinohara Shozo—a disciple of Fukuzawa—had wished in the same paper on November 13, 1884 that someone should set up a "Datsuakai" (Leaving Asia Society) as a counterpoise to the "Koakai" (Raising Asia Society) established in 1880. Sone Toshitora, a naval officer and poet, was one of the founders of the Raising Asia Society. He worked closely with a Chinese colleague, Wang Tao, and a Vietnamese diplomat, Nguyen Thuat, whom he met in Shanghai in 1883, to jointly put together a book titled *Hoetsu koheiki* (Account of the Franco-Vietnamese war).[31] Composed in literary Sinetic by those who shared a script but not a spoken language, this narrative was an early example of Asian intellectual solidarity against European imperialism. Another Chinese diplomat, Wu Tingfang, contributed to Sone Toshitora's efforts to forge a common cultural ecumene and political sphere that encompassed Japan, China, Korea, and also Vietnam.

Fukuzawa, on the other hand, likened the movement of civilization to the spread of measles. Resorting to a cost-benefit analysis of embracing the communicable disease named civilization emanating from the West, he concluded that Japan might as well come to terms with a process that seemed inexorable. China and Korea were making a futile attempt to arrest the natural law of its spread. If either country were able to carry out massive reforms on the scale of Japan's Meiji Restoration, they might hope to rise to the challenge of the times. Since the prospects of such an outcome were bleak, Japan might as well dissociate itself from the dismal fate of its Asian neighbors.[32] What was the "Asia" that Fukuzawa was so anxious to leave behind and others had wanted to raise? His discomfort, as Urs Matthias Zachmann has shown, was with late nineteenth-century Europe's representation of Asia. It was the "Western Orientalist discourse on Asia" that Japan had to "leave" to decenter Europe as subject.[33]

While a modernizing Japan sought to extricate itself from unequal treaties imposed by the West, the late nineteenth century saw a new spurt in the colonial conquest of territories across other parts of Asia. Besides Japan, only Thailand managed to retain its formal sovereignty. King Chulalongkorn, who reigned from 1868 to 1910, traveled to Java and India exploring inter-Asian connections in his diaries while noting the power that the British wielded in Calcutta.[34] Despite having to cede suzerainty over principalities in Laos in 1893 and the provinces of Battambang and Siem Reap in Cambodia to the French in 1904 as well as the northern Malay states of Kelantan, Trengganu, Kedah, and Perlis in 1909 to the British, Thailand managed to remain independent at its core in return for concessions on trade and extraterritoriality to Western powers.

Having consolidated their Raj in India, the British completed their subjugation of Burma as a result of a third Anglo-Burmese War that commenced in 1885 and annexed it as a province of British India. The sultanates in the Malay Peninsula fell one by one into an expanding British Empire beginning with Perak in 1871. Having established their control over Cochinchina in southern Vietnam, the French launched an expedition in 1866 led by Doudart de Lagrée and François Garnier to navigate the Mekong as a possible route to China. From 1873, they turned their attention to the Red River in northern Vietnam and finally acquired Tonkin as a French protectorate as a result of a military offensive that began in 1885. The Dutch colonial presence had been largely limited to the populous island of Java since the seventeenth century. The last three decades of the nineteenth century witnessed the conquest of most of the outer islands of the Indonesian archipelago. The Dutch and the French shared with the British a common conception of modern European sovereignty. Eric Tagliacozzo has shown how the border between the Dutch and British Empires in Southeast Asia came to be drawn more rigidly in the fifty-year period from 1865 to 1915.[35] The precolonial states of Asia had far more flexible notions of sovereignty and territory. A fierce war was fought over decades by the Dutch from the early 1870s against one such state, the Sultanate of Aceh, on the island of Sumatra.

The Spanish had started early in their mission of colonial conquest. They expanded from their base in Luzon in the late nineteenth century to some of the other islands of the Philippines until they were replaced by the United States in 1898. In February 1888, José Rizal, celebrated author of the novel *Noli ma tangere* (Touch me not) published the year before, had arrived in Japan. The book, a paradigmatic example of the imagination of the nation in Asia, had received high praise in Europe and had been banned in the Philippines.[36] During his month-and-a-half sojourn, Rizal was impressed by the accomplishments of the industrious Japanese. He fell in love with a young aristocratic Japanese woman, O-sei-san, who became his guide on his tours through Tokyo. She also tutored him in Japanese painting even though the brilliant writer had limited artistic talent. His friend Juan Luna, a mercurial prize-winning painter, was enthusiastic about Japanese art, which he believed was "as advanced as that of Greece and Italy" and urged more study of "that country whom we resemble so much." Rizal was pleased enough to be mistaken for a Japanese. He would go on to compare Japanese and Tagalog variations on the fable of the monkey and the tortoise and speculate about the Japanese people's possible Malay origins. His Asian romance was short lived, however, as Europe beckoned the young proponent of Filipino patriotism.[37]

On April 13, 1888, Rizal boarded the SS *Belgic* in the port of Yokohama. On the transpacific voyage, he was befriended by Suehiro Tetcho, a literary figure equal in stature to the redoubtable Fukuzawa Yukichi. The Meiji gentleman found in the Manila gentleman not just an overqualified interpreter in his conversations with Europeans but also a symbol of hope for Asia. Suehiro recorded their journey together in a comic travelogue *Oshi no ryoko* published in 1889. Rizal and Tetcho traveled by rail across the United States from San Francisco to New York. They then crossed the Atlantic by ship to Liverpool. Settling down to study in the British Museum, Rizal saw off Tetcho in London as the Japanese author and future parliamentarian continued his round-the-globe voyage through Europe, the Indian Ocean, and China back to Japan. Bred in the modern European intellectual tradition, Rizal made sparse nameless mentions of his Asian romance and friendship of 1888. The encounter with Rizal, on the other hand, inspired Suehiro Tetcho to dream about Japanese expansion in the southern seas and Asian independence in a series of political novels including *Nainyo no daiharan*. Through a careful case study of Rizal's Japanese interlude and the encounter between Rizal and Tetcho, Caroline Hau and Takashi Shiraishi advance an interpretation of Asianism as a "network formed through intellectual, physical, emotional, virtual, institutional, and even sexual contacts, or some combination thereof."[38]

This early link in an Asian network did not die with Tetcho and Rizal. Suehiro Tetcho, who unlike Fukuzawa opposed Japan's war against China in 1894–1895, succumbed to cancer in February 1896. In December of that year, the Spanish colonial masters executed José Rizal, who was the inspiration behind the revolutionary Filipino movement for independence. Rizal's poetic farewell, "Mi ultimo adios," lent poignancy to his martyrdom, which posthumously elevated him to the status of the pioneering figure in Asian resistance. Both Katipunan, the radical movement led by Andrés Bonifacio, and the first Philippine republic headed by Emilio Aguinaldo looked toward Japan for support when faced with Spanish and then American aggression between 1896 and 1899. José Rizal's comrade Mariano Ponce served as a key Filipino emissary in Japan from June 1898 until March 1901.

Having promised to aid the Filipino nationalists inspired by their martyr José Rizal and led by Emilio Aguinaldo, Commodore George Dewey sank part of a Spanish fleet in Manila Bay before turning American guns against those fighting for independence. A British imperial poet born in India exhorted Americans to "take up the White Man's burden" to serve the "needs" of their "new-caught, sullen peoples, Half-devil and half-child."[39] Rudyard Kipling sent the poem to his friend Theodore Roosevelt in November 1898 as the debate raged over US policy toward the Philippines and published it in February 1899 at the onset of the American war against Filipino freedom fighters. The decision to incorporate the Philippines as a US colony did not go uncontested in Washington and passed by just a single-vote majority in the Senate. President William McKinley explained that he had been guided by the Almighty one night in reaching that decision. He could not take the "cowardly and dishonorable" course of returning the Philippines to Spain or "turn them over to France or Germany—our commercial rivals in the Orient" or "leave them to themselves" as "they were unfit for self-government." As a result, there was nothing to do "but to take them all, and to educate the Filipinos, and uplift and civilize and Christianize them." William James had been closer to the mark when he denounced the American treatment of the Aguinaldo movement as "piracy positive and absolute." It was the connection of the Philippines to China that proved the most salient in the US decision in favor of colonization. The acquisition of the Philippines as a colony was seen as a boon to American capitalism with Manila as a staging post for the "open door" to the lucrative China market. It proved to be of some strategic value too. McKinley ordered US troops to join British, Russian, and Japanese forces to crush the Boxer Uprising in China. During the presidential campaign of 1900, the Republican Club of Massachusetts put out a leaflet urging American voters to tell William Jennings Bryan, McKinley's Democratic opponent and critic of the Philippine policy, to "Remember Pekin!"[40]

If the surface phenomena of wars and geopolitics of the late 1890s in East Asia were to be foregrounded, it would be hard for historians to locate a basis for imagining an idealist utopia named Asia. Japan's war against China in 1894–1895 was one such conflict. Yet this tussle between a young nation and an old empire provided the background for the Hundred Days' Reforms of 1898 in China. Any resentment against Japan's aggression in 1894 and the humiliating Treaty of Shimonoseki in 1895 was counterbalanced by the reformers' recognition of the imperative to emulate Japan. "We and the Japanese are like lips and teeth," Kang Youwei wrote. Zhang Taiyan deployed the same metaphor to call for a union with Japan as a bulwark against the aggressive imperialist designs of Western powers. Kang Youwei and his intellectual disciple Liang Qichao reissued Tarui Tokichi's book *On the Great Eastern Federation,* described by Craig A. Smith as "probably the first major text on Asian unity that was widely available in Chinese." In his influential *Datong Shu,* Kang advocated "abolishing state boundaries and evolving from division to unity" as his vision of an Asian federation, which would be a stepping-stone to global harmony. When the reforms failed and the empire struck back at the reformers, Tokyo became a diasporic space that provided not just a refuge but a political base for reformers including Kang Youwei and Liang Qichao. Japanese scholars of China associated with the journal *Chinese Progress* ensured that the Chinese reformers found a home away from home in Japan.[41] The Toa Dubunkai, an Asianist organization, was established in 1898. Okuma Shigenobu, Japan's prime minister, and Inukai Tsuyoshi, education minister, both leading lights of this organization, helped establish *datong* schools and lent support to the Chinese reformers in exile.

Revolutionaries had been put on the run even before the reformers. Sun Yat-sen's republican dream would have had little chance of realization without the safe haven he found in Japan and the support he was able to garner among the overseas Chinese in Southeast Asia. On a cold winter night in 1899, Mariano Ponce of the Philippines was invited to dinner in Tokyo at the home of Inukai Tsuyoshi, leader of the Shimpoto (Party of Progressives) in parliament. There he met Sun Yat-sen and sought support for the armed struggle in the Philippines. The Chinese leader in exile asked his Japanese friends Miyazaki Toten and Hirayama Shu to arrange a dispatch of arms by sea. The bonds that were forged embraced the political and the personal. In 1898, Ponce married Udagawa Okiyo, the daughter of his Japanese hosts in Yokohama. Much like Rizal, Ponce had spent much time in Europe and engaged with intellectual currents circulating in the West, but his affections lay with Asia. He confessed in a letter to the Japanese editor of the *Orient* that he had lived in Europe for a decade but did not feel happy till he returned to Asia. He felt enormous love for the region of the world where he was born. Ponce's friendship at first sight with Sun Yat-sen in 1899 would last until his death in 1918 on his way to see the Chinese leader.[42]

The Boxer Uprising in 1900 witnessed not only Japan lining up alongside the Western powers but soldiers from colonial India being pitted against the Chinese rebels. The British Indian Army was a mercenary force that was deployed to secure imperial interests around the globe. What went through the minds of Indian soldiers as they were deployed against fellow Asians is a subject that is beginning to receive scholarly attention. Anand Yang's reading of a Hindi narrative, *Thirteen Months in China,* by Gadadhar Singh, an Indian subaltern who fought to repress the Boxer *bidroha* or revolt, reveals multiple layers of identity and a markedly ambivalent attitude. As a Rajput, Gadadhar was a loyal soldier fighting on behalf of his colonial masters. Yet as a Hindustani, he felt "a sense of Asian kinship with the enemy Chinese." His characterization of the unbridled loot carried out by the international expeditionary force as "atyachar" (oppression) deviated sharply from Western triumphalist accounts of the same events. Gadadhar was reluctant to accept European definitions of civilization and the outrages in the name of civilization against barbarism, declining to agree with the Western view that the Chinese were "uncivilized." "From such experiences," Yang concludes, "developed subaltern sentiments about the empire and civilization he collaborated with and a budding awareness of racial and cultural kinship between China and India—and even the rest of Asia—that anticipated the rising discourse about civilization and pan-Asianism in the decades to come."[43]

If the Indian subaltern exhibited ambivalence, the Indian elite's response to the Boxer phenomenon was somewhat mixed. There were some who had imbibed, if not internalized, the European discourse on civilization. The *Kerala Samachar,* for instance, deemed the Boxers to be "a danger to civilization." The *Maratha* associated with the anti-colonial politics of Bal Gangadhar Tilak, by contrast, saw it as a "patriotic movement incensed by the audacious inroads of foreigners into China." In his analysis of the Boxer Uprising and India, C. A. Bayly has located the "new imperialism of the 1890s" in "the generation of new world-scale mythologies of past crises and future dominance." Rabindranath Tagore, who had in 1881 favorably reviewed Theodore Gottlieb's book denouncing the opium trade, now endorsed the critique of British policy toward China in Goldsworthy Lowes Dickinson's book *Letters from John Chinaman*.[44] In an essay in *Bangadarshan,* Tagore lamented that in China, the West's bestiality had even discarded the cloak that covered its shame.[45]

Across Asia at the turn of the twentieth century, scholars and intellectuals began to lament the loss of their own countries. In due course, this sentiment would broaden into a sense of shared grief. In some instances, Asians participated in the Western subjugation of other Asians. Indian soldiers were deployed by the British to put down resistance in China and Southeast Asia. At the same time, intra-Asian links that were manipulated to bring about the fall of Asia came in for harsh criticism from the late nineteenth century onward. On the final day of the nineteenth century, Tagore composed a poem on "the last sun of the century" setting "amidst the blood-red clouds of the West and the whirlwind of hatred." Deploring what he saw around him as the "drunken delirium of greed," he urged his own country to remember that "what is huge is not great and pride is not everlasting."[46]

CHAPTER 2

Intimations of an
Asian Universalism

T HE YEAR WAS 1903. Abanindranath Tagore removed a huge
European oil painting from the wall of his studio and sold it to the
wealthy art collector Rajendranath Mallik. This was to create space for
an Asian work of art to be executed by Yokoyama Taikan. The chosen
theme was "Raas-Leela," the love play of Radha and Krishna on a full-
moon night. Abanindranath described the scene to Taikan. A young girl
modeled the wearing of a sari. The placement of jewelry was made clear
from pictures of old idols. Taikan crouched on the floor and began work.
First, he did a drawing on silk with coal and then began applying color.
Within a few days, the painting was near completion. The sky shone
with moonlight, but Taikan was not satisfied. Every day, he removed the
cloth cover from the unfinished work and said something was missing.
One morning, he arrived to find that the women at home had collected
fresh *shiuli,* a fragrant white autumnal flower, on a plate and some had
blown across the room. Taikan picked up the flowers and scattered them
on his painting in great delight. Putting them back on the plate, he then
picked up one flower in his left hand and, looking at it closely from all
angles, began applying its white and orange colors to his work of art. The
moonlit night soon came alive with a rain of flowers from the sky and the
breeze dropped them in the midst of the dance of "Raas-Leela." Taikan
planted a *kadam* flower in Radha's hand, draped a garland of *shiuli* flowers

2.1 Raas-Leela (1903) by Yokoyama Taikan (Reproduced from a copy of *Rupam: An Illustrated Quarterly Journal of Oriental Art,* no. 10, April 1922, in the Fine Arts Library, Harvard University)

round her neck, and curled a bunch around Krishna's flute as well. At last, the painting was hung on the wall after Taikan had framed it himself, decorating it with the border of a *baluchari* sari. A party was thrown for friends to come and watch "Raas-Leela" (figure 2.1).[1]

The process of mutual understanding and learning through artistic conversations across Asia unfolded gradually. A disheveled Taikan wearing a straw hat would roam the bazaars of Calcutta, furiously sketching every detail that caught his eye. Used to the rich colors of Mughal and Persian paintings, Abanindranath's eye could not at first see the smoky touch of Taikan's coal on silk, dusted away with a feather to be topped with a light brush of ink. In time, he began to appreciate this style. Yokoyama Taikan and Shunso Hishida embraced Indian themes in their works. Abanindranath offered descriptions based on the *shastras* so that they could paint Indian deities. Taikan's painting of the goddess Kali and Hishida's of Saraswati—both adorned with white lotuses—were bought

2.2 Saraswati (1903)
by Shunso Hishida
(Reproduced from a copy of
*Rupam: An Illustrated Quarterly
Journal of Oriental Art,* no. 10,
April 1922, in the Fine Arts
Library, Harvard University)

by a family elder, the feisty patriot Sarala Devi's mother Swarnakumari
Devi (figure 2.2).

Taikan taught Abanindranath the art of slow drawing, how to etch a line
slowly. In return, the Indian imparted to the Japanese guest the technique
of Mughal painting. Having observed Taikan soak his paintings in water,
Abanindranath took the plunge himself and was impressed with the
"beautiful effect" it had on his canvas. From that moment onward, the
Japanese "wash" became an intrinsic element in Indian painting.[2]

Okakura Tenshin had described Taikan as someone who had brought
into the artistic field represented by the Nippon Bijutsuin school "his wild
imagery and tempestuous conceptions." This was displayed in his 1898
painting *Kutsugen Wandering on the Barren Hills* "amongst wind-blown
narcissus—the flower of silent purity—feeling the raging storm that gathers

in his soul."[3] The fresh white autumn flowers of Bengal appear to have had a soothing effect on the artist who had followed Okakura's trail to India from the land of the peony, lotus, and chrysanthemum.

THE ARTISTIC BOND FORGED between Yokoyama Taikan and Abanindranath Tagore presaged the fusion of Indian nationalism and Asian universalism during the swadeshi movement of 1905. In January of that year, the Russian surrender to General Nogi Maresuke of Japan in Port Arthur galvanized anti-colonial sentiment across the length and breadth of the Asian continent. The Asian resistance truly began in the eyes of Benoy Kumar Sarkar at that moment with a determined and successful effort to meet force with force. The "political enslavement of Asia by Eur-America engendered also the cultural chauvinism among the scientists and philosophers of the West in regard to the East" and "a vast body of *idolas*" had been manufactured under the aegis of a racialized colonial despotism. "The more Port Arthurs Asia can possess to her credit side," Sarkar contended, "the more easy it will be for Young Asia to purge the world of the occidental *idolas* and usher in the Renaissance of the twentieth century."[4] Turning the tables on the cultural and intellectual plane was facilitated by a dramatic Asian victory in the political and military domain.

The historian Ranajit Guha has argued in the context of colonial India that a willingness to resort to *bahubol* or physical force against colonial rule from about 1905 was the litmus test of rejecting "a servant's education" in the domain of culture.[5] One of the earliest intimations of an Asian universalism had emanated from the context of the fin de siècle colonial conquest of the Philippines and armed resistance against it. These early networks of Asian solidarity were not strong enough to thwart the military might of the United States directed against the Philippines at the turn of the twentieth century. Yet it is worth noting that Japan had emerged as the hub of these connections between East, Southeast, and South Asia before its spectacular victory over Russia in 1905.

Since the 1880s, Japanese intellectuals, such as Sone Toshitora, had begun to articulate a vision of Asian universalism that found full expression from the turn of the twentieth century onward. The events of 1905 made Japan the focal point of an Asian universalist moment. Chinese reformers and revolutionaries, including Kang Youwei, Liang Qichao, and Sun Yat-sen, had already congregated in Tokyo from the late 1890s. It was from Japan that Liang embarked on his eight-month-long lecture tour in the United States during 1903 and forged links with the Chinese overseas community across the Pacific. In the United States, he was dismayed to find economic inequality and racial discrimination. By 1905, he was playing host in Japan to the Vietnamese anti-colonial leader Phan Boi Chau. Japan's dramatic victory over Russia in 1905 enthused young Asians in China, Vietnam, Indonesia, Philippines, India, Iran, and Turkey. Tokyo became a magnet drawing in a steady stream of Asian students. In April 1907, both Liang and Zhang Taiyan, a Chinese scholar of Buddhism, were present in Japan when young Japanese, Chinese, Indians, Vietnamese, and Filipinos formed an Asian Humanitarian Brotherhood, also known as an Asian Solidarity Association, in Tokyo. The currents of Asian and Islamic universalisms mingled in Japan with the arrival of Abdurresid Ibrahim from the Ottoman Empire and Mohammed Barakatullah from India.

An Asian Ecumene

Even as the infant republic of the Philippines was absorbed as a colony by the American republic turned empire, a charismatic Japanese ideologue traveled in December 1901 to the capital of the British raj with an Asian dream. Okakura's Asianism has been often interpreted as an answer to the Japanese turn away from Asia and toward Europe at the height of the Meiji project of modernization. His perspective on Asia was qualitatively different from but not an absolute contrast to that of Fukuzawa's. Whereas Sone Toshitora's view of Asia in the 1880s encompassed China, Japan, Korea, and Vietnam, Okakura's embraced India as well and presented a bolder conceptual challenge to both Europe's depiction of Asia and self-congratulatory European versions of global history. In an inversion of Hegel, Okakura sought to place Asia rather than Europe as the end of history. Assigning to Asia the idealism of "love for the Ultimate and Universal," he was constructing a utopia at a time when Europe bore the marks of the anti-idealist reality of the present. Okakura's Asia, therefore, came to function as "a cipher for utopian discontent with the present, thereby joining a globalized fin-de-siècle discourse beyond the particularism of the East/West binary."[6]

The main purpose of Okakura's journey to India was to invite the Hindu sage Swami Vivekananda to come to Japan. Vivekananda had made a brief stopover in Japan on his way to the United States in the summer of 1893. "Japan is the land of the picturesque!" he exclaimed on seeing Tokyo, Kyoto, and Osaka. He was much impressed with Japan's modernization of its army and navy, its factories, its steamers, and other engineering feats. He wanted a number of Indian young men to visit Japan and China every year. In Japan, he found India to be "still the dreamland of everything high and good." He saw Japan's temples, but this man of religion launched into a tirade against India's priest craft and its abominations of untouchability and prejudices regarding food habits and travel. He urged India's youth to come out of their "narrow holes and have a look abroad."[7] Two months later, he gave a stirring address to the World Parliament of Religions in Chicago proclaiming the equal truth of all religions and calling for an end to the scourge of religious fanaticism.

Okakura wanted to bring this inspirer of the youth of India and proponent of a universalistic religion of humanity back to Japan for an international conference. Vivekananda's American disciples Josephine McLeod and Sara Bull supplied the initial link between the bohemian Japanese and the ascetic Indian. Okakura came to see Vivekananda in his monastery at Belur across the river from the Kali temple in Dakshineswar on January 6, 1902. Vivekananda's failing health prevented him from accepting Okakura's invitation to travel once more to Japan. But he joined Okakura and Prince Oda on a visit to the principal Hindu temples and Buddhist pilgrimage sites in north India. He was relieved that the temples, usually unwelcoming of foreigners, did not obstruct the entry of his Japanese guests. Swami Vivekananda passed away on July 4, 1902, not before observing with some concern and a hint of possessiveness unusual in a life of renunciation how his devoted Irish disciple, Sister Nivedita, had warmed to Okakura as the embodiment of an Asian dream.

In the first decade of the twentieth century, Nivedita served as a unique bridge between the scientist Jagadish Chandra Bose and the sannyasi Vivekananda, the so-called moderate and extremist strands in India's anti-colonial politics, and above all, the Rammohun Roy and Ramakrishna Paramhansa streams in Bengali intellectual and social history represented by Rabindranath Tagore and Swami Vivekananda. A quintessential swadeshi internationalist, she would play a key role in linking Indian nationalism with Asian universalism. Having met Okakura in Vivekananda's Belur *math,* she introduced him to the talented Tagore clan of Calcutta. Surendranath Tagore, another of Rabindranath's many talented nephews, has left a vivid account of his first encounter with Okakura at a party hosted by Sara Bull. He found the Japanese visitor to be "a sturdy figure of medium height, clad in a black silk kimono on which was printed or embroidered his family crest, a simple white flower of five petals." Holding "a bamboo-and-paper fan decorated with a sprig of foliage done in sepia" in his hand and wearing "Japanese cloth socks and grass sandals" on his feet, he "sat at ease, with a profound gravity of expression, incessantly smoking Egyptian cigarettes." The vivacious Nivedita did most of the animated talking until she contrived to arrange a one-on-one conversation between Okakura and the young Tagore in an adjoining veranda.[8]

Nivedita believed Okakura could inspire India's idealistic youth to lead a project of national renewal. Even though Surendranath had no instant answer to Okakura's query about what he could do for his country, the young man became the Japanese ideologue's friend and guide on an exploration of India. Okakura's attempt to get land to accommodate pilgrims in Bodhgaya met formidable obstacles before achieving some success. An elephant ride in search of the ruins of Nalanda on a hot summer's day turned out to be a journey to nowhere, as Surendranath's "Calcutta Hindi" was incomprehensible to the local Biharis. But the duo had a better time visiting the Golden Temple in Amritsar, the Taj Mahal in Agra, Akbar's capital Fatehpur Sikri and his tomb at Sikandra, the places of worship on Mount Abu, and the port in Bombay where they collected drinks from a Japanese ship. What impressed Surendranath the most was "how smoothly Okakura glided into the landscape of the remote Bengal village . . . his Taoist robes striking no discordant note in the province of the *aul* [mendicants] and the *baul* [singing devotees]."[9]

Underlying Okakura and Nivedita's landmark intellectual partnership of 1902 was a highly charged emotional spark. Nivedita, who had been administered the vow of celibacy by Vivekananda, was a striking presence in Calcutta's social circles appearing in her flowing white gown, her coiffured hair, and a garland of *rudraksha* beads adorning her neck. In the painter Abanindranath's trained eye of the beholder, Nivedita was the epitome of beauty. The artist had seen the handsome Vivekananda, but he was not a patch on Nivedita who glowed like a "majestic moon" in a galaxy of stars.[10] Okakura's wanderings across the subcontinent eventually took their toll in the form of an attack of malaria and neuralgia of the head. Nivedita moved him to her home and nursed him back to health in the early autumn, having herself recovered from a bout of illness and the traumatic bereavement of Vivekananda's passing. As Okakura lay sick on a long basket sofa in her sitting room, Nivedita spent long hours into the night bathing his head and giving him massages. Okakura felt at home and told her how "whole fields of love, of which he had been unaware" had opened before him. These protestations led Nivedita to reflect on the attractions and perils of the man-woman relationship in a series of letters to Josephine McLeod. Even though she would "always feel a love and tenderness" for Okakura, or Nigu, as she called him, in the end she decided to let him go and free herself from his spell.[11] In any event, her work of editing and revising Okakura's book had been accomplished and the product of a Japanese-Irish collaboration in India was to see the light of publication as *The Ideals of the East* from London in 1903.

Okakura was well versed in the art and art history of both Europe and North America where he had been sent on a study tour of art education in the West by the Japanese government in 1886 and 1887. Respectful though he was toward his mentor Ernest Francisco Fenollosa, he departed from the Hellenistic bias in the interpretation of Japanese art to recognize the influences from China. On his return from the West, Okakura was appointed director of the New School of Art at Ueno, Tokyo, before resigning in 1897 to set up the Nippon Bijitsuin or Hall of Fine Arts at Yanaka in the outskirts of Tokyo. Nearly forty artists rallied to him led by the renowned Hashimoto Gaho and including the younger Taikan, Kanzan, Sessei, and Kozan. In *Ideals,* Okakura identified the "broad expanse of love for the Ultimate and Universal" as "the common thought-inheritance of every Asiatic race, enabling them to produce all the great religions of the world, and distinguishing them from those maritime peoples of the Mediterranean and the Baltic, who love to dwell on the Particular, and to search out the means, not the end, of life."[12]

The flamboyant rhetoric of the author Okakura embellished by his editor Nivedita requires careful interpretation. If Fukuzawa had wanted to move away from the disparaging European discourse on Asia, Okakura represented the creative urge to wrest that discourse away and supply it with a new Asian authorship. Adept at reading early modern European maps of Asia, Sanjay Subrahmanyam flaunts a lack of nuance in grasping modern Asian texts about the continent's own identity. Quoting a flowery passage from Okakura's chapter on "the range of ideals," Subrahmanyam makes exaggerated claims about inclusion and exclusion in the oneness of Asia, going to the extent of hurling a hard to substantiate charge of "Islamophobia" against Okakura.[13] The passage in question spoke of "the old energy of communication" that "lived yet in the great moving sea of the Tartar hordes" and how the "great Mongol outburst" under Timur and Genghis Khan overspread both China and India, tinging the latter's "Mussulman Imperialism with Mongolian polity and art." Okakura went on to argue on the next page of the same chapter,

> Arab chivalry, Persian poetry, Chinese ethics, and Indian thought all speak of a single ancient Asiatic peace, in which there grew up a common life, bearing in different regions different characteristic blossoms, *but nowhere capable of a hard and fast dividing-line* [emphasis added]. Islam itself may be described as Confucianism on horseback, sword in hand. For it is quite possible to distinguish, in the hoary communism of the Yellow Valley, traces of a purely pastoral element, such as we see abstracted and self-realized in the Mussalman races.

Turning from western to eastern Asia, Okakura applied the same method of interpretation to Buddhism as he had to Islam.[14]

Acknowledging the deep intellectual and cultural debt owed to China and India, Okakura claimed that it was "the great privilege of Japan to realize this unity-in-complexity with a special clearness." The march of history had "left to China no landmarks, save her literature and ruins." In

India, the "grandeur of Asoka—ideal type of Asiatic monarchs"—lay "almost forgotten among the crumbling stones of Bharhut and Buddha Gaya." The "historic wealth of Asiatic cultures" could be "consecutively studied through its treasured specimens" only in Japan, which was a living "museum of Asiatic civilization." Tang culture and Indian art, for example, were richly represented in the temples of Nara. Perhaps in waxing eloquent about Japan's "unbroken sovereignty" and the Japanese as "an unconquered race," Okakura had tempted fate.[15] These attributes would be stripped away in the aftermath of the dropping of two atom bombs in 1945.

The substance of Okakura's book was a chronological study of the evolution of Japanese art through the ages culminating in the Meiji era. Okakura held up as the finest modern specimens drawing on Asia's past in technique and subject matter Kano Hogai's representation of "Kwannon, the Universal Mother, in her aspect of human maternity," Hashimoto Gaho's picture of Chokaro as "an image of the playful attitude of fatalism," Kanzan's "Funeral Pyre of Buddha" destined to "fill the world with its light of supreme renunciation," and Taikan's "Kutsugen Wandering on the Barren Hills."[16] A second manuscript by Okakura edited by Nivedita in 1902 contained a more direct call to Asia's anti-colonial resistance against the West. Certain to fall foul of the repressive capacity of the colonial state, this book, titled *The Awakening of Asia,* was first published in Japan, decades later in 1938.

In 1903, Okakura sent Hori San to study Sanskrit in Rabindranath Tagore's Bolpur school and the artists Taikan and Hishida to Calcutta. Art played the central role in the awakening that Okakura and Nivedita had sought. George Nathaniel Curzon's decision to partition Bengal triggered the swadeshi (own country) movement in 1905. Having learned the technique of the Japanese "wash" from Taikan, Abanindranath Tagore painted an arresting image of the mother nation in that style. Nivedita was taken by it. Initially conceived as *Bangamata* (Mother Bengal), the painting was at her suggestion retitled as *Bharatmata* (Mother India). Nivedita did not fail to notice its broader Asian inspiration. She wrote in her critical appreciation,

The curving line of lotuses and the white radiance of the halo are beautiful additions to the Asiatically conceived figure with its four arms, as the symbol of the divine multiplication of power. This is the first masterpiece, in which an Indian artist has actually succeeded in disengaging as it were, the spirit of the motherland—giver of Faith and Learning, of Clothing and Food,—and portraying Her, as she appears to the eyes of Her children.[17]

The iconic swadeshi image was not devoid of a *bideshi* (foreign country) touch (figure 2.3).

2.3 Bharatmata (1905) by Abanindranath Tagore (Reproduction courtesy of Victoria Memorial Hall and Rabindra Bharati Society, Kolkata)

Looking and Journeying East

On April 1, 1906, friends gathered at the jetty on the river in Calcutta and chanted "Bande Mataram" ("I bow to you, Mother") in one voice as they bid farewell to sixteen students departing by ship for Japan and the United States. The students responded by jointly raising the slogan hailing the mother nation that had been adopted as the mantra of the swadeshi movement.[18] Fifteen of the students were Bengalis and only one from north India, B. D. Pande, who was on his way to learn leather technology. Rathindranath Tagore, son of Rabindranath, was a member of the group headed to the agricultural university at Urbana-Champaign in Illinois. The students were sponsored by the National Council on Education, an institution established by the swadeshi movement to challenge the hegemony of British colonial education. The swadeshi desire to nationalize education and promote indigenous industries did not preclude acquiring knowledge from abroad, especially Japan.

Manmatha Nath Ghosh from Jessore district in Bengal, who wrote a vivid travelogue, had chosen his destination to learn from the labor-intensive industries of Meiji Japan. The ship on which he and his fellow students traveled followed the usual easterly route of that era from Calcutta to Rangoon, Penang, Singapore, and Hong Kong before arriving in Yokohama. The Burmese capital of Rangoon was dominated by Indian migrants just as the cities of the Malay Peninsula bore a strong Chinese imprint. In Penang, a border of sorts was crossed as Tamil Muslim money changers boarded the ship to supply passengers with straits dollars in place of rupees. Manmatha was thrilled after close to a month's voyage to reach "the land of the rising sun."[19]

Manmatha had a quick orientation in Tokyo where he was impressed with the helpful attitude of the police in marked contrast to what he had been used to in India and met students from various Asian countries at a meeting of an Oriental association. He spent the first six months serving as an apprentice in a small button-making factory in Kobe. He then spent a year in Osaka mastering the technique of manufacturing celluloid. The owner of this exclusive home-based production unit was at first reluctant to share his trade secrets but relented after reflecting on the history of India's gifts to Japan of religion and culture. Manmatha woke up at the crack of dawn and worked as hard as his industrious Japanese hosts through the day. In time, he became an intrinsic part of this family-based enterprise. Alongside experimenting with camphor, a key ingredient in the making of celluloid, he learned artificial leather making, crafting handles of umbrellas and walking sticks, and the exquisite art of making combs. He visited the commercial museums in various cities of Japan and lamented the lack of institutions to promote commerce and industry in colonial India. Full of admiration for Japan on this score, he was not able to acquire a taste in Japanese cuisine or approve of their habit of collective bathing au naturel.[20]

Manmatha had come to Japan with a scholarship for two years but ended up spending a third year studying and negotiating discounts for purchasing camphor on which Japan had a virtual monopoly. This was necessary for his plans to manufacture celluloid in India. Just as his family was getting anxious about his extended stay, his wife asked him to learn a Japanese craft that he could teach her. Manmatha managed to get himself admitted to a girls' school for artificial flower making and emerged from it a graduate in that specialized subject. Just before his return, he was able to witness a grand naval review in Kobe where he saw Admiral Togo Heihachiro and was much impressed by the humble public demeanor of the great military hero who had sunk the Russian fleet in the Bay of Tsushima in May 1905.[21]

That world-shaking event had electrified people across the whole of Asia and resulted in a rapid increase in the flow of students and political activists to Japan. In 1896, there were just over a dozen Chinese students in Japan. The number rose to about 1,300 in 1904 and shot up to 8,000 by 1905. In 1907, a hundred Chinese women were enrolled in the Practical Women's School in Tokyo. Manmatha was one of fifty-four Indian students in 1906, up from just fifteen in 1903, but that number would cross the one-hundred mark by 1910. Students from various countries of Southeast Asia and West Asia congregated in Japan as well.[22] Tokyo had emerged as an Asian anti-imperial metropolis before revolutionaries on a global itinerary forged diasporic spaces of anti-colonial activism in European capitals, such as, Berlin and Paris.[23]

By the autumn of 1905, the two key leaders of Vietnamese anti-colonialism—the revolutionary monarchist Phan Boi Chau and the republican Phan Chu Trinh—were both in Japan. By 1906, Phan Boi Chau had managed to bring the scion of the Nguyen dynasty, Prince Cuong De, as well to Japan. With a poetic declaration "To All Comrades I Go East," Phan Boi Chau had left his political base in the Nghe An province and traveled in disguise by ship to Hong Kong and then on to Shanghai. After the Japanese naval victory over Russia on May 28, 1905, he was able to make the sea crossing to Japan. Phan Boi Chau's meetings with Japanese political leaders Inukai Tsuyoshi and Okuma Shigenobu and the Chinese reformer in exile Liang Qichao impressed on him "the problem of rivalry between Europe and Asia."[24] He had lengthy "brush conversations" relying on classical Chinese calligraphy with Liang on whose advice he launched the Dong Du (Go East) movement encouraging young Vietnamese to study in Japan. Three thousand copies of his pamphlet calling for crowd-funding these students were printed for him by Liang.

The strategic emphasis on education abroad was very much part of the means to Phan Boi Chau's end of fomenting revolution at home. Once he became acquainted with the thought of Giuseppe Mazzini by reading Liang's Chinese biography of three heroes of Italian unification, he affirmed the Mazzinian doctrine that "education and insurrection should go hand in hand."[25] In 1907, Chau became a founding member of the Asian Humanitarian Brotherhood or Asian Solidarity Association in Tokyo, giving him an opportunity of meeting Korean, Filipino, and Indian political activists in addition to Chinese reformers and revolutionaries and their Japanese sympathizers. The aim of this society, as proclaimed in its charter, was "to fight against imperialism and to achieve the independence of Asian peoples who have lost their sovereignty." Committed to the unity of "Chinese, Indian, Annamese, Burmese and Filipino brethren," this Japan-based association paid special attention to the unity and independence of China and India, which together could raise "a protective shield over Asia."[26] Its membership was open to all anti-imperialists, regardless of whether they were nationalists, republicans, socialists, or anarchists. The martyr José Rizal was adopted as the unifying symbol for recovering the lost countries of Asia from Western imperialist domination. The Japanese government, however, was keen to shed the humiliation of inequality by entering into equal treaties with European countries. The Anglo-Japanese alliance of 1902 was followed by a Franco-Japanese understanding in 1907. This signaled the start of the hounding of Vietnamese exiles. With Phan Boi Chau's expulsion from Japan in 1909, his Dong Du experiment came to an end.

Sun Yat-sen had been expelled from Japan even earlier, in 1907. He set up his political base in Penang from where he plotted the armed uprising in Canton in 1910 and the ensuing fall of the Qing Empire in 1911. His talented associates from his days of Japanese exile, Hu Hanmin and Wang Jingwei, ably assisted him in harnessing some of the subaltern energies among the overseas Chinese. Wang became a hero of Chinese patriotic lore of that time for his attempt to assassinate the prince regent in Beijing in 1910. Kang Youwei and Liang Qichao had led the intellectual effort at an Asian renaissance in Japanese exile. Kang forged an Indian connection by spending some time in Darjeeling at the beginning of the twentieth century. In 1908, he was in the streets of Istanbul as crowds celebrated the restoration of the 1876 reformist constitution of the Ottoman Empire.[27] He had little regard for Sun Yat-sen. Miyazaki Toten's efforts at mediating their differences came to nothing. In the course of the first decade of the twentieth century, Liang emerged from the shadow of both his teacher Kang and of Confucian ideas of imperial legitimacy. His critical intellectual engagement with the United States ensured that his vision of Asian universalism always had a global dimension. But it was the successful mobilization of what Tim Harper has called the "village abroad" that enabled Sun Yat-sen to emerge in 1911 as the founding father of the Chinese republic.[28] Japan figured as a potential leader of an Asian resurgence in Sun's conception during the early years of the republic in 1912–1913. In his speeches in Japan during February and March 1913, he identified the Western powers as posing the real threat to China. "If there was no Japan," Sun believed, "then there would be no talk of future prospects for China. In East Asia, the revolution accomplished by my generation was due to Japan's strength."[29]

In 1905, the Ottoman reformer in Egypt Mustafa Kamil had written about Japan as a model for the rest of Asia. The Ottoman-Meiji ties went back to 1889 when Sultan Abdul Hamid had sent a large ship named *Ertugrul,* which tragically sank in 1890 after a grand reception in Yokohama. The

Japanese sent two war vessels to Turkey carrying the survivors of the ship-wreck. From November 1908 to June 1909, Abdurresid Ibrahim visited Japan and took part in Asianist confabulations. He nursed an ambition of conferring the honor of Islam on the people of Japan. Selcuk Esenbul has shown the intricacies in the relationship between Japan and Turkey as well as Buddhism and Islam. Halide Edip, a Turkish nationalist femi-nist, was one of many women to name her son Togo after the famous Japanese admiral who had sunk the Russian fleet. Mehmet Akif, future composer of Turkey's national anthem, depicted his friend Ibrahim preaching Islam in the form of the Buddha in his epic poem *Safahat* (Pas-sages). During his 1908–1909 sojourn, Ibrahim took part in the setting up of Ajia Gikai (Asian Congress) and in gatherings of Toa Dobunkai (East Asia Common Culture Society) now being led by Konoe Atsumaro. In Japan, Ibrahim met Mohammed Barakatullah, an Indian supporter of the Ottoman Empire and professor of Hindustani at Tokyo Imperial University. Hailing from the princely state of Bhopal in central India, Barakatullah had journeyed through the United Kingdom and the United States to Japan to attempt a modus vivendi between Asia and Islam. In 1909 with the help of Hasan Hatano Uho, a Japanese convert to Islam, he launched the journal *Islamic Fraternity,* which circulated in Southeast Asia. On his return voyage from Japan, Ibrahim went to China, the Dutch East Indies, and British India spreading the twin messages of Asian soli-darity and Islamic fraternity.[30]

In paying an obituary tribute to Mustafa Kamil in 1908, the Bengali swadeshi leader Aurobindo Ghose pointed out how the Ottoman reformer balanced the "religious solidarity of Islam" as "a moral asset" with "the distinct existence of Egyptian Nationality." "Asia is not Europe and never will be Europe," Aurobindo wrote in another essay titled "Asiatic De-mocracy." He acknowledged that much of Europe's political history will repeat itself in Asia but that Asia would "transmute it in her own tem-perament." In his view, after Christianity betrayed its early promise, the Prophet Muḥammad had "tried to re-establish the Asiatic gospel of human equality in the spirit." If European democracy emphasized "the rights of man," Asiatic democracy based itself on "the *dharma* of humanity." Au-robindo came out in support of his compatriot Bipin Chandra Pal's vision of "the possibility of China and Japan overthrowing European civilization." India's freedom, he asserted, was "necessary to the unity of Asia," and he looked forward to "the smiting down of European pride, the humiliation of Western statecraft, power and civilization and its subordination to the lead of the dominant Asiatic." In elaborating on "the Asiatic Role," he viewed Asia as "the custodian of the world's peace of mind, the physician of the maladies which Europe generates." He saw the calm, contemplative, self-possessed "spirit of Asia" taking "possession of Europe's discoveries" and correcting "its exaggerations, its aberrations by the intuition, the spiritual light that she alone can turn upon the world."[31]

Asian Rendezvous in Calcutta and Boston

As Japan became the cynosure of Asian eyes from 1904 to 1905, the Japanese visionary of the oneness of Asia found a base in the Museum of Fine Arts in Boston, first as adviser between 1904 and 1909 and then as curator of Asian art from 1910 onward. In 1906 appeared Okakura's *Book of Tea,* giving historians an opportunity to speak of a gentle Teaist strand of Asian universalism to be distinguished from the more aggressive variants. Teaism was defined as "a cult founded on the adoration of the beautiful thing among the sordid facts of everyday existence." The "subtle charm" of tea made sure that it did not have "the arrogance of wine, the self-consciousness of coffee, nor the simpering innocence of cocoa." But Okakura refused to be a "polite Teaist" while criticizing the unfavorable Western attitude toward understanding the East. It was rare to find, he wrote—referring to Sister Nivedita without naming her—the perspective of the author of *The Web of Indian Life* enlivening "the Oriental darkness with the torch of our own sentiments." He was outspoken in his criticism before calling on "the continents" to stop "hurling epigrams at each other":

> European imperialism, which does not disdain to raise the absurd cry of the Yellow Peril, fails to realize that Asia may also awaken to the cruel sense of the White Disaster. You may laugh at us for having "too much tea" but may we not suspect that you of the West have "no tea" in your constitution?[32]

Akira Iriye sees Teaism as evoking the shared civilizational "beauty" of Asia, helping its people "to regain their self-confidence so that they would once again be able to contribute to the world's civilization."[33]

Okakura made a second visit to India in 1912, ten years after his first. Sister Nivedita had passed away in Darjeeling in 1911, but he was once more welcomed in Calcutta by the Tagore family she had brought into his life. At the dock, Surendranath "clambered on board" while the ship was still moving to be greeted by a surprised and smiling Okakura: "Still the same!" Behind the smile, there seemed to be the shadow of an illness.[34] During his first visit, Abanindranath would visit him at Surendranath's home where Okakura sat facing a bronze lotus bearing cigarettes that he lit one after the other. On this occasion, he frequently visited the Jorasanko studio where he expounded on tradition, observation, and originality in art to Nandalal Bose and other students of Abanindranath with the help of three match-sticks. He was impressed with the progress made by Indian artists in a decade. A visit was arranged for him to see the thirteenth-century Sun Temple in Konarak. Okakura wanted to also see the Jagannath temple in Puri where foreigners were generally barred. The artists brainstormed and their Japanese guest obtained a grand entry into the temple and a darshan of the deity. The trip to Konarak was the high point of his second visit to India from an artistic point of view.[35] On a personal level, he was enchanted by Priyamvada Devi Banerjee, a widowed niece of the essayist Pramatha Chaudhuri, the husband of Rabindranath's niece Indira, sister of Suren-dranath. Having met her in Surendranath's home, Okakura continued an epistolary romance with Priyamvada upon his departure for Japan and the United States.

Rabindranath Tagore had been away in Britain with his poems of *Gitan-jali* and missed seeing Okakura in 1912. Boston was the venue of their next meeting in February 1913. There is circumstantial evidence to suggest that Tagore had come in late January and early February to visit Okakura, who was then instrumental in getting him invited to give a series of lectures at Harvard for which he returned after a trip to New York.[36] The letter of invitation was issued by James Haughton Woods, an assistant professor of philosophy, who knew Okakura and had sought his intervention in helping Dharmanand Kosambi, an Indian scholar of Buddhism, who had been having trouble in his intellectual collaboration with a senior scholar of Sanskrit and Pali, Charles Rockwell Lanman. Okakura was also known to Abbott Lawrence Lowell, then president of Harvard. The objections of some faculty members concerned about the supposed "plague of swamis" coming to Harvard from India were overcome, allowing Tagore to deliver three lectures in Emerson Hall in February 1913 and two more in April. Among the themes addressed was the relationship between the individual and the universal. Taken together, the lectures, published later in the year as *Sadhana: The Realization of Life,* represented an effort to find the grounds for a philosophical exchange between East and West.

"Babu Rabindra came yesterday with his son and his charming daughter-in-law," Okakura wrote to Priyamvada on February 4, 1913. "I am hoping to make their short stay here as little of a bore as possible, though of course being a stranger myself, I cannot do much. Their presence here makes me feel that you are not far from me." The concept of Asia figured in their conversations. After Tagore's departure following his first set of lectures, Okakura wrote again to Priyamvada on March 3, 1913, "Your uncle has left for Chicago and I feel a sudden loneliness."[37] Okakura had been warmly embraced by Boston's intellectual and cultural elite since 1904, being feted at the soirees hosted by Isabella Gardner at her newly constructed palazzo close to the Museum of Fine Arts. He had held exhibitions of the paintings by Yokoyama Taikan at the home of Sara Bull at 168 Brattle Street, Cambridge. Yet his self-identification as a stranger and feeling of loneliness on the departure of his friend whom he had encountered only fleetingly was not a mere affectation and must be seen as evidence of an affective bond forged in the name of Asia.

Having left for Japan, Okakura was not present in Boston at the time of Tagore's April lectures at Harvard and was felled by Bright's disease in September 1913. He missed seeing his friend Rabindranath Tagore become the first Asian to win the Nobel Prize for Literature in November of that year. Even after Okakura's death, Boston continued to be a global venue for theorizing on Asian art. The Ceylonese art critic Ananda Coomaraswamy arrived at the Museum of Fine Arts in 1916 after having been a member of the inner circle of the Bengal school of artists between 1909 and 1913. A woodcut print by Nandalal Bose titled "The Artists' Studio, Jorasanko" in the museum's collection shows three Tagore brothers, A. N. Tagore, G. N. Tagore, and S .N. Tagore, along with A. K. Coomaraswamy and N. L. Bose lounging about with their hookahs on the southern veranda of one of the Tagore mansions in Calcutta. Coomaraswamy's joint work with the late Sister Nivedita titled *Myths of the Hindus and Buddhists* was published in 1913. Well versed in the nuanced relationship between art and swadeshi from his Calcutta days, Coomaraswamy propounded from his Boston perch his grand theory on Asian art that "envisioned a great cultural region connecting India with Southeast and East Asia." His interpretation of modern Indian art was now placed within "a monumental interregional terrain of ancient Asian cosmopolitanism."[38]

In Search of Young Asia

O N A WARM DAY in June 1915, the young Indian sociologist Benoy
Kumar Sarkar waited in his hotel lobby in Tokyo for Yone Noguchi,
professor of English literature at Keio University. The poet Noguchi had
spent six months in England during 1914 being celebrated by the literati
in London and Oxford. Sarkar noted that the English had engaged in a similar craze ("*matamati*") with "Rabi-babu," Rabindranath Tagore, the year before. Sarkar set off with Noguchi by tram and then train to his village home
some seventeen or eighteen miles outside the capital. The poet's wooden
cottage in the midst of a forest and fields looked like a kakemono work of
art. His study and an adjoining room for guests had Japanese paintings on
the walls while the bookshelves contained works of English poetry and
criticism. Sarkar noticed a photograph of the English poet laureate Robert
Bridges, a handwritten congratulatory message from William Butler
Yeats, and a small bust of Francis Thompson. Sarkar learned that Noguchi
had received a letter from Rabindranath Tagore saying that he would be
visiting Japan soon and that the main purpose of his visit would be to have
conversations about Japanese literature and art.[1]

Sarkar thought Indians should be aware that Noguchi could partially fill
the void left by Okakura's passing two years earlier, even though he was not
a profound philosopher or pundit. The way Noguchi had articulated the
inner meaning of Japanese literature in *The Spirit of Japanese Poetry* had
convinced Sarkar that the literary critic belonged to the same intellectual

family as the art critic. Sarkar recommended Noguchi's essays in *Through the Torii* to his Indian readers to get a sense of his attitude and opinions, especially "What is the Hokku poem?" and "Again on Hokku." He recognized that an element of exaggeration tended to creep into the dissemination of such works of interpretation. Yet Noguchi was committed to the contemplativeness and restraint that were the essence of Asian literature and art. "Japanese poetry," Noguchi had written, "at least the old Japanese poetry is different from western poetry in the same way as silence is different from voice, night from day." In Sarkar's view, Goldsworthy Lowes Dickinson, in his book *Appearances,* had got Japan quite wrong, having been misled by the sight of some banks and shops, electric lights and train stations, a few professors and businessmen in hats and coats, into portraying the whole of Japan as "Eur-America's mofussil." To understand the true Japan, it was necessary to find interpreters like Noguchi and to independently view the interior and exterior of Japanese society with eyes open. Sarkar quoted two poems, "The Poet" and "The Lotus," from Noguchi's collection *Pilgrimages.* The first was an example of the power of his poetry:

> The roses live by eating of their own beauty and then die:
> He too is fed on his own poem.
> His poem? Yea, his very flesh in the grasp of the moment!
> What a cry of the Soul and flesh in the grasp of the moment!

"The Lotus" revealed his introspective nature:

> The one lotus whiter than prayer,
> Before me rose fall as a dream,
> With the Sunlight fallen through the clouds,
> The flower smiled the sorrow of Heaven.

This sounded to Sarkar like the melody of Tagore's *Gitanjali.*

Sarkar could hear in Noguchi the voice of the new Japan that had not lost its originality under the influence of Eur-America. On the India-Japan relationship, it could still be said in the words of Dwijendralal Roy:

Uthilo jekhane Buddha-atma mukta korite mokshadwar
Aajio juria ardha jagat bhakti-pranata charane janr

(Here arose Lord Buddha Great who opened Nirvana's gates above
Half the world still kneel before him worshipping in fervent love)[2]

Even in the twentieth century, Sarkar saw Japan as a part of the Indian universe (*Bharat-mandal*) and Noguchi as born of the same mother as Rabindranath. "*Gitanjali*" and "*Pilgrimages,*" he proclaimed, "are excavations from the same mine." This was not, however, the only melody of the inhabitants of Asia; other tunes were also Asia's own and Sarkar did not want those to be lost from view.[3]

Noguchi's wife brought tea. Sarkar noted that it came sans milk and sugar. "Have you read Okakura's *Book of Tea?*" the poet asked, telling his guest that the ceremony of tea had been performed before it was served." Noguchi and Sarkar talked about music and art as they took a walk through the bamboo groves of the village and spent some time in a local temple. On their return, Sarkar found that Noguchi's wife had lit evening lamps in the freshly washed yard. A Japanese dinner featuring fish, cooked rather than raw, followed. Unable to master the art of chopsticks, Sarkar took the help of a spoon. The conversation continued following the meal. By the time Sarkar bade goodbye to the Noguchi couple, the moon had risen in a cloud-capped sky.[4]

The Birth Giver of Young Asia

The success of the republican revolution in 1911 had enabled Chinese revolutionaries and reformers in Japanese exile to return to their homeland. The "father" of that revolution, Sun Yat-sen, retained his Japanese connections, which he renewed through occasional visits. For public intellectuals and political activists from colonized Asia, the attraction of Tokyo as a diasporic city space for anti-colonial action grew during World War I. To be sure, Berlin and Istanbul also emerged as diasporic spaces for the congregation of global revolutionaries as Germany and Ottoman Turkey ranged themselves against the British and other Western empires that dominated

Asia. Yet Tokyo as an Asian anti-imperial metropolis had a special appeal to Asians who were eager since 1905 to fuse nationalisms with a larger conception of Asian universalism. Despite the penchant of the Japanese state to curry favor with Britain, France, and the United States, Tokyo welcomed a steady flow of academic and political visitors from colonized Asia between 1915 and 1918. Sojourners and seekers of knowledge or asylum from India included the redoubtable swadeshi leader Lala Lajpat Rai, the poet Rabindranath Tagore, and the revolutionaries Rashbehari Bose, Narendranath Bhattacharya (before he became M. N. Roy), and Taraknath Das. The cultural ethos of Asianism cultivated since 1905 became the foundation for efforts at mounting interreferential and interconnected revolutionary action between 1914 and 1918.

The keenest observations on the rise of "young Asia" came from the energetic, globe-trotting Indian intellectual Benoy Kumar Sarkar, based on his extended visits to Japan and China during 1915–1916. While offering deep insights into quotidian life in both countries, he sought out and interacted with every major Japanese and Chinese intellectual and political figure of that time in Tokyo, Shanghai, and other major cities. While placing Japan's 1905 military victory in a broader Asian and global historical context, he also delved into the promise and frailty of the republican experiment in China. A scholar with a deep political commitment, he prepared the intellectual field in which interdependent revolutionary action against Western empires could take root across Asia. He also emerged as the foremost theorist of the concept of "young Asia" that inspired an entire generation to take a resolute stand against Western imperial power. The Bengali word *"nabin"* could be rendered as either "new" or "young." The invocation of youth signaled a rebirth of Asia after a century of temporary aggression and illegitimate usurpation by Eur-American imperialists. Liberated from a sorry recent past and an oppressive present, the young could lay claim to the future. The adjective "young" was deployed in two senses: the youth of Asia were exhorted to craft a young, self-confident Asian continentalism. Whereas Lala Lajpat Rai chose *Young India* as the title of his 1916 book and Mohandas Karamchand Gandhi of his 1919 political journal, Sarkar decided to unfurl the intellectual banner of young Asia.

Born in 1887, Benoy Kumar Sarkar was a brilliant student who read history and literature at Presidency College, Calcutta. As a young man, he enthusiastically joined the swadeshi movement in 1905 and played an innovative role in mass mobilization in his home district of Malda. By reinterpreting a local performative musical tradition named *gambhira,* he was able to connect a folk element to the imagination of the Bengali and, by extension, Indian nation.[5] He emerged as one of the finest examples of the colorful cosmopolitan, rooted in local learning and patriotic activism while embarking on a global intellectual quest. In 1914, he traveled to Egypt, Ireland, and England and then boarded the *Philadelphia* in November to cross the Atlantic from Liverpool to New York. Lala Lajpat Rai, the preeminent leader of swadeshi nationalism in the Punjab, and the renowned scientist Jagadish Chandra Bose along with his wife, Abala, were fellow passengers on the transatlantic voyage. The ship was also the venue of his meeting with a young Austrian woman, Ida Stieler, whom he would marry in November 1922.[6] As part of his efforts to forge Asian connections in America, Sarkar traveled with Lala Lajpat Rai to Boston where he introduced the Indian leader to Masaharu Anesaki from the University of Tokyo who had come as a visiting professor to Harvard.[7] After half a year in the United States, he embarked on his Pacific crossing and arrived in Japan on a ship named *Tanyo Maru* from Honolulu in early June 1915.

Benoy Kumar Sarkar's major English works have been receiving belated scholarly attention from historians. These interpretations have ranged from the sophisticated analysis of his internationalism and futurism by Manu Goswami to a superficial misreading of him as a "Hindu nationalist" by Nile Green.[8] Sarkar's travel writings in Bengali, by contrast, have remained neglected even though they are arguably the best sources for understanding the affective bond forged with an entity called Asia. In 1915–1916, Sarkar spent three months in Japan, nearly ten months in China, and again four months in Japan. His essays on Japan were published during those years in the journals *Grihastha, Upasana,* and *Prabasi* among a profusion of articles in Bengali journals on Asia in the late nineteenth and early twentieth centuries.[9] Sarkar's Japan travelogue appeared as a book titled *Nabin Asiar Janmadata Japan* (The birth giver of young Asia, Japan) in 1923. In his introduction to the book version, Sarkar mentioned that Indians often ask,

"Are the Japanese friends or enemies of Asia?" The problem with this line of inquiry would become apparent if one asked similar questions as to whether the Germans or the English or the French were friends or enemies of Europe. The answer regarding Japan would be the same as any to those types of questions. He discussed this matter at various places in his *ketab* (book), which contained a sprinkling of Persianate words bringing the written register of Bengali prose close to both Hindus and Muslims. By 1923, Tokyo was "no longer the only capital of free Asia"; Ankara was "also a new center of this freedom." Kemal Ataturk had emerged as the defender of Asia's western gate. To Japan went the credit of being the *deekshadata* (giver of initiation) and *shikshaguru* (mentor) of "young India, young China, young Afghanistan, young Iran and young Egypt." Sarkar noted that Indian literature had only a few books about foreign lands authored by Asians or Indians.[10] He certainly followed the pioneers of earlier times to enrich that genre during the early twentieth century.

On the ten-day voyage across the Pacific, Sarkar noticed the social distance between the American and Japanese passengers, many of whom were returning from the world's fair in San Francisco. A *kodan* (traditional Japanese oral storytelling) on the Russo-Japanese War seemed akin to a *kathak* (performative narration of stories by bards) on the swadeshi movement in the Barisal district of Bengal. Sarkar conversed in English with Baron Ito, son of Prince Ito Hirobumi, the Meiji statesman and viceroy to Korea who had been assassinated in 1909. On arrival in Japan, he faced the practical difficulty of the language barrier in the streets of Yokohama and Tokyo. "For English-educated Indians," Sarkar commented wryly, "Englishstan and Yankeestan are merely extensions of Hindustan." The influence of Eur-America was not as noticeable in Japan as he had been led to expect, and the Japanese "seemed to be relatives of Indians."[11] For the next three months, Sarkar launched into a systematic study tour of all aspects of Japanese life, its social norms and learned institutions, based on varied interactions with its prominent and ordinary citizens. His writings formed the intellectual basis for interreferential political and revolutionary action across young Asia at a moment of European imperial crisis. If the swadeshi links were primarily cultural suffused with an anti-colonial spirit, World War I afforded the opportunity for youthful daring on both intellectual and political planes.

The first institution on Sarkar's itinerary was Tokyo Imperial University where he visited the library and museum. He chatted with Professor Kazutoshi Ueda about Japanese language and linguistics. Professor Junjiro Takakusu had brought a collection of Indian materials for the museum. By *Bharatvarsha*, the land of India, the Japanese understood the entire *Bharatmandal*, the Indian universe, including Siam, Burma, Indochina, Persia, Java, and Sumatra. Sarkar had already met Tokyo's professor of Buddhist literature, Masaharu Anesaki, at Harvard, where in his role as visiting professor he had been busy propagating the peace-loving credentials of Japan. An Indo-Japanese association with the prime minister Count Okuma Shigenobu as president issued four bulletins a year, two in English and two in Japanese. It counted some 500 members led by the scholar of Buddhist literature Bunio Nanio and the Tokyo University professors Takakusu and Anesaki. Steering clear of politics so as not to offend the British, eminent Japanese citizens were keen to learn about India.[12] After visits to the war museum and the art museum in Ueno Park, Sarkar took in Ginza, which with its department stores Mitsukoshi and Maruzen and big banks could be "regarded as Tokyo's Chowringhee," Calcutta's main thoroughfare. The biggest bazaar selling fresh produce in Tokyo appeared similar to Bengal's mofussil village *hat* or the *chak* in Allahabad. Sarkar believed he discovered the true identity of the Japanese in their handicrafts, cottage industries, and family-based businesses. Japanese lacquer work and silk embroidery left him suitably impressed.[13]

A visit to the editorial office of *Kokka* provided the occasion for a conversation about art. The editor, Seiichi Taki, taught art history at Tokyo University and had visited India. Sarkar saw Nandalal Bose's painting *Koikeyi* (a Ramayana character, Rama's stepmother) on Taki's wall. A few works of Abanindranath Tagore and Nandalal Bose had been featured in an issue of the magazine a few years ago. Under Okakura's influence, according to Taki, young Japan had these days become admirers of the new Indian art and some were even imitating Abanindranath's artistic style. Taki himself found modern Indian art to be too soft and feminine but praised the Indian artists' command of lines and sense of color. Sarkar was taken to the performance of *noh* plays by Noguchi and described *noh* as Japanese *gambhira* in sharp contrast to Dickinson's analogy with Greek drama. Both seemed to have sprung from the same inspiration and followed a similar evolution from medieval to modern times. Preaching morals and theorizing on quotidian life through plenty of satire and humor were the hallmarks of both genres.[14] At a Tuesday evening gathering of writers, Sarkar found that the impending visit of Tagore had created quite a stir. The Japanese translation of *Sadhana* based on Tagore's 1913 Harvard lectures had sold thousands of copies. The Japanese did not appreciate the Nobel-winning *Gitanjali* as much. At another venue, Sarkar met Hattori Unokichi, a scholar of Chinese philosophy and literature, who had spent time at Peking University and was poised to go to Harvard in place of Anesaki. Sarkar wondered whether James Haughton Woods's plans to bring professors from India to Harvard would bear any fruit.[15]

Sarkar noted that the venerable prime minister Okuma Shigenobu had emphasized education in the mother tongue when he founded Waseda University. At the same time, Waseda had appointed to its faculty Tsubouchi Shoyo, a translator of Shakespeare into Japanese, with whom Sarkar discussed education and literature. Sarkar observed the high standing of three elders in Japanese society and among foreign visitors—Okuma Shigenobu, Inazo Nitobe, the author of *Bushido,* and Baron Shibusawa Eiichi, the captain of finance and industry. Having encountered Shibusawa at a meeting of the Japanese Association Concordia, Sarkar sought him out for an interview in his office. He learned that the restructuring of banking and finance had been the key first step in the economic modernization of Japan.[16]

Indians needed to come to Japan, in Sarkar's opinion, only to see that it was possible to accept the work patterns of Eur-America without adopting Eur-American airs. Reflecting on international relations, Sarkar considered Japan to be quite isolated. The Western allies were currently busy slaying Germany in the European Kurukshetra (epic battlefield). Once that was accomplished, Asia's new Abhimanyu would have to face attacks from ten sides, much like Arjun's son who was encircled by the Kauravas in the Mahabharat epic. Citing Ichiro Tokutomi, the editor of *Kokumin* (established in 1890, the same year as the Imperial Diet), Sarkar assessed that the Anglo-Japanese alliance lacked depth and may not last long.[17]

Once he ventured out of Tokyo, Sarkar identified even more similarities between Japan and India. In the streets, hotels, and markets of Tokyo,

Nikko, Matsushima, and Sapporo, he looked upon Japanese men and women in the same way as he had Marathi speakers in the streets of Poona. In Japan, he had come to truly appreciate that despite the difference of language, unity was deeply implanted in the heart of Asia. The politeness and dignity that he saw among the Japanese and Muslims were the products of "a thousand-year long Asiatic custom and practice." The discovery of similarity in difference continued once an eleven-hour journey brought him from Tokyo to Kyoto, Japan's Delhi, with its seventeenth-century Kano art and the Nishi Honganji Buddhist temple. Upon arriving in Nara, the Sarnath of Japanese Buddhism, Sarkar wondered, "Was there no difference between eighth-century Japan and India?" It was only the sight of the factories and municipality of Osaka that led Sarkar to deploy an English analogy—"Asia's Manchester." But even in its vicinity, he found an occasion to spend a night at a Buddhist monastery run by a young Japanese scholar who had visited the explorer of Tibet Sarat Chandra Das in Darjeeling.[18]

By mid-August 1915, Sarkar mused, "What have I seen in Japan?" His reflections in answer to that question underscore a dramatic contrast between his travel experiences in Asia and Eur-America:

> In England and America, I understood the language of the people—I could converse with them in their mother-tongue. Yet I felt oddly out of place [khapchhara] in those societies. They too were unable to accept me as one of their own. I have not understood the language of the men and women of Japan . . . yet standing on any street in any city or village I have felt as if I have been watching the scenes of Calcutta. . . . In their gait and look, their posture, their manner of speech, their laughter and humor, their modest and respectful demeanor, their customs of greeting and serving guests, in all these matters I have found India. . . . In its heart and mind Japan is a part of Asia—it has only imported some scraps of iron from Eur-America.[19]

Sarkar was admitted into the circle of scholars and artists in New York and Boston during 1914–1915 and 1917–1919, partly facilitated by Edwin Seligman, a professor of historical political economy at Columbia University, and Max Weber, the cubist artist and critic. Yet it was his feeling "oddly out of place" recorded candidly in his Bengali writing that was depicted in Florine Stettheimer's oil painting *Studio Party, or Soiree* (1917–1919) (see figure 3.1).

In it, Sarkar's still figure is placed as an exotic fig leaf in front of Florine's nude self-portrait on the wall of her studio, the venue of an animated avant-garde soiree. "The awkwardness of Sarkar's pose," Manu Goswami has commented, "belies the centrality of his placement."[20] For Sarkar, it was not a pose; he felt awkward or *khapchhara* in this milieu. The intellectual engagement with Eur-America and the affective bond with Asia represented distinct modes of internationalist belonging of a colonized Indian intent on shaping a new global future.

Before leaving Japan, Sarkar addressed the three criticisms that were directed against the birth giver of new Asia: first, Japan was not a true friend of India; second, Japan had colonized Korea; and third, Japan was complicit in Eur-America's aggression against China. While acknowledging the fact of Japanese imperialism, Sarkar saw it in the context of the existence of Western concessions and extraterritoriality in China's treaty ports and Western spheres of influence and spheres of interest in Manchuria, Mongolia, and Tibet. The reality of power relations in the region made it impossible for Japan to simply remain grateful for civilizational gifts received from China and Korea in the past. It did not behoove those unable to defend themselves to envy someone who had successfully done so. Sarkar was not in favor of Asians echoing the charges of Eur-America against Japan's rise to the status of a "first-class power" and the ambition to be a "world power."[21]

A twenty-six-hour journey from Osaka to Pusan marked the transition from Japan's *janmabhumi* (homeland or land of birth) to *bhogbhumi* (land possessed). Sarkar had arrived once more in unfree Asia. He feared that Korea would suffer the fate of Ireland as a colony next door and reckoned Japan might face a Korean problem much like England's Irish problem.[22] From Korea, Sarkar went on to Manchuria to see for himself Mukden and Port Arthur, venues of battles in 1904–1905 won by General Nogi and Admiral Togo as historically significant in modern times as the ancient Greco-Persian battles of Marathon and Thermopylae. In Port Arthur, he met Count Otani, the Buddhist scholar of the Honganji sect in Kyoto, who

3.1 Studio Party, or Soiree (1917–1919) by Florine Stettheimer with Benoy Kumar Sarkar at the center below Florine Stettheimer's self-portrait (Transfer from Beinecke Rare Book and Manuscript Library, Gift of Joseph Solomon to the Florine and Ettie Stettheimer papers, Yale Collection of American Literature, Yale University Art Gallery)

was living in exile after getting embroiled in a financial scandal at home. Otani had visited India thrice in addition to traveling in China and Turkestan and held a lengthy discussion with Sarkar on the land routes and sea-lanes along which Buddhism had spread from South to East Asia. But it was 1905 as a temporal threshold in modern history that enchanted the Indian visitor much more. In a final chapter titled "Bande Port-Arthuram," he wrote that the one who had proclaimed "the East is East and the West is West" was blinded by an awful superstition. Port Arthur had brought home the clear realization that this mark of difference was "a matter of only one century." "Before the nineteenth century," Sarkar asserted, "concepts such as east and west had no currency in human society." The travelogue closed with a ringing proclamation about the future: "Having acquired new knowledge, the people of Asia will once again stride the world as human beings within the twentieth century. The way in which *Prachyamanab* [human beings of the east] excelled in secular life by productively engaging with the interplay of *bishwashakti* [world forces] until the sixteenth and seventeenth centuries indicated they will regain that high status from the twenty-first century."[23]

China and the Intellectual Power of Asians

The 522-mile journey from Mukden to Peking was made in twenty-two hours. What struck Sarkar on his arrival was China's *durdasha* (misfortune). Everywhere, he could see the domination of the foreigner. As in Japan, he proceeded to keep a record of his trip in Bengali and published some of it in the form of three articles in *Prabasi,* a fragment in *Dhaka Review o Sammilan,* and one essay in *Grihastha.* The travelogue was completed in its entirety by June 1916 and published in full as a book titled *Bartaman Juge Chin Samrajya* (The Chinese Empire in the present age) in 1921. In his introduction to the book, Sarkar noted that much had been turned upside down in China and the world in the five years since his journey. What was just a traveler's diary was also the repository of ingredients for studying the science of civilization and theory underlying the humanities. Nearly every travelogue was at one level just description, but authors tended to have a predilection for analysis and criticism as well. Sarkar supplied his own commentary and interpretation in good measure along with vivid description of what he saw. He dedicated the book to Kang Youwei and Liang Qichao, who deserved the reverence of young Asia.[24]

Residing in a hotel run by Westerners in the Legation Quarter of Peking, Sarkar went for dinner at a Chinese Muslim restaurant. He noted that there were as many as 20,000 Muslim families in Peking. He visited the main mosque in the Muslim neighborhood where as soon as he pronounced "*La Ilaha Il Allah,*" Chinese voices completed the affirmation with "*Muhammd u Rasul Allah.*" The Sanskrit language, the Devanagari script, and an image of Buddha in a fourteenth-century inscription near the Great Wall naturally thrilled Sarkar. The whole of Asia, he wrote, must become the domain of inquiry for Indian historians. Among the Chinese intellectuals Sarkar met in Peking was Yan Fu, who had studied at Cambridge and translated Herbert Spencer and Adam Smith into Chinese. Another day, the Edinburgh-educated author of *The Spirit of the Chinese People,* Ku Hung-ming (Gu Hongming), sought Sarkar out in his hotel and held a lengthy discussion on Confucianism.[25]

Unlike a handful of other Indian visitors who tended to limit themselves to coastal cities, Sarkar traveled into the rural interior of China.[26] He set off by train from Peking for the 300-mile journey to Honan (Henan) Province. The hectic and noisy activity at the stations with hawkers selling grapes, pears, and apples while loudly bargaining with the travelers had a ring of familiarity. The mud walls of huts and the fields of maize and millet reminded him of Bihar. The flickering kerosene lanterns after dark were similar to those seen in Indian villages. The linguistic difference seemed to be of little consequence. If Bengalis of Calcutta could regard the Marathas of Poona and the Tamils of Madurai as their brothers, why should they not call Chinese their brothers as well? Getting a little carried away, Sarkar declared China to be like a province of India. More to the point, he concluded, "The whole of Asia is one. If one is to disbelieve the unity of Asia, one would first have to lose faith in the unity of India." Yet Sarkar was not a proponent of a unitary state either in China or in India. The existence of multiple European states took nothing away from the fundamental unity that underpinned the idea of Europe. China, he believed, was pursuing the mirage of so-called unification and would be much better off as a con-glomeration of a number of independent provinces.[27] A federal India and a federal China, Sarkar seemed to argue, could happily reside in a unified concept of Asia.

After surveying the *Bharatmandal* (Indian universe) crafted by Indian and Chinese pilgrim scholars in Honan (Henan), including the White Pagoda and the cave temples, Sarkar departed for the neighboring Hupei (Hubei) Province. Once the train crossed the hilly terrain of the Honan-Hupei border into the plains, the fishermen's boats and peasant cottages were reminiscent for Sarkar of the scenes of east Bengal. On reaching the city of Hankow (part of present-day Wuhan) some 750 miles southwest of Peking, that idyll was broken. Sikh policemen were to be seen in the British concession. The Chinese saw Indians mostly in their roles as gatekeepers, watchmen, and armed guards. It was evident to Sarkar that the Chinese public "suffered oppression" at their hands. "Wherever in China there were neighborhoods based on foreign concessions," Sarkar found, "there was some degree of resentment against Indians."[28]

Sarkar chose to return east by steamer down the great Yangtze River. Along the banks, he saw green paddy fields but also foreign concessions at several urban settlements. It took two days to reach Nanking, the revolutionary center of the Chinese republic. Continuing to observe the vastness of China's landscape and people on either side of the river, Sarkar reached his destination Shanghai, which he found more glittering than Calcutta or Bombay. In Shanghai, he learned a new term—comprador—the Chinese intermediaries in the system of racialized capitalism. Sarkar met Tang Shaoyi, a thoroughly modern man who told him in unequivocal terms that it was the duty of every Asian to safeguard the glory of Asia. Tang Shaoyi had visited India for eight months in 1904 as plenipotentiary of the Qing government and saw many commonalities between the societies of Bengal and South China.[29]

After a quick trip to Hangchow, Sarkar settled down for a seven-month stay in Shanghai. He spent most of his time rummaging through books. He mused about the conditions of foreign oppression in China that he felt were probably worse than complete subjugation. At a Saturday gathering in an elite Shanghai club, Sarkar encountered Wu Tingfang, the witty author of *America through the Eyes of an Oriental Diplomat,* who inquired about theosophy and expressed a desire to visit Madras at war's end.[30] Wu Tingfang wrote the introduction to Sarkar's book *Chinese Religion through Hindu Eyes: A Study in the Tendencies of Asiatic Mentality,* the product of his research in Shanghai. The book was dedicated to the memory of three ancient scholars: Kumara-Jiva, who pioneered the translation of Buddhist texts into Chinese at the turn of the fifth century; Xuan Zhang, who spent sixteen years from 629 to 645 in India and spread the knowledge he acquired on his return to China; and Kobo Daishi, who studied Indian texts in China from 804 to 806 and disseminated what he learned in Japan. "Neither historically nor philosophically," Sarkar stated in the opening paragraph of his preface, "does Asiatic mentality differ from the Eur-American." Only after the Industrial Revolution of the nineteenth century had "the alleged difference" been broached and "then grossly exaggerated." The "pseudo-scientific theories or fancies regarding race, religion, and culture" that "vitiated" the present were "unknown to the world down to the second or third decade of the 19th century."[31] This was Sarkar's opening salvo in the devastating critique of the comparative method of Orientalism that would be the hallmark of his scholarly works in subsequent years.

To contest the hubris of European Orientalism, Sarkar called for a new movement of educated Indians to travel and reside abroad. Historically, Asia was neither more nor less outward looking or inward looking than Europe. Sarkar rejected the sweeping claims made by Lowes Dickinson in *Appearances* and Herbert Giles in his Hibbert Lectures titled *Confucianism and Its Rivals* that the Hindus were steeped in religion while the Chinese were not. The chronological scope of Sarkar's book *Chinese Religion through Hindu Eyes* covered nearly a millennium and a half from the fourth century BCE onward. He contended that "an idea of Asiatic unity" was encapsulated in the Japanese term *San-goku* (three countries), which was rendered in English as "Concert of Asia." "Asiatic Culture is one," Sarkar claimed, "but is richly varied." It had changed over time "from epoch to epoch" and across space from India to China and Japan. He was impatient with "such poetic and sonorous expressions as 'unchanging East.'" Scholars had yet to learn that "Asiatic history" was "as dynamic and as good a record of changes as the history of Europe."[32]

Having made the case for historical change of the same order in Asia as in Europe, Sarkar spelled out a "three-fold basis of Asiatic Unity" or "foundation of Asiatic consciousness." First, there was a living faith in an eternal order regulating a balance in the universe among human beings and nature. Second came a shared "conception of Pluralism" as a corollary to the "cult of World-Forces or Nature-Powers." The "third basis of Asiatic Mentality" was "the spirit of Toleration or the conception of 'peace and good-will to all mankind.'" Sarkar confused the argument about pluralism somewhat by a digression into polytheism. However, he conveyed a compelling case for a "psychological groundwork" that made "Asiatic Unity a philosophical *necessity* in spite of ethnological and linguistic diversities."

The book ended on a tantalizing note. It had not traced the "practical idealism, romantic positivism and assimilative eclecticism," which had been "the inspiration of eight hundred million souls during the last thousand years." "I stop," Sarkar concluded, "at the threshold of the great Asiatic Unity."[33]

For insights into the psychology of intimacy evoked in early twentieth-century Asian encounters, one has to fall back on Sarkar's Bengali travel writing rather than his erudite scholarship in English. He candidly acknowledged the role of power in shaping his responses to China and Japan. He had been willing to accept more from Japan, including quickly learning Japanese words, than he had in the course of a much longer stay in China. If he had been partial in favoring one side, it was the Chinese. He had been able to regard the Chinese as relatives more than the Japanese. Yet the Chinese were not able to influence him. Had China been as powerful as the United States, every aspect of Chinese life would have found recognition across the globe and he would have become a true Chinese in three days.[34]

Even more fascinating was what Sarkar had to say about Chinese Muslims and the role of Islam in undergirding Asian unity. Theorizing on this subject had come a long way from Okakura's emphasis on the Buddhist arc. Sarkar felt a much closer affinity to Chinese Muslim society than Chinese Buddhist society. He could understand that time was needed to get to know Confucius. But what might explain his greater intimacy with Muslims rather than Buddhists, given the history of the spread of Buddha's teachings from India to China? On his voyage in the western Indian Ocean, he had felt a bond with Muslim fellow passengers, more so than with Parsis, and wished he could disembark with them to make the pilgrimage to Mecca. Once he reached Egypt, the Muslims there embraced him as a visitor from Hindustan. The warmth of their welcome made him sad when he had to leave Cairo. He had felt the same close kinship with the Muslims of Persia. In Japan and China, he had seen Buddhists and understood their historical relationship with India. "But the music that sprang from my heart strings as soon as I encountered Muslims here," he wondered, "why did it not sound on the same strings when I met the Chinese and Japanese Buddhist worshipers of Sakyasingha?"[35]

Following conversations with him, Chinese Muslims could gather that Sarkar was not a Muslim but had come from a Muslim country. In Egypt, too, he had seen how a non-Muslim from a Muslim land had been accepted as a relative. "Muslims have kept Asia truly united," Sarkar observed, "by tying this thread of brotherhood." It was no doubt possible to establish human relationships anywhere in the world. But what could explain the special property of the special way in which he considered Chinese, Iranian, and Egyptian Muslims to be his very own? "May be," Sarkar answered, "India (I cannot remember the four corners of that vast country, let me speak of Bengal) or Bengal is not just Hindustan, it is also Musalmanstan." From a historical perspective, Hindustan was the land of Hindus, Parsis, Jains, Christians, Sikhs, and Muslims. But for all practical purposes in the Bengali mind, "Bharatvarsha" was "Hindu-Musalmanstan." In a lyrical passage, Sarkar went on to describe how from their birth, Hindu friends played with Muslim friends and children of both faiths grew up together. After that, in bazaars, shops, and markets, in grazing pastures and agricultural fields, in religious fairs and religious practices, "in festivities and in distress, in famines and in cemeteries," Muslims were companions of Hindus and Hindus were companions of Muslims. The blood and breath of Hindus and Muslims were inextricably mixed. "The bond forged by this companionship, dwelling together and brotherhood," Sarkar believed, "was unbreakable." It was impossible for human beings of flesh and blood to forget this attachment. Cerebral reasoning, philosophical discourses, and historical scholarship might reveal the relationship of Hindus and Buddhists as well as Parsis and Vaidiks. But could discoveries of the head, Sarkar asked, create the chains of enchantment strung by pulls of the heart? How could Buddhists hope to find the place that Muslims occupied in the Bengali Hindus' heart? And for this reason, Bengali Muslims preferred to die by the banks of the Ganga and Brahmaputra than by the Tigris or the Nile.[36] Far from harboring Hindu nationalist sentiments of the sort later propagated by V. D. Savarkar or "downplay[ing] Islam as little more than a crude medieval political force preventing an Asian unity," as claimed by Nile Green,[37] Sarkar was an eloquent and passionate proponent of Hindu-Muslim equality and unity. He was a scholar who believed Islam undergirded Asian unity and also noted "the contributions of Islam to European civilization."[38]

On his return to India, he would become an ardent supporter of Deshbandhu Chittaranjan Das's 1923 Bengal Pact between Hindus and Muslims.[39]

Long before the slogan "*Hindi-Chini Bhai-Bhai*" (Indians and Chinese are brothers) was raised in the 1950s, Sarkar gave a particular spin to the precise nature of this brotherhood. He considered China to be India's "*masir bari*," the home of the mother's sister. He had embarked on his global voyage believing that he would not find any country like India. China had astonished him by being similar to India in many respects. He was for now enjoying this insight in solitude but wanted many more Indians to make this journey of discovery. The Egyptians, the Chinese, and the Iranians were all beckoning young India, saying, "Brother Hindustani, Asia is yours."[40]

The final chapter of Sarkar's travelogue was devoted to an interpretation of political revolution in China—a subject on which he also wrote in his English articles. He used the Bengali term *samrajya* for empire and *swaraj* for republic. Kang Youwei was for him China's Rammohun Roy, the great early nineteenth-century social reformer, even though he and Prince Ito Hirobumi of Japan came half a century after Roy. The time lag could be easily explained. "The nose of India," Sarkar wrote, "protrudes into the vast Indian Ocean." Naturally, India was the first Asian country to have to negotiate European modernity. Kang Youwei was born in Kwangtung, "China's Bengal," and was fortunate to have excellent students, notably Liang Qichao. Even though Sun Yat-sen had acquired an international reputation, Kang Youwei was more highly respected within China in Sarkar's estimation. The Yunnan rebellion of 1916 was not merely a schism against the increasingly authoritarian Yuan Shikai who had wrested the levers of the republic from Sun Yat-sen, forcing him once again into Japanese exile. The involvement of Tsai Ao and Liang Qichao in Yunnan's declaration of independence from Peking gave it a modern ideological tendency in dialogue with Europe.[41]

Pioneering the comparative study of Chinese and Indian empires, Sarkar queried young China's characterization of the anti-Manchu republican revolution of September 1911 as "anti-foreign." It was a politically expedient move that did not gel with historical reality. Sarkar drew an "interesting parallel" between the Mongol and Manchu Empires of China and the Afghan and Mughal Empires of India. Even though the first Muslim sovereigns had come as conquerors, there was "a great *rapprochement* between the Hindus and the Mohammedans in language, music, painting, architecture, folk customs, etiquette, and phases of social life." Sarkar cited numerous examples to show that "the distinction" was "all but obliterated" in political and military affairs. Similarly, while it was true that "the Mongols and Manchus came into China from outside," they "did not regard China as their '*colony*' but made it their *patrie,* the center of all their affections and dreams." Sarkar made a further insightful comparison of the structure and ideology of Chinese and Indian empires:

> As with the Holy Roman Empire in Europe and the Moghul Empire in India, in China also the *de facto* independence of the Provinces and the formal vassals was never regarded as inconsistent with the *de jure imperium* of the *hwangti, sarvabhauma* or "world sovereign."

China, quite as much as India, was "a 'pluralistic universe' in spite of the 'fundamental unity' of cultural 'ideals' pervading the entire area." The internecine wars and revolts that erupted were "neither racial nor religious, but fundamentally territorial or provincial." Just as the rule of Muslim sovereigns in India was "not an alien rule," so also the rule of the Mongols and the Manchus in China was "not a foreign rule."[42]

"Revolutions constitute the assertion of new stronger forces," in Sarkar's definition, "and all history is the document of these assertions."[43] The turbulence in China in the aftermath of the republican revolution was not so different from what happened in France after the French Revolution. Sarkar wanted Asia and Europe to be judged by the same measure. Before leaving China, he recorded the death of Yuan Shikai on June 6, 1916 and speculated on the future direction of the Chinese republic. He could see that the fate of the whole of Asia along with China's hinged largely on the eventual outcome in Europe's twentieth-century Kurukshetra.[44]

Asian Encounters during a European War

The search for new imaginations of Asia was matched by efforts to turn the continent into a connected field of political resistance to Western imperialism. Exactly at the same time as Benoy Kumar Sarkar made his voyage across the Pacific in May 1915 for his scholarly exploration of Japan and China, a Bengali revolutionary was finding his way from Calcutta across the Bay of Bengal and the South China Sea in search of political refuge in Japan. The passenger manifest of the *Sanuki Maru* that sailed from Calcutta on May 12, 1915 included the name of one P. N. Tagore, who claimed to be a nephew and secretary of Rabindranath Tagore and that he was traveling ahead to make arrangements for the poet's forthcoming visit. The previous day, Basanta Kumar Biswas, a young man who had hurled at bomb at Charles Hardinge as he ceremonially entered Delhi on an elephant on December 24, 1912, had been hanged in a Punjab prison. Rashbehari Bose had supervised that daring plot to assassinate the British viceroy but had managed to elude the dragnet of intelligence operatives. In February 1915, he masterminded a string of mutinies in British Indian garrisons all the way from Lahore to Singapore. Leaks in the conspiracy meant that the uprisings were not properly synchronized and crushed with a heavy hand.[45] With the police closing in on him, Rashbehari Bose adopted the disguise of the fictitious P. N. Tagore. The *Sanuki Maru* brought him to Kobe via Singapore and Shanghai in about three weeks.[46]

Exploiting the war crisis, Indian freedom fighters were keen to foment armed insurrections in India by smuggling in German and Turkish arms. The Ghadar global network of revolutionaries stretched from the west coast of the United States through Berlin and Istanbul to myriad port cities in Asia. One group made its way to the capital of the Ottoman Empire in May 1915 and had an audience with the sultan and Enver Pasha, leader of the Young Turks in 1908 and now war minister. After receiving their promises of support, Mahendra Pratap and Mohammed Barakatullah made their way to Afghanistan, where on December 1, 1915, they proclaimed themselves president and prime minister, respectively, of a provisional government of free India. A vacillating Afghan emir and the lack of effective German support undermined their efforts from India's northwest. Taraknath Das and M. P. T. Acharya went from Istanbul in the direction of Palestine and Egypt to stir disaffection among Indian soldiers in the Suez zone. The British Indian army suffered a debacle in the Mesopotamian campaign at Kut-al-Amara between November 1915 and April 1916.[47] This should have provided a real opportunity for those trying to wean away Indian soldiers from their loyalty to the colonial masters, but the moment was lost.

There seemed to be better prospects for Indians abroad at the other end of the continent in East Asia. Lala Lajpat Rai was in Japan in the latter half of 1915 after his visits to the United States and Turkey. He adopted a "don't ask, don't tell" policy when he met Rashbehari Bose in the guise of P. N. Tagore. Lajpat Rai and Rashbehari Bose were befriended by Shumei Okawa, who had been inspired by Okakura's books to take forward the Asianist cause.[48] On December 27, 1915, the Indian Association held a meeting at the Seiyoken restaurant in Tokyo ostensibly to celebrate the coronation of the Taisho emperor. Lajpat Rai offered his good wishes to the imperial family and called on Japan to play a leading role in the liberation of Asia. Okawa was able to assemble a number of important Japanese guests, including Masaharu Anesaki, recently returned from his stint at Harvard, and Masayoshi Oshikawa, a member of the Imperial Diet. Both spoke in support of the quest for Indian freedom. However, the day after this successful event, the Japanese government under pressure from the British ordered the deportation of Rashbehari Bose and another Indian revolutionary, Herambalal Gupta, who had come from the United States. Toyama Mitsuru, the leader of the Kokuryukai, gave the Indians protection. They were then taken to Nakamuraya, a restaurant in Tokyo, where the owners, Aizo and Kokku Soma, kept them in hiding. Gupta later returned to the United States while Rashbehari Bose married one of the Soma daughters, Toshiko, in 1918 and acquired Japanese citizenship in 1923. The Nakamuraya curry with its Indian flavor would become a featured item on the restaurant's menu for decades to come.[49]

Another Indian revolutionary, Narendranath Bhattacharya, traveling under the assumed names Reverend C. A. Martin and Mr. White, had been trying to arrange arms shipments since April 1915 from Batavia and Manila in support of Jatindranath Mukherjee or Bagha Jatin (Tiger Jatin). Jatin died after a battle with British police outside Balasore in Orissa on September 10, 1915. "Martin" then traveled to Japan where he met Rashbehari Bose and Sun Yat-sen. He broached with the latter a plan to smuggle arms from Yunnan to eastern India with German help. With the Japanese government close on his heels, "Mr. White" moved to Shanghai and sought German assistance in his plans. He seemed to have mistakenly believed that Sun Yat-sen had a role in the Yunnan insurrection. Narendranath Bhattacharya eluded British operatives tracking his movements and managed to return to Japan before crossing the Pacific in May 1916. Upon arrival in San Francisco the next month, he was taken under the wings of Dhan Gopal Mukerji at Stanford who suggested that he change his name to the humanistic and casteless Manabendra Nath Roy or M. N. Roy for short. The name change symbolized the beginning of a new trajectory in his political development.[50]

Rabindranath Tagore's visit to Japan, postponed in August 1915, eventually began on May 29, 1916. As he disembarked the *Tosamaru* in Kobe, his Japanese friends Yokoyama Taikan, Katsuta Shokin, Sano Jinnosuke, and Kawaguchi Ekai were on hand to welcome him. The artists Taikan and Katsuta had visited Calcutta, Sano had taught jujitsu in Santiniketan, and Kawaguchi was well traveled in Bengal and Tibet. Tagore was not very taken by the urban sprawl of Kobe or Osaka even though he was warmly received in the garden house of Maruyama, owner of the *Asahi Shimbun* newspaper in Osaka. His mood lifted once he found himself in the midst of "a cyclone of affectionate welcome" upon reaching Tokyo by way of Mount Fuji.[51] A large crowd had gathered at the station and Tagore was taken in a decorated carriage drawn by six gray horses to Taikan's residence near Ueno Park. The streets were lined with people who shouted, "Banzai, banzai" as the poet passed. On June 5, 1916, Tagore settled down comfortably in his friend Taikan's home. The young artist Mukul Dey accompanying Tagore was especially thrilled to see Taikan and his art at close quarters. He organized an exhibition of paintings of the Bengal school at the Nippon Bijutsuin which received favorable notice in the Japanese press.[52]

Tagore delivered his first formal lecture at Tokyo Imperial University on June 11, which was followed the next day by a grand reception in Ueno Park attended by 200 Japanese citizens led by the prime minister, Okuma Shigenobu. Tagore chose to speak at the reception in Bengali and was interpreted by Kimura, who had spent eight years in Calcutta. Count Okuma imagined the poet had spoken in English but following Kimura's translation agreed with Tagore that Japan risked losing its ancient Bushido and it would be against its innate nature to fully embrace modern Europe. The Buddhist scholar Takakusu spoke in honor of the distinguished visitor.[53]

Japanese beauty and hospitality charmed Tagore. Even Japanese poetry evoked images, not music, for Tagore. He was impressed with the sparse quality of Japanese art and poetry. In his travelogue *Japan Jatri* (Traveler to Japan), he gave a couple of Bengali renderings of three-line Basho poems:

Purono Pukur,	*(Old Pond,*
Banger Laph,	*Frog's Jump,*
Jaler Shabda.	*Water's Sound.)*
Pocha Dal,	*(Rotten Branch,*
Ekta Kak,	*One Crow,*
Sharatkal.	*Autumn.)*

Tagore was struck by the Japanese readers' ability to visualize poetry.[54] In private correspondence, he noted that the Japanese had achieved excellence in visual rather than aural faculties.[55] Tagore made it a point to visit Okakura's home and was warmly received by his family (see figure 3.2).

While staying as a guest of the Japanese merchant and art patron To-mitaro Hara in Hakone, Tagore turned his attention to drafting lectures that he had been invited to deliver in the United States. He occasionally traveled to Tokyo for speaking engagements. Japan's expedition on the path of nationalistic imperialism worried and repulsed Tagore. "What is dangerous for Japan," Tagore declared, "is not the imitation of the outer features of the West, but the acceptance of the motive force of western nationalism as her own."[56] In Japan, Tagore had a thoughtful sounding board for his ideas in Charles Freer Andrews. On being read a draft of Tagore's lecture "The Cult of Nationalism," Andrews suggested that Tagore was confusing the distinct concepts of nation and state.[57] Tagore declined to take that criticism on board. Yet Andrews, to whom Tagore dedicated his book *Nationalism* (and also *Personality*), had a point. World War I, which Tagore saw as "the war of retribution" was in origin a conflict between European nation-states. Another of Tagore's traveling companions, William

3.2 Rabindranath Tagore with the family of Okakura Tenshin, 1916 (Reproduction courtesy of Rabindra Bhavana, Visva Bharati)

Pearson, introduced the French scholar activist Paul Richard to the poet. Paul and his wife, Mirra, had been editing Aurobindo's journal *Arya* in Pondicherry and their paths crossed with Tagore's in Japan. The Richards were swept up by the intellectual and political currents advocating Asian unity. At Pearson's insistence, Tagore contributed a foreword to Paul Richard's book *To the Nations.*[58]

Yone Noguchi observed that the large audience listening to Tagore's rebuke of Japan for embracing the tenets of European nationalism was "distinctly divided into two opinions." Tagore criticized not only Japan but also the "spirit of extermination" that was "showing its fangs in another manner" in California, Canada, and Australia "by inhospitably shutting out aliens through those who themselves were aliens in the land they now occupy." According to Noguchi, what Tagore presented to "the well-balanced intellectual Japanese minds" was the following:

> How can we properly check the western invasion? Again, how can we keep our own beauty and strength grown from the soil a thousand years old and let them realize the fullness of their nature, not curtailing all that is best and true in them at the threatened encroachment of foreign elements? After all, he only presents this great momentous question; and like any other prophet, he does not answer the question. Only pointing the way by his inspired hand unseen but sure; it is our work to solve.[59]

Some Japanese intellectuals were no doubt willing and eager to engage with the Tagorean critique. But the enthusiastic crowds were missing when Tomitaro Hara bade farewell to his guest as he boarded the *Canada Maru* for his transpacific voyage on September 7, 1916.[60]

Within days of the poet's departure, a young Indian revolutionary from the United States arrived in Japan by the *Tanyo Maru* on September 11, 1916. In August 1915, he had presided over an International Students' Reunion in Berkeley that had brought together Indian, Chinese, and Japanese students in the United States. On his arrival in Japan, Taraknath Das immediately got in touch with Rashbehari Bose and Sun Yat-sen to explore the possibility of arms shipments from China to India. His efforts on that front in Peking and Shanghai did not bear fruit, but he achieved more success as a public intellectual than as a secret revolutionary. In March 1917, Das published from Shanghai a short book titled *Is Japan a Menace to Asia?* His reasoning in answering that question was not much different from what had been offered by Benoy Kumar Sarkar toward the end of his Japan travelogue. He invoked Tagore in his preface to buttress his view of Japan as a potential leader in the fight for Asian liberation. Tang Shaoyi, former prime minister of the Chinese republic, wrote an introduction in which he endorsed Das's conclusion that Japan was "a menace to European aggression in Asia." However, Das had made it clear that the Indian people would "never welcome the Japanese or any other yoke in place of the present one." Ichiro Tokutomi, editor of the *Kokumin Shimbun* and a member of the upper house of Japan's Imperial Diet, contributed an appendix, and the book sold well in Japan. The pro-British Shanghai journal the *Far Eastern Review* noted its significance as a political document even while criticizing it as a sophisticated Asian version of Boxerism.[61]

On board the *Tanyo Maru,* Taraknath Das had been befriended by two American women—Ellen La Motte, niece of the business tycoon Alfred du Pont of Delaware, and Emily Chadbourne, sister of the Chicago-based industrialist Charles Crane. They continued to meet in Shanghai and Tokyo. Das tutored Ellen and supplied her with materials on the problem of opium that eventually resulted in two books by La Motte on that subject in the early 1920s.

In Japan, Das published another book, *Isolation of Japan in World Politics,* in June 1917, calling on the Japanese to disown their alliance with Britain and rally to the cause of Asian independence. Shumei Okawa wrote an introduction to this book, which came out in Japanese. La Motte and Chadborne carried the manuscript to New York for publication in English. Despite knowing Okuma Shigenobu, Toyama Mitsuru, and Inukai Tsuyoshi, Das as an American citizen could not avoid being hounded by the British and being served an extradition order by the United States once it entered the war in April 1917. He had to face trial in the Hindu-German Conspiracy Case against Ghadar activists. Heading back to San Francisco on the *Siberia Maru,* he wrote in the journal of a Japanese fellow passenger: "Japan, China and India should cooperate for Asian Independence. All Asian nations should regard Japan as the leader of Asia, but Japan must prove by her actions that she is striving to free Asia."[62] In September 1920, Taraknath Das wrote a lead article in the inaugural issue of the *Independent Hindustan* calling for friendly ties between China and Japan as well as "American support against British and other imperialisms in Asia." His concluding exhortation had strong echoes of Benoy Kumar Sarkar's rhetoric: "It is the proud privilege of all, particularly of Young Japan, Young China and Young India, nay, Young Asia, to work unceasingly for bringing about a Sino-Japanese understanding as the first and foremost requisite for Asian Independence."[63]

Young Asia's Futurism

Several variants of Asian universalism were articulated during World War I. For Indian and Chinese revolutionaries, Japan was a base or a refuge for political action. Among scholars and intellectuals, Benoy Kumar Sarkar had come to Japan and China mainly to learn while Rabindranath Tagore journeyed to Japan and the United States primarily to teach his ethics of the imperative to rise above the nation. The poet philosopher was not always able to navigate his way around the pitfall of making an East-West or Asia-versus-Europe dichotomy even though he was always careful to offer caveats and invariably dedicated to keeping the lines of transcontinental communication and conversation open. It was Sarkar who set about dismantling the comparative sociology of knowledge that during the nineteenth century had constructed the Orient as the inferior other of the Occident.[64] He did so in a series of remarkable lectures and essays on his return to the United States after spending more than a year in Japan and China.

Sarkar's first essay titled "The Futurism of Young Asia" in a book bearing that name published from Berlin in 1922 was initially delivered as a lecture at Clark University in the United States in February 1917 and printed as an article in the reputable *International Journal of Ethics* from Chicago in July 1918. It supplied the leitmotif for the entire volume—namely, "war against colonialism in politics and against '*orientalisme*' in science." Immanuel Kant's three critiques in the late eighteenth century of pure reason, applied reason, and judgment were creative and "led to 'a transvaluation of values.'"

The "diverse intellectual currents among the Turks, Egyptians, Persians, Hindus, Chinese and Japanese of the twentieth century" taken together "should be called the 'critique of Occidental Reason.'" How could political and military triumphs of Europe over Asia lasting no more than a century and a half "entitle the sociologist to propound the jingo cult of difference between the East and the West"? That was, in Sarkar's considered view, "the first question in the Critical Philosophy of Young Asia."[65]

China was "said to have been 'opened' by the Treaty of Nanking" at the end of the Opium War in 1842. The "futurists of Young Asia" remembered the event very differently as "the first term in a series of the law of the gun in China." A "systematic mal-application of the comparative method" by researchers and a dissemination of their opinions widely through "movies, theaters, and journals" had turned Asia into "a synonym for immorality, sensuousness, ignorance, and superstition." The modern present was no doubt "the age of pullman cars, electric lifts, bachelor apartments, long distance phones, Zeppelins and the 'new woman.'" However, the Eur-American scholars in "their Oriental studies" mistakenly assumed these to have been "the inseparable features of the Western world all through the ages." Modernization, as Sarkar saw its denouement, was "neither the mono-poly of the whites, nor a very complicated and difficult process." Japan had certainly picked it up quite easily between 1853 and 1905. "Young Asia does not want sympathy or charity," Sarkar declared. "The demand of Young Asia is justice—a justice that is *to be interpreted by itself* [emphasis added] on the achievements of its own heroes."[66]

Dwelling on the "fallacies of neo-liberalism," Sarkar warned Asians not to believe in "the *ignis fatuus* of Western good-will." He accused "Western liberals" of being "ignorant of the conditions of foreign commerce and empire in Asia." How could they "forget the fact that justice in home politics has ever gone hand in hand with injustice and tyranny abroad"? His clarion call to cosmopolitanism was grounded on "the principle of race equality in international relations." He stated the demand of young Asia in unequivocal terms:

> The New Asia wants the New Europe and the New America to admit, as principle, that their peoples must not by any means command greater

privileges in the Orient than the oriental peoples can possibly possess within the bounds of the Occident. . . . The doctrine of international reciprocity is the first article of faith in the gospel of Young Asia. . . . Young Asia wants Eur-America to realize that democratic emotions and ideals are not the monopoly of occidental race-psychology.

Sarkar gave a number of examples to support his claim about the deep roots of the spirit of democracy in Asia. The Koran taught Muslims that the hand of God was with the multitude. China had its Rousseau in Mencius who placed the people and national gods on a higher plane than the king. The great epic *Mahabharata* advocated resistance against arbitrary rulers, including execution of the tyrant.[67]

Sarkar's theorizing of Asia as a concept on par with Europe was conducted in the metropolitan centers of what he called Eur-America. It was distilled out of the experience of travel and study across Asia and beyond during World War I. In the immediate aftermath of this cataclysmic conflict, the idea of Asia propounded by anti-colonial thinkers and activists would have to contend and come to terms with other universalisms of both the religious and secular assortments.

CHAPTER 4

Multiple, Competing, and Overlapping Universalisms

"WE HAVE BOTH now the opportunity of a lifetime," Mahatma Gandhi wrote in one of his essays titled "Hindu-Muslim Unity," published in *Young India* on May 11, 1921. "The Khilafat question will not recur for another hundred years. If the Hindus wish to cultivate eternal friendship with the Mussalmans, they must perish with them in the attempt to vindicate the honor of Islam."[1] By emphasizing the religious distinction in defining majority and minority, the British had sought to drive a wedge between their Hindu and Muslim subjects since the late nineteenth century. By showing solidarity with Muslims on the question of the caliphate, Gandhi hoped to bridge the divisions being cunningly promoted by the colonial masters. Under Gandhi's leadership, Indian anti-colonial nationalism became a mass movement during the global Islamic universalist moment from 1919 to 1922. If the euphoria over Japan's military victory in 1905 had linked Indian nationalism with Asian universalism, the anguish over Ottoman Turkey's military defeat in 1919 connected Indian nationalism with Islamic universalism. The Bolshevik revolution in October 1917 and the collapse of the Russian Empire opened the alluring prospect for anti-colonialism to forge another dimension of transnational solidarity with communist internationalism at war's end. Vladimir Ilyich Lenin's pronouncements on the colonial and national questions elicited thoughtful and sometimes enthusiastic Asian responses. As for the Wilsonian doctrine of national self-determination, Asian nationalists sought to make some strategic use of it to gain political leverage but figured out soon enough that its scope was strictly limited to Europe. The idea of Asia was refashioned during the 1920s in competition and overlapping with multiple universalisms vying for allegiance.

By March 1920, the khilafat question had become for Gandhi "a question of questions" or "an imperial question of the first magnitude" that overshadowed "the Reforms and everything else."[2] The reference here was to the Montagu-Chelmsford reforms of 1919—so named after the secretary for state for India and the viceroy—which had sorely disappointed Indian nationalist opinion across the board by offering meager concessions at the local level while buttressing British power at a unitary center. If the constitutional reforms fell woefully short of Indian expectations, a committee chaired by Sidney Rowlatt had recommended in July 1918 the perpetuation in peacetime of wartime ordinances that provided for detention without trial and other measures that made a mockery of professions about the rule of law. The first of these Rowlatt bills, or "lawless laws" as Gandhi described them, was enacted in March 1919. Hindus and Muslims joined in a mass movement or satyagraha against it. After civilians were killed in police shooting in Delhi, Swami Shraddhanand, a Hindu leader from the Punjab, was invited to address a mass gathering from the pulpit of the Jama Masjid after Friday prayers on April 4, 1919.[3] The resistance in the Punjab led by Saifuddin Kitchlew and Satyapal elicited brutal repression from the colonial state, including the notorious massacre of hundreds of innocent men, women, and children at Jallianwala Bagh in Amritsar on April 13, 1919. In this explosive scenario came news of Lloyd George's broken pledge not to deprive Turkey of its lands in Asia Minor and Thrace and instead to impose harsh terms at the peace talks in Paris. The first all-India khilafat conference in Delhi on November 23, 1919 expressed gratitude to Gandhi and other Hindus for taking up the khilafat question. "To ask India to celebrate peace while the Khilafat question remains unsettled," Gandhi said presiding over a joint session of Hindus and Muslims at the conference on November 24, "is like asking France to celebrate peace, pending the settlement of Alsace-Lorraine. That Turkey is outside India does not affect the comparison."[4] Gandhi was perfectly comfortable with an extraterritorial anti-colonial sentiment mingling with territorially based patriotism.[5]

Once the brothers Maulana Shaukat Ali and Muhammad Ali were released from internment in December 1919, they became Gandhi's closest political allies in preaching the message of noncooperation with the British government throughout the country. The Khilafat Committee formally adopted Gandhi's noncooperation program on May 28, 1920 before the Indian National Congress did so by a large majority at its special Calcutta session presided over by Lala Lajpat Rai in September. Another legendary leader of the older generation, Bal Gangadhar Tilak, had already blessed the green flag of the khilafat before his death on August 1, 1920. The Congress called for the redress of the two wrongs—the British atrocities in Punjab and British perfidy regarding the khilafat. In October 1920, Swami Shraddhanand appeared in Burma, a province of British India since 1886, to be welcomed by Muslims and Buddhists into the Shwedagon pagoda for a meeting in support of the khilafat movement. The Buddhist leader U Ottama preached unity among all the religious communities.[6] Buddhist, Hindu, and Muslim universalisms could peacefully coexist and reinforce one another at a moment when anti-colonial nationalism was not hamstrung by notions of rigid territoriality. The noncooperation resolution of the Congress was ratified at the annual Nagpur session in December 1920. It was with the support of pro-khilafat Muslims that Gandhi captured the leadership of the Indian National Congress and turned it into a mass political organization.

The mass mobilization of Indians now took place, as Ayesha Jalal has shown, under the sign of two symbols—"the *al-Hilal* or crescent of the Islamic *khilafat* and the *charkha* or spinning wheel of the Indian National Congress." She has also underscored that Gandhi's lieutenant, Maulana Abul Kalam Azad, "took strong exception to the term 'pan-Islamism,'" a position that was shared by the great poet philosopher Allama Muhammad Iqbal. In his 1920 essay "Masl-i-Khilafat wa Jazirat al-Arab," Azad pointed out that "Muslims subscribed to the ideal of universal brotherhood and had a non-territorial conception of nationality." Wrongly dubbed "pan-Islamism," such a broad conception had its origins in early Islam and the

Koranic revelation itself, not in Sultan Abdul Hamid's claim to the khilafat in the late nineteenth century.[7] A strenuous objection to the prefix "pan" attached in colonial discourse to Islamism and Asianism was common to proponents of Islamic and Asian universalisms alike. These spatial imaginations now expanded from revolutionary political action of the 1910s to encompass broader mass movements of the 1920s. What was shared by multiple universalisms of this era was a steadfast refusal to see the nation-state as a natural political unit.

Asianism, Islamism, Communism

Woodrow Wilson's racism has become a focal point of attention and condemnation since 2020. His championing of white supremacy was well known a hundred years ago in 1919–1920, but at that time, such an attitude meshed well with the global power dynamics that buttressed Western imperialist domination. Japan's advocacy of a racial equality clause in the founding principles of the League of Nations fell on deaf ears. The arguments in its favor were rehearsed at meetings of the Universal League for the Equality of Races in Tokyo and marshaled by the Frenchman Paul Richard in a short book, *The Dawn Over Asia,* which was translated into English by Aurobindo and published from Madras in 1920.[8] Paris was not Madras. The newly minted "first-class power" of Asia was still second class in the metropolitan centers of Europe. If this was the state of affairs inside the formal portals of negotiations, it was a forlorn hope that anyone would take serious notice of a petition listing "Demands of the Annamite People" composed and circulated by Nguyen Ai Quoc, the future Ho Chi Minh, in Paris on June 18, 1919.

Even Asian ideologues deeply skeptical of Japanese versions of Asianism were not prepared at this time to abandon the quest for a more generous form of Asian solidarity. Perhaps the most insightful among such figures was Li Dazhao who spent several years between 1913 and 1916 in Japan and studied at Waseda University. On his return to China in 1916, he worked at first as a journalist and then from 1918 as a librarian at Peking University. If Leon Trotsky could envision a republican United States of Europe, Li Dazhao allowed himself to entertain the possibility of a United

States of Asia. Enamored of the Bolshevik revolution, Li offered a redefinition of Asianism in February 1919. Rejecting "Greater Asianism" (*Da Yaxiyazhuyi*) as a camouflage for Japanese aggression against China, Li proposed "New Asianism" (*Xin Yaxiazhuyi*) that would build an Asian union on the foundation of national liberation. "Looking at the world situation," he wrote, "the Americas will surely become an American Union, Europe will become a European Union and we Asians should also form such an organization, which will be the foundation for a World Union."[9] Li Dazhao counted Mao Zedong as one of his students, played a leading role in the May Fourth Movement, and emerged as one of the founders of the Chinese Communist Party (CCP) alongside Chen Duxiu in 1921. If Li Dazhao envisioned a federation of new Asia, the young Mao Zedong realized that China itself had to be a federation of its multiple regions. In September 1920, he argued from his Hunan base in favor of the "self-determination of the people of the various provinces" and pooling of republican sovereignties of "the 27 small Chinas."[10]

In the aftermath of World War I, Moscow beckoned those Asians who could not get a hearing in the corridors of power in the capitals of western Europe. Lenin was not wholly free of a weighty European intellectual tradition flowing from Montesquieu and Adam Smith through Hegel and Marx that propagated a blinkered view of an ahistorical Asia. As Wang Hui puts it, Asia represented "a political type defined as the antithesis to the European nation-state, as well as a social type defined as the antithesis to European capitalism or a transitional space between prehistory and history proper."[11] Even in his characterization of Russia as an Asiatic country, Lenin had imbibed some of the stereotypical notions about the backwardness of Asia. Yet he saw revolutionary potential in such conditions of backwardness and his variant of the doctrine of national self-determination was far more capacious than the one advocated by Woodrow Wilson. His "Thesis on the Colonial and National Questions" adopted at the Second Congress of the Communist International in June 1920 saw a key revolutionary role for the oppressed masses in colonized Asia. He permitted a supplementary thesis by M. N. Roy changing Lenin's proposal for a temporary alliance with bourgeois democratic forces in the colonies to one with national revolutionaries.

For Indian revolutionaries based in Afghanistan, there was no great difficulty in switching allegiance from Germany and Turkey to Soviet Russia. Men like Mohammed Barakutullah and Obaidullah Sindhi now looked the Moscow way and proposed an ideological marriage of Bolshevism and Islamism. The fickleness of Afghan support ensured that the *hijrat* from India to a neighboring Muslim land, theorized by Abul Kalam Azad as an alternative to jihad, ended in unmitigated disaster for the migrants and left men like Obaidullah in the lurch.[12] The Second Congress of the Comintern was followed by a "Congress of the Peoples of the East" in Baku on the Caspian Sea in early September 1920. Standing on the cusp of Europe and Asia, Grigory Zinoviev called on the peoples of the East to wage a true jihad, or holy war, against their oppressors, especially the British imperialists. Enver Pasha made an appearance in Baku even though he was restrained from playing the stellar role he coveted for himself. The erstwhile Young Turk gradually lost faith in an alliance with the Bolsheviks. He died fighting against the Soviet regime alongside Muslim rebels near the Afghan frontier in August 1922. If the bond between Islam and Bolshevism had broken in central Asia, its prospects were still alive in Southeast Asia. The Sarekat Islam founded by Oemar Said Tjokroaminoto in 1912 was the main vehicle for Indonesian anti-colonialism against Dutch rule between 1919 and 1922. At the Fourth Congress of the Comintern in November 1922, Tan Malaka made an impassioned plea in German for a modus vivendi between communism and Islamic universalism, which signified anti-imperialist resistance across the globe.[13]

The khilafat movement in India had a large measure of success during 1921. Energized by Gandhi's somewhat rash promise of swaraj (self-rule) within a year, the boycott of British goods and institutions proceeded apace. In Bengal, a broad foundation of Hindu-Muslim unity was laid under the leadership of Deshbandhu Chittaranjan Das. At the All-India Khilafat Conference at Karachi in July, Maulana Mohammad Ali Jauhar called on Indian soldiers not to serve the British Empire. He and six of his compatriots were arrested the next month and charged with sedition. Before being sentenced to two years in prison in the Karachi case, Mohammad Ali successfully used the court as a stage to communicate his vision of intertwining Indian nationalism with Islamic universalism. Indians seemed to move quite easily from championing the cause of the khilafat to celebrating the military exploits of Mustafa Kemal Ataturk. The revolutionary poet Kazi Nazrul Islam composed his stirring ballad "Kemal Pasha" in October 1921.[14] The Indian National Congress called for a boycott of the visit by the Prince of Wales in November. The shutdown was especially successful in Calcutta and resulted in the imprisonment of Chittaranjan Das and his young lieutenant Subhas Chandra Bose. With Das, the president-elect, in jail, the Congress met for its annual Ahmedabad session in December under the presidency of the khilafatist leader Hakim Ajmal Khan. The year ended without Gandhi being able to redeem his pledge to deliver swaraj. In early February 1922, he suddenly called off the noncooperation movement upon receiving news of an incident of violence in a village named Chauri Chaura in the United Provinces of northern India.

Although Muslims were united on the matter of *hakimiyat,* or divine sovereignty of Allah over the entire universe, they were divided on the question of khilafat, or temporal sovereignty. Until 1920, Kemal had seemed open to the prospect floated by one of his generals of a federation or a "United States of the Ottoman Caliphate." When the Turkish Grand National Assembly decided to abolish the sultanate and appoint a new *khalifa* shorn of any temporal authority in November 1922, Muhammad Iqbal saw it as an appropriate exercise of collective *ijtihad* (independent reasoning) and intellectual freedom.[15] The Indian National Congress met in Gaya for its annual session a month after the crucial decision taken by the Turks. In his presidential address on December 26, 1922, Deshbandhu Chittaranjan Das envisioned "the participation of India in the great Asiatic Federation," which he saw in "the course of formation." "I have hardly any doubt," he went on to say, "that the Pan-Islamic movement which was started on a somewhat narrow basis has given way or is about to give way to the great Federation of all Asiatic people. It is the union of the oppressed nationalities of Asia." This was the first articulation of the vision of an Asiatic federation from the highest echelons of the Indian National Congress. Das had prefaced this call with an enunciation of his ideal of nationalism. "Nationalism in Europe," Das explained, "is an aggressive nationalism, a selfish nationalism, a commercial nationalism of gain and loss. The gain of France is a loss of Germany, and the gain of Germany is a loss of France. . . . That is European nationalism; that is not the nationalism of which I am speaking to you to-day." He contended that no nation could fulfill itself until it realized "its identity with Humanity."[16]

The swing in the pendulum back from an emphasis on Islamic to Asian universalism for oppressed nationalities was understandable in light of the rapid changes in Turkey. At Lausanne in June 1923, the Turks gave up any claims to temporal and spiritual authority over the holy places in the Arabian Peninsula. October saw the formal transformation of the empire into a republic. When the Indian National Congress convened in December 1923 for its annual session in Cocanada, the president, Muhammad Ali, gave a spirited address on India as "a federation of faiths." His lingering faith in the relevance of the khilafat question, however, seemed out of step with the times. Once Kemal Ataturk finally abolished the khilafat in March 1924, the time had come to once more look and travel east, even though Muslim universalism continued to have a long afterlife well beyond Ataturk's peremptory decision.

Asian Understandings and Misunderstandings

The year 1924 was of some importance for a series of Asian crossings and conversations. "I go to China in what capacity I do not know," Rabindranath Tagore wrote to Romain Rolland on February 24, 1924. "Is it as a poet or as a bearer of good advice and sound common sense?" Tagore's hesitation regarding which of his multiple identities to privilege would have some bearing on his reception in China. He had been invited to deliver a series of addresses by the Peking Lecture Association (Jiangxueshe), which in the recent past had hosted John Dewey, Bertrand Russell, and Hans Driesch. Tagore carefully selected his travel companions. The scholar of comparative religion Kshitimohan Sen and the artist Nandalal Bose joined him from Visva-bharati, and from Calcutta University came Kalidas Nag. Nearly eight years after his first easterly voyage, Tagore boarded the *Ethiopia* in Calcutta on March 21, 1924, having expressed the hope that their visit would "reestablish the cultural and spiritual connection between China and India."[17]

The *Ethiopia* followed much the same route in 1924 that the *Tosamaru* had in 1916. The poet was hosted by the business magnate Abdul Karim Jamal in Rangoon. In addition to the enthusiastic reception given by Indians of diverse religious and linguistic backgrounds, Tagore was warmly welcomed in a Chinese school run by Lim Ngo Chiang. A large crowd gathered in Penang to carry Tagore in a procession accompanied by music to the home of P. K. Nambiar, a local lawyer. Sitting on his bed in a corner of his cabin, Tagore had by then composed two of the six lectures he was slated to give in China. A brief stop at Port Swettenham enabled him to take a tour of Kuala Lumpur. The poet's secretary, Leonard Elmhirst, noticed "a political consciousness" in the Malay Peninsula that had not yet taken "an aggressive form." In Singapore, Tagore disembarked the *Ethiopia* and boarded the Japanese ship *Atsatumaru* for the next stage of his journey.[18]

Eight years earlier, Tagore had been impressed by the work ethic of Chinese laborers in Hong Kong harbor and forecast the future rise of China. On this occasion during his halt for three days at the home of a Surati merchant named Nemazi, an emissary from Canton arrived bearing a graciously phrased letter of invitation from Sun Yat-sen dated April 7, 1924. "Dear Mr. Tagore," the founder of the Chinese republic wrote, "I should greatly wish to have the privilege of personally welcoming you on your arrival in China. It is an ancient way to show honor to the scholar. But in you I shall greet not only a writer who has added luster to Indian letters, but a rare worker in those fields of endeavor wherein lie the seeds of man's future welfare and spiritual triumphs." Whether poorly advised or exercising poor judgment of his own, Tagore declined the invitation citing time constraints. Had he accepted Sun Yat-sen's invitation, he would have found how Canton in 1924 had become the confluence of a diverse band of Asians seeking freedom. In Hong Kong, the Singaporean Chinese scholar Lim Boon Keng, vice-chancellor of the newly established Amoy University, came to see Tagore, laying the foundation for future interactions between the Chinese and Indian literati.[19]

Shanghai, not Canton, turned out to be Tagore's gateway to China on April 12, 1924. The young poet Xu Zhimo was on hand to receive him along with a large crowd of admirers. In a city dominated by merchants and soldiers, Tagore foregrounded his identity as a poet because his help is needed "at the time of awakening, for only he dares proclaim that the winter . . . that keeps the human races within closed doors" was going to end and the doors would open. "Age after age in Asia," he went on, "great dreamers have made the world sweet with the showers of their love. Asia is again waiting for such dreamers to come and carry on the work not of fighting, not of profit making, but of establishing bonds of spiritual relationship."[20] He did not like what he saw of the use of Indian soldiers by the British against the Chinese in Shanghai and wrote an article condemning that practice for *Prabasi*.[21] He traveled to Hangchow (Hangzhou) and Nanking (Nanjing) before making his way to his destination, Peking, which he reached on April 23, 1924. There was an "outburst of enthusiasm in the Chien Men Station, on the day he arrived, such as has never been accorded, to any other foreign guest."[22]

The following day, Liang Qichao welcomed Tagore at a grand reception. He would introduce the poet at another of his major lectures as well (figure 4.1). "The meaningless idolatry of hero-worship," Liang said, "is common amongst the peoples of Europe and America." For the Chinese who had "not yet acquired this fashionable habit," the "one great central idea" was that Tagore came from a country that was "our nearest and dearest brother—India." The claim was "not a mere matter of courtesy" but as Liang explained in some detail had "its foundation in history."[23] The formal English translation of Liang's words misses the intimacy and affection expressed by the Chinese savant for the Indian poet. He appears to have spoken with great spontaneity as follows:

> Ha ha! Our old brother, affectionate and missing, for more than a thousand years, is now coming to call on his little brother. We, the two brothers, have both gone through so many miseries that our hair has gone grey and when we gaze at each other after drying our tears we still seem to be sleeping and dreaming. The sight of our old brother suddenly brings to our minds all the bitterness we have gone through in our separate beds for all these years. Ah, ah, we must hold his [Tagore's] hands tight and not let go; we must hug him and kiss him again and again. We must pour out the hot tears we have carried from our mother's womb and soak his huge lovely white beard in them.[24]

Not everyone was as warm and effusive as Liang in embracing Tagore.

4.1 Rabindranath Tagore and Liang Qichao with Kshitimohan Sen and Nandalal Bose, Beijing, April 1924 (Courtesy of the Liang family)

Amartya Sen suggests that Tagore himself may have been partly responsible for eliciting a critical response by a mistaken choice of what aspect of his persona to present in China. A message that struck a chord among a sensitive section of the European literati disenchanted with the crass materialist excesses and brutal nationalist conflicts of the 1910s did not appeal to a rising generation of Chinese intellectuals challenging encumbrances from the past and keen on embracing a materialist modernity in the early 1920s. Sen is also skeptical of the view that the organized left, especially the Communists, orchestrated the opposition to Tagore.[25] Yet Guo Moruo launched a preemptive attack on Tagore as early as October 14, 1923 in *Creation Weekly,* before he could have known what the poet was going to present in China. An admirer and translator of Tagore's poetry during his years as a student in Japan, Guo Moruo was now concerned that Chinese youth might be misled by what he saw as Tagore's spiritualism. Mao Dun refused to welcome him on the day of Tagore's arrival. Chen Duxiu was another scholar activist who had been inspired by Tagore and translated some of his poetry. In 1924, he organized the distribution of handbills at Tagore's lecture venues describing the Indian poet as the upholder of ancient civilizational values that were anachronistic and best discarded in modern times. Xu Zhimo was too embarrassed to translate these propaganda leaflets for Tagore, but the Bengali poet learned of their contents from Japanese friends. Lu Xun attended one of the lectures and sneered at the Chinese on the stage for wearing Indian headgear. There seems little doubt that these Chinese intellectuals displayed all the dogmatic zeal of fresh converts to a new religion called communism in fighting their battles against Tagore and his Chinese hosts.

Tagore gave anywhere between thirty and forty informal talks and some half dozen formal lectures during his month and a half in China. In introducing himself to his Chinese audience, he spoke of three movements that had cast a formative influence on his life. The first was a "revolutionary" religious movement introduced by "a very greathearted man of gigantic intelligence, Raja Rammohan Roy." The second was "the literary revolution" pioneered by Bankim Chandra Chatterjee who "lifted the dead weight of ponderous forms from our language." The third was a national movement that proclaimed it was a mistake to be "indiscriminate in our rejection of the past." "This was not a reactionary movement but a revolutionary one," Tagore asserted, "because it set out with a great courage to deny and to oppose all pride in mere borrowings." Turning to Kshitimohan Sen, he said how he got acquainted with the mystic poets of the thirteenth to the seventeenth century through Sen's study and "was amazed to discover how modern they were." His friend Nandalal Bose would be able to confirm how the art movement begun by Abanindranath was "growing in vitality." As for music, he could speak for himself: "My songs have found their place in the heart of my land, along with her flowers that are never exhausted, and that the folk of the future, in days of joy or sorrow or festival, will have to sing them. This too is the work of a revolutionist." Having presented his modernist and revolutionary credentials, Tagore described his religion as "a poet's religion" whose touch came to him through "the same unseen and trackless channels" as "the inspiration" of his music.[26]

In China, Tagore articulated the principles he believed ought to undergird Asian unity. "In Asia we must seek our strength in union," he suggested, "in an unwavering faith in righteousness, and never in the egotistic spirit of separateness and self-assertion. . . . In Asia we must unite, not through some mechanical method or organization, but through a spirit of true sympathy." He was quite open to accepting truth when it came from the West. "The West came," in Tagore's telling, "not to give of its best, or to seek our best, but to exploit us for the sake of material gain. It even came into our homes robbing us of our own. That is how Europe overcame Asia." The responsibility of Asians, therefore, was to rise from their stupor and prove that they were not beggars. Copying and imitating the West would not do. "We want to find our own birthright," Tagore proclaimed. To students who wanted progress, the poet suggested that there need not remain "forever a gulf between progress and perfection." "If you can bridge this gulf with the gift of beauty," he urged, "you will do a great service to humanity."[27]

The criticisms he received rankled sufficiently for Tagore to cut short his stay in Peking. On May 18, 1924, Tagore took his leave at a final meeting in a university setting. He saw it as "a gathering of intimate friends" and he had "never been so happy nor so closely in touch with any other people." He could see that some had been afraid that the poet was importing the "spiritual contagion" from India that might weaken their "vigorous faith in money and materialism." He assured them that he had "not convinced a single skeptic that he has a soul, or that moral beauty has greater value than material power."[28] The modernist intellectual Hu Shih, who had some experience in building solidarity among Asian expatriates in the United States on the eve of World War I, applied some balm on behalf of the hosts saying that Tagore and his party had "succeeded nobly and admirably in their task" and that he had "become a warm admirer of the poet and his friends."[29]

Despite the controversies generated by Tagore's visit in the realm of politics, Gal Gvili has persuasively argued that the brief sojourn along with the Tagorean influence more generally served as "a vehicle for the Chinese envisioning of pan-Asian poetics." The understanding of transregional connections as emotionally stimulated was reflected in Xu Zhimo's poetry and Wang Tongzhao's literary criticism that absorbed Tagore's sensitive evocation of religious sensibility. In Xu Zhimo's poem "Sunrise over Mount Tai" ("*Tai shan richu*"), the debt to Tagore is obvious. Gvili finds "the ideal of pan-Asian poetics" in its "most realized form" in the work of Bing Xin, who grasped intuitively Tagore's conception of the harmony between the individual soul and the universe and gave expression to it in an "inter-personal poetic form," for instance, in her 1925 poem "Yearning" ("*Xiang si*"). Yet to interpret Tagore as a poet of Asian spirituality against Western materialism, as Gvili does, is to take a blinkered view of his literary genius.[30] Unfortunately, Tagore did not get the Nobel Prize for his greatest poetry and Chinese poets, translators, and critics in the 1910s and 1920s were limited to English versions of his Bengali poems, mostly from *Gitanjali*. Tagore was perfectly aware of this limitation and said to his Chinese audience,

> I am gratified to hear from you that you are convinced that I am a poet because I have a beautiful grey beard. But my vanity will remain unsatisfied until you know me from my voice that is in my poems. I hope that this may make you want to learn Bengali some day. I hope yonder rival poet, taking notes opposite me, will consider this seriously. I will admit him into my class and help him so far as I am able.[31]

Tagore's finest modern poetry celebrating life, love, women, and the wonders of this world was to be composed later in 1924 and in early 1925 to appear in his book *Purabi,* which he rendered as *The East in Its Feminine Gender*.[32]

Tagore's visit also facilitated interactions in the domain of art. He had imagined his China based on Chinese works of art, "marvels of beauty" shown to him by his Japanese host in 1916. These had convinced him that the Chinese were "a great people."[33] During the 1924 visit, his artist companion Nandalal Bose had opportunities to meet Chinese painters like Qi Baishi, Chen Banding, and Yao Mangfu. Nandalal was disappointed to find some of the higher arts of China to have "become infected by the Western virus," but he also praised "marvelous paintings." He dismissed the value of the present that Tagore received from the titular emperor Puyi as no more than "the seal impressed on it." He collected a few beautiful old rubbings along with prints, postcards, and books, including biographies of great painters. He created picture postcards with his own sketches, took photographs, and created a work of art as a gift for the dancer Mei Lanfang, who performed his famous *Goddess of the Lo River* on the occasion of Tagore's farewell from Peking.[34]

Tagore traveled from Peking to Taiyuan (Yangku) in Shansi (Shanxi) Province and then to Hankow (today's Wuhan) in Hupei (Hubei) where he addressed a large gathering. He journeyed by steamer, as Benoy Kumar Sarkar had done in 1915, from Hankow to Shanghai, enjoying the river cruise. He arrived in Shanghai on May 28 and bid farewell to China the next day. On May 26, 1924, the US Congress had enacted the Johnson-Reed Act, widely referred to as the Orientals Exclusion Act, imposing stringent immigration restrictions on Asians. The year 1924 was an election year in the United States, and President Calvin Coolidge promptly signed the exclusionary law. After Tagore's departure, his friends in Shanghai established an Asiatic Association later that year. "There is on foot an important movement to establish Asiatic concord through the common culture of Asiatic nations," the *Christian Science Monitor* of Boston reported from Shanghai. "Inspiration for the movement is acknowledged to Tagore, whose teachings permeate the issued declaration."[35]

After crossing the sea from Shanghai to Kobe, Tagore settled in at the Imperial Hotel in Tokyo for a monthlong stay. Japan was reeling from the aftereffects of devastating earthquakes in September 1923 and January 1924. Tagore's Japanese hosts were angry about the exclusionary law in the United States contravening the so-called gentlemen's agreement of 1917. Tagore met Rashbehari Bose and his family, who made sure that the poet felt comfortable in Japan.[36] Tagore's message of the intrinsic relationship between beauty and hospitality had a friendlier reception in Japan than in China. In Japan, the Asian universalist turn in the domain of art was alive and well. Nandalal Bose had the privilege of being hosted by Kampo Arai as well as Tagore's friend Yokoyama Taikan and was introduced to masterpieces of Japanese art. In an address to women, Tagore recalled his 1916 visit to Dr. Naruse's university where his audience had appeared to him like "a field of white flowers bending their heads gracefully before the spring breeze." He likened Japanese hospitality to "a silent shower of beauty."[37] "I have deep love for you as a people," Tagore told the Japanese, "but when as a nation you have your dealings with other nations you can also be deceptive, cruel and efficient in handling those methods in which the western nations show such mastery." He urged his hosts to exorcise the demon called Nation in the interest of peace.[38] Sun Yat-sen would deliver much the same message on his trip to Japan six months later.

For now, Sun Yat-sen was in Canton trying to forge a concordat between communism and nationalism. Canton in 1924 became the crossroads for Indian, Indonesian, and Vietnamese revolutionaries under the auspices of a mission of the Comintern headed by Mikhail Borodin. During the first congress of the Kuomintang (KMT) (Guomindang, GMD) in late January 1924 attended by Chinese Communists in their individual capacity came the shattering news of the death of Lenin. The Borodin mission is usually seen as brokering a tenuous understanding between the KMT (GMD) and the CCP by bringing men like Wang Jingwei of the KMT (GMD) left and Li Dazhao, one of the founders of the CCP, onto a shared platform. Under its roof, however, a wider effort at Asian liberation was being mounted by key activists who had relocated from Europe to Asia. M. N. Roy, who had been close to Borodin since their time together in Mexico at the close of World War I, was now his associate in Canton. Tan Malaka, the dynamic Indonesian anti-imperialist, arrived in December 1923 and articulated his dream of *Aslia,* a coming together through a global socialist network of Asian peoples who had lost their countries to the West. He played a major role in convening the first Pan-Pacific Labor Congress in June 1924, bringing together in Canton subaltern workers from port cities of South and Southeast Asia under British, French, Dutch, and American rule. Late in the year, Nguyen Ai Quoc of Vietnam, now using the name Le Thuy, quietly moved into the mansion housing the Borodin mission.[39]

On November 12, 1924, Sun Yat-sen traveled north from Canton toward Peking in an attempt to unify China's south and north through diplomacy rather than a full-fledged military expedition. His call for a new national assembly found resonance among enthusiastic audiences in Shanghai. Before moving farther north, Sun made a quick journey with his wife Soong Ching-ling across the sea to Japan where he had spent many years in revolutionary exile (figure 4.2). A year before on November 16, 1923, he had written a letter to his friend Inukai Tsuyoshi upon receiving news that he had joined the cabinet. In it, Sun had described England and France as "the leader of the oppressors" and India and China as "the core of the oppressed." Japan was "an unknown quantity." He urged that Japan must help China and that Japan must recognize Soviet Russia.[40] This was in line with the thinking of Rashbehari Bose, who had written an article in June 1923 titled "First Recognize Russia" and urged Russo-Japanese collaboration in support of Asian anti-imperialists. Before leaving Shanghai, Sun Yat-sen cabled Inukai Tsuyoshi and Toyama Mitsuru asking to meet them in Kobe. Unable to leave Tokyo, Inukai sent a member of the Diet, Kazuo Kojima, as his representative. Toyama and Sun Yat-sen met after eight years in the Oriental Hotel in Kobe. If conditions improved in China and there was no anxiety about infringement by other countries, Toyama is said to have conveyed to Sun Yat-sen, it would be natural for Japan to surrender the special concessions it had in China. Such a conditional offer from an old comrade bitterly disappointed the Chinese leader.[41]

On November 28, 1924, Sun Yat-sen delivered his most important political address at Kobe Prefectural Girls' School on the significance of greater Asianism (*Da Yaxiyazhui*) in the resistance against Western imperialism. Liberating the phrase from the pejorative meaning Li Dazhao had associated with it, Sun's speech spelled out the full range of supranational solidarity from Russia to Japan and Turkey to India that might be harnessed by Asian anti-colonial movements.

The address opened in a very conventional way, describing Asia as "the cradle of the world's oldest civilization." European countries had grown so powerful in the last few centuries that three decades ago, there was

4.2 Sun Yat-sen and Soong Ching-ling with Japanese hosts, Kobe, November 24, 1924
(Wikimedia Commons)

"no independent country in the whole of Asia." The tide then began to
turn with Japan's repudiation of the unequal treaties forced on it and its
defeat of Russia in 1905. The "colored races in Asia, suffering from the
oppression of Western peoples" regarded the Japanese victory as their
"own victory." Since the suffering of the Asiatic peoples living in West
Asia was more immediate and intense than that of those living farther
east, they were more prompt in responding to the news. That transformative event gave hope to the peoples of Asia and sparked "a series of
independence movements—in Egypt, Persia, Turkey, Afghanistan, and
finally in India."[42]

These stirrings in Asia had been noticed in the West. Sun Yat-sen made
an unnamed reference to the writings of an American author as a prelude
to his discourse on the meanings of civilization. The writer in question was
the white supremacist Lothrop Stoddard whose 1920 book *The Rising Tide
of Color against White World Supremacy* had in Mark Mazower's words "really
caught the international mood."[43] Stoddard was an alumnus of Harvard
having earned his BA and PhD in history from this august institution. His

other institutional affiliation in the early 1920s appears to have been none other than the Ku Klux Klan and his racist book had won praise from President Warren Harding. The "renascence of the brown and yellow peoples of Asia" and "the frightful weakening of the white world" during World War I, according to Stoddard, had "opened up revolutionary, even cataclysmic, possibilities." His opinion that "colored migration" was "a *universal* peril, menacing every part of the white world" influenced the debate about Asian exclusion in America. "There is no immediate danger of the world being swamped by black blood," he concluded. "But there is a very imminent danger that the white stocks may be swamped by Asiatic blood."[44] Stoddard followed up his warnings about being inundated by the tide of color with a 1922 book titled *The Revolt against Civilization: The Menace of the Under-Man*. In it, he cited Grigory Zinoviev's speech at Baku in 1920 to raise the specter of "Russian Bolshevism's Asiatic goal."[45]

"This American scholar," Sun Yat-sen remarked in his 1924 speech, "considers the awakening of the Asiatic peoples as a revolt against civilization." In Sun's view, there were civilizations and civilizations. Resorting to a bit of deft strategic essentializing, he proposed a typology of civilizations drawing on a Confucian dichotomy between the kingly way (*wangdao*) and the despotic way (*badao*)—the one based on the rule of right and the other on the rule of might. Europe on its imperialist mission had chosen the latter path. European civilization in its social context had become "the cult of force, with aeroplanes, bombs, and cannons as its outstanding features" that had been "repeatedly deployed by the Western peoples to oppress Asia." There was another kind of civilization whose fundamental characteristics were "benevolence, justice and morality." For a thousand years, according to Sun Yat-sen, China had been "supreme in the world," enjoying a status comparable to contemporary Britain and the United States. Sun differentiated China's tributary system from the extractive imperialism of the West. China exercised influence flowing from its rule of right, not compulsion, to earn respect from its tributaries.[46]

The contrast between the two forms was clearly delineated in conceptual terms. "The rule of Right always influences people with justice and reason," Sun Yat-sen stated, "while the rule of Might always oppresses people with brute force and military measures." Recognizing the conundrum that imperialists face when they impose dominance without hegemony, Sun noted that people "oppressed by force never submit entirely to the oppressor State." Egypt and India had always "entertained the thought" of freedom from Britain. "If Great Britain becomes weaker some day," Sun Yat-sen prophesied, "Egypt and India will overthrow British rule and regain their independence within five years." To realize greater Asianism, it must be built on the pillars of benevolence and virtue. "Only by the unification of all the peoples in Asia on the foundation of benevolence and virtue," Sun declared, "can they become strong and powerful."[47]

Three countries came in for special mention as exemplars of subjugated Asia. Japan and Turkey were "the only two independent countries" and therefore "the Eastern and Western barricades of Asia." The critique of the rule of might did not entail renunciation of armed struggle to uphold the rule of right. "If we want to regain our rights," Sun Yat-sen said categorically, "we must resort to force." There was a third country that was trying to "separate from the White peoples in Europe" and Europeans had come to consider as "a poisonous snake or a brutal animal." This was Russia whose recent civilization Sun considered similar to "our ancient civilization" and "in accord with the principles of benevolence and justice." He acknowledged that oppressed peoples were to be found in Asia and Europe. Sun's greater Asianism sought "a civilization of peace and equality and the emancipation of all races." In conclusion, Sun Yat-sen tossed a challenge to his Japanese audience:

> Japan today has become acquainted with the Western civilization of the rule of Might but retains the characteristics of the Oriental civilization of the rule of Right. Now the question remains whether Japan will be the hawk of the Western civilization of the rule of Might, or the tower of strength of the Orient. This is the choice which lies before the people of Japan.[48]

In interpreting Sun Yat-sen's Asianism, the twenty-first-century Chinese scholar Wang Hui has seen it as "antithetical" to the Japanese version of greater East Asianism. Wang categorizes Sun Yat-sen with Lenin and Li Dazhao in whose perspective "what makes Asia Asia is not any cultural essence abstracted from Confucianism or any other civilization, but rather the special position of Asian countries in the capitalist world-system."[49] This formulation misses a nuance or two. There was at this time no singular Japanese variant of Asianism and there were several Asian discourses on civilization ready to contest European and American exclusions of Asia from the scope of the civilized. In 1924, a nod in the direction of communist internationalism could coexist with a residual faith in Japan's potential to continue to serve as the fount of Asian universalism.

Although Sun Yat-sen signed a last political testament drafted by Wang Jingwei before his death, the Kobe speech was Sun's final major public address. His death in Peking on March 12, 1925, followed soon on June 16 by the passing of Deshbandhu Chittaranjan Das, removed two shining stars from the political firmament of Asia. In his last speech in Faridpur on May 2, 1925, Das had envisioned a free federation of Indian states in a larger federation of free nations, which was different from Sun Yat-sen's dream of unifying China through a military and diplomatic northern expedition. Das declined the overtures of the Comintern more emphatically than the ambivalent Sun. But on the question of the unity of the oppressed peoples of Asia, their views had been remarkably similar.

Elusive Asian Revolutions

Bolshevism's ties to Asianism and Islamism unraveled during 1926–1927. The Partai Komunis Indonesia had found a niche within the mass-based Sarekat Islam in the early 1920s. It launched an abortive revolution in November 1926 without adequate national or international support, in the face of ruthless Dutch repression, that proved to be a major long-term setback for radical politics. The Communists had occupied a similar position within the GMD in China since 1924. After Sun Yat-sen's death, their relations remained rocky during the military maneuvers and coun-termaneuvers of 1926. Li Dazhao's execution in Beijing, on April 28, 1927, removed the most talented Communist leader at a critical moment. The future of the united front depended to a large extent on the Communists' ability to maintain good relations with the nationalist left led by Wang Jingwei in Wuhan after their falling out with Chiang Kai-shek in the spring of 1927. More adept at revolutionary theory than revolutionary practice,

M. N. Roy bungled this relationship, bringing the Mikhail Borodin mission to an ignominious end.[50]

Asianism in Japan faced challenges of its own during the mid-1920s. Between 1923 and 1926, Rashbehari Bose, assisted by Anand Mohan Sahay, had been urging Japan to take a more generous approach to Asia, especially China. In March 1926, Rashbehari published a sharply critical essay on the Japanese attitude in the journal *Gekkan Nippon*. "The most regrettable thing," he wrote, "is that the Japanese intellectuals who go overboard about the freedom and unity of Asia based on the broad common interests of the colored people show disdain for the Chinese." "Japan, where are you headed?" he asked in another essay in an echo of Sun Yat-sen's question. In early August 1926, he took active part in the Pan-Asiatic Congress held in Nagasaki where he tried to play a mediating role between contending views and interests. Among several stresses and strains that afflicted this gathering was the question of Korean participation and the credentials of Korean participants. The Chinese delegates demanded a resolution calling for the abrogation of the unequal treaties between Japan and China as the basis for unity against Western imperialism. The principal Japanese organizer, Juntaro Imazato, a member of the Diet, was persuaded to accept a version of such a resolution. Rashbehari Bose held the balance between the Japanese and Chinese positions as well as the views expressed on behalf of Korea, the Philippines, and Vietnam. Rising to speak in the final session, he recorded the names of fifteen distinguished contributors to Asia's awakening, including Turkey's Kemal Pasha, Japan's Toyama Mitsuru and Inukai Tsuyoshi, China's Sun Yat-sen, and India's Mohandas Gandhi, Motilal Nehru, and Rabindranath Tagore.[51]

In July 1927, Rabindranath Tagore set off on another voyage of discovery to Southeast Asia. He described this journey as a "pilgrimage to see the signs of the history of India's entry into the universal."[52] Tagore left a vivid record of his quest for a different universalism through his letters that were published as *Java Jatrir Patra* (Letters of a traveler to Java). The linguist Suniti Kumar Chattopadhyay complemented Tagore's literary masterpiece with a learned travelogue titled *Dweepmaya Bharat* (Island India). A visual evocation of the voyage can be found in Surendranath Kar's works of art. Tagore disembarked the French ship *Amboise* in Singapore where he had a conversation with the Chinese literati in addition to engaging with the Indian diaspora. It is here that he first met Tan Yun-shan, who later became the first head of Cheena Bhawan (China House) in Santiniketan.[53] In Penang, Tagore wrote a foreword to Lim Boon Keng's English translation of Qu Yuan's ancient classic *The Li-Siao: An Elegy on Encountering Sorrows*.

During the 1927 voyage, Tagore was especially fascinated by the Southeast Asian variants of the great Indian epics the *Ramayana* and the *Mahabharata*. The Southeast Asian negotiations with Indian cultural forms and products were regarded throughout by Tagore as a creative process conducted by active historical agents. There was no sense of hierarchy in his analyses of the many versions of the *Ramayana* and *Mahabharata*. "India's true history reflected in the many stories of the *Ramayana* and *Mahabharata* will be seen more clearly," he wrote, "when we are able to compare with the texts that are to be found here [in Southeast Asia]."[54] In Karangasem on the island of Bali, some learned men arrived with a set of coconut leaf manuscripts—one of them the "Bhishmaparva" (chapter on Bhishma) of the *Mahabharata*. The chapters of the *Mahabharata* extant in Bali included the "Adiparva," "Viratparva," "Udyogparva," "Bhishmaparva," "Ashramaparva," "Mushalparva," "Prasthanikparva," and "Swargarohanparva." The Balinese were keen to hear from Tagore stories of the missing chapters of the *Mahabharata*.[55] From Karangasem, Tagore traveled to the Gianyar Regency to be engaged in further discussions of the Indian epics by his host.

The Southeast Asian versions of the *Ramayana* and the *Mahabharata* inspired Tagore to offer insightful environmental interpretations of the epics. "In the *Ramayana* here," Tagore wrote, "Ram and Sita are brother and sister and they were married." This version of the *Ramayana* led him to notice some striking similarities between the *Ramayana* and the *Mahabharata*. First, two marriages could then be seen to be at the center of the two epic stories and both were invalid according to "Aryan" principles. The concept of a brother-sister marriage was not unknown in Buddhist histories, but it was outside the bounds of the Hindu shastras. The marriage of one woman with five brothers as depicted in the *Mahabharata* was equally strange and contrary to the rules enunciated in ancient law books. Second, both marriages were enacted as a result of a display in the skill of archery or the use of weapons, however irrelevant that might have been in the context of the eligibility or compatibility for the marriages. Third, the brides were not born of human mothers. Sita was the daughter of mother earth and picked up at the edge of a plowed field; Krishnaa (or Draupadi) was conceived and arose through the performance of a *yagna,* a devotional sacrificial rite of fire. Fourth, the main protagonists of both epics lost their kingdoms and were sent into forest exile with their wives. Fifth, each narrative tells the tale of the wife's humiliation and its revenge.[56]

Having made his argument about the centrality of the metaphor of marriage in both epics, Tagore proceeded to offer an interpretation of the stories featuring weapons of war as an allegory for a key feature of India's environmental history. The inner meaning of the *Ramayana* was located in the episode of *haradhanubhanga,* Rama's ability to rise to the challenge and deploy the mighty divine bow for the purpose of winning, protecting, and recovering Sita. The spread of settled agriculture from the eastern part of Aryavarta to the south had not been an easy process. The *Ramayana* narrated the historical conflict between the agricultural plains and the forests. Echoes of that conflict could also be heard in the burning of the Khandava-vana (Khandava forest) in the *Mahabharata.* This was not about randomly setting alight trees in the forest but a determined assault calculated to destroy the human adversaries who had chosen the forest as their refuge. Indra came to the rescue of those who venerated him, attempting to put out the fire with a thundery shower of rain.[57]

The counterpart of the *Ramayana's haradhanubhanga* is the *Mahabharata's lakshyabheda.* Arjuna had won Krishnaa (or Draupadi) by unerringly piercing the target—seen by him only as a reflection in a pool of water—with his arrow. His feat signified success in uniting with the beloved through an intense quest for devotion. Krishnaa, who emerged from a sacrificial fire, represented a principle that divided India. The five Pandava brothers accepted her; the Kauravas heaped insult on her. The Brahmin Dronacharya was the commander of the Kauravas' army while Krishna was Arjuna's char-ioteer on the battlefield of Kurukshetra. Just as Rama had learned the art of war from Vishwamitra, Arjuna earned his spurs from Krishna, the philosopher of righteous war. Krishna was Krishnaa's friendly protector who had answered her call and saved her when the Kauravas had tried to dishonor her in their court. The forest through which Rama roamed with Sita was the forest of the non-Aryans. The forest to which the Pandavas had returned with Krishnaa was the forest of the Brahmins. Krishnaa's bountiful plate was the source of grain for the guests of the forest. To the tension between forest and agricultural plains in India was added the tussle between Vedic religion and the dharma of Krishna. In Lanka, the citadel of non-Aryan power, the Aryans triumphed. Kurukshetra, the bastion of the antagonists of Krishna, witnessed the victory of the Pandava devotees of Krishna. In all history, Tagore argued, the apparent battle over material resources is ever accompanied by a deeper struggle over theory or doctrinal faith. The expansion of agriculture had a more powerful parallel in the broadening of the mind seeking truth. Those wedded to narrow conventions of the past clung to Vedic mantra as the ultimate at a time when those traveling on the wider path embraced the supreme being with loving devotion. By the time Buddha started preaching his *dhamma,* the Brahmin-Kshatriya conflict of opinion had cleared the ground for his message to receive a positive response.[58]

There was one other keen insight that Tagore gleaned from the epic story of the *Ramayana.* The field of agriculture could be ruined in two different ways—first, an unruly disruption from without and second, one's own uncaring attitude. When Ravana abducted Sita, it was still possible for Rama to be reunited with her. But when Rama's callous indifference led to the Rama-Sita split, mother earth opened up to take her daughter back. The twins born to Sita in exiled neglect had been named Lava and Kusha. The etymological meaning of Lava, Tagore noted, was "to cut" or "sever." And Kusha represented the reeds that grew on marshy frontiers and destroyed cultivable crops. He asked the pundits to ponder the significance of the birth of Lava and Kusha at the same time.

Upon reaching Java, Tagore was enchanted by the extent to which stories of the *Ramayana* and *Mahabharata* had been internalized and interpreted by the Muslim Javanese. As he watched a dance performance in Suryakarta of the fight between Indrajit, the educated demon prince of Lanka, and Hanuman, the heroic monkey, Tagore was impressed by the tasteful and innovative costumes designed for the dancers. Hanuman was not portrayed in Java as a comic character, as was usually the case in Bengali popular theater. The Javanese rose to the challenge of capturing the "humanity" (*manushyatwa*) of Rama's ally from the animal kingdom. In contrast to the Bengali penchant for the length of Hanuman's tail and the expressions of his burned face, the Javanese conveyed the greatness of Hanuman exemplified in his spirit of dedicated service and sacrifice. Indrajit, too, was a picture of beauty. Their war dance was choreographed to an exquisite musical harmony and achieved a perfect balance between beauty and strength. The characters of the epics were more alive and better known in Java, Tagore asserted, than in India.[59]

Tagore found that the Javanese had made the stories of the *Ramayana* and the *Mahabharata* completely their own. Dance was their favored language of expression. In Suryakarta, two women played the roles of Arjuna and one of his more obscure antagonists, Subal. The sultan's brother himself played the role of Ghatotkacha. In Indian versions, Ghatotkacha was the son of Bhim, the second Pandava brother, and a demon named Hirimba. In the Javanese tale, Ghatotkacha married Bhargiva (Bhargavi), Arjuna's daughter, and they had a son named Shashikiran. The Javanese dance did not depict Ghatotkacha as a warrior but rather his wistful longing for his beloved Bhargiva who was far away. In the climax, he flew away in search of the woman he loved. The Javanese did not attach false wings to Ghatotkacha in the manner of angels in the European artistic tradition. A piece of cloth was sufficient to allude to the movement of flying in the dance. The Javanese seemed to have imbibed Kalidasa's injunction in his drama *Shakuntala—rathabegam natyati*—the movement of the chariot had to be expressed through the dance and not by a chariot.[60]

In Yogyakarta, a Dutch scholar explained to Tagore that Yogya was a variant of the original name Ayodhya. The sultan's family performed the story of the killing of the great bird Jatayu in the *Ramayana*. Jatayu's wings had been clipped as the gallant bird rushed to the aid of Sita when Ravana abducted her. Rhythmic movement and imagery formed the basis of Javanese aesthetics in the performative arts. Tagore lamented the lack of more comparative studies of the epic. "One day some German scholar will do this work," he wrote. "After that by protesting against or substantiating that thesis we will earn Ph.D.'s in the university."[61] Tagore pursued the Buddhist and *Ramayana* connections further in Siam on his return journey to India. His poem "Siam," composed on October 11, 1927, gave a final expression to his search for traces of Indian universalism in Southeast Asia:

> Today I will bear witness
> to India's glory
> that transcended its own boundaries
> I will pay it homage
> outside India at your door.[62]

Tagore made a final visit to East Asia on his way back from the United States in 1929. By then, it was the continued discriminatory policies and practices of the West that prevented internal fissures in Asia from breaking out into the open. Tagore was especially grateful for the shelter of Japanese hospitality in May 1929, after a humiliating encounter with US immigration officials in Los Angeles. The captain and crew of the Japanese ship *Taiyo Maru* observed the poet's sixty-eighth birthday on May 6, 1929, with a grand celebration. On board the ship, Tagore composed a poem titled "A Weary Pilgrim" for the *Asahi Shimbun:*

> Send thy welcome signal,
> O Rising Sun,
> Open the golden gate at the ancient
> Shrine of the East
> Where dwells the spirit of Man,
> Great as the grass that blesses the lowly dust,
> And meek as the mountain under stars.[63]

Once in Tokyo, he called for Japanese statesmanship to be conducted with sympathy and understanding toward its weaker neighbors.[64]

Tagore's stopover in Vietnam on his way home in June 1929 was reminiscent of his mixed reception in China five years earlier. Once again, the poet seemed to have admirers and detractors in almost equal measure. Quite a few literary and political figures embraced Tagore in their quest to find a place for Vietnam in a larger anti-colonial entity named Asia. His critics derided what they saw as his elitism and opulent lifestyle, symbolized by his willingness to drink champagne, which set him apart from subaltern or underground Asian networks. Soon after his departure for India, two poems were published in the journal *Duoc Nha Nam* (Vietnamese flame) giving him a stellar position in a shared Asian cultural ecumene. The second poem would have warmed Tagore's heart:

> A thousand autumns as the bearded wise man
> I have long heard words about you [Tagore]
> Only now can I see you here
> You are a star of the Asian sky.[65]

This was just before dark clouds of the Great Depression appeared on the Asian firmament.

CHAPTER 5

Asia in the Great Depression

"IN THE EXTREMES of honor and of serfdom accorded to its Womanhood," the planners of an All-Asian Women's Conference proclaimed on Christmas Day, 1929, "Asia is one." Okakura's claim at the turn of the twentieth century was now being significantly modified by the votaries of a women's Asia. In a document on the need for such a conference, they expressed concern about "the tides of Western influence" sweeping across Japan, Turkestan, and India. "The power to sift what is essential, what is appropriate for Asia from this surging life can only be wisely gained," they maintained, "if ASIA AS ASIA gets together to review her own uniqueness, if she takes stock of her own assets of civilization." One of the early responses to this call came from Rabindranath Tagore. He wrote on March 2, 1930, "The consolidation of the cultural consciousness of the Orient is the preliminary step for the enrichment of world culture and as women are the fundamental custodians of the cultural life it will be most valuable for them to meet and strengthen their understanding of the gifts that Asia has to offer to the world."[1]

A letter of invitation went out on March 12, 1930, addressed to "Sisters in Asia" signed by an impressive array of fourteen distinguished Hindu, Muslim, Christian, and Parsi women leaders from different regions of India led by the poet and freedom fighter Sarojini Naidu.[2] The city of Lahore, "a meeting place of all races" and the site of the recent Congress pledge to strive for complete independence, was chosen as the venue. The delegates gathered on January 19, 1931, for their weeklong conference in Lahore's specially decorated Town Hall Gardens, which witnessed "lively scenes" and the women in their "beautiful national costumes—rendered more beautiful in the artistic settings, presented a spectacular sight." Sarojini Naidu, the president, was still languishing in prison for her part in Mahatma Gandhi's civil disobedience movement. It was decided that a leader from a different country would take turns in presiding over the sessions each day. Daisy Bandaranaike of Ceylon presided over the first session. The conference opened with a Vedic hymn:

> United in progress
>> United in speech, united in thoughts
> Let our minds approach Thee
>> With the same objects before us in this great gathering.

When the inaugural session closed with Tagore's prayerful song that would later become India's national anthem, "Asia" replaced "Bharat" (India) in the final verse:

> Lo, the night breaks into dawn, the
>> Eastern sky is glowing red at the approach of sunrise,
> The birds break into song, the blessed breeze blows the breath of
>> New life.
> In the young sunlight of Thy mercy
>> Smiles sleeping Asia.
> Bowing her head at Thy feet
> Glory, Glory, Glory! Lord of Universe
>> Lord of destiny of Asia
> Glory, Glory, Glory, Glory unto Thee for evermore.[3]

Even though invitations had been sent to thirty-three countries eliciting many messages of support, delegates from just a few—Afghanistan, Burma, Ceylon, Japan, and Iran—were able to attend in person. Two delegates had arrived from Java but, belonging to the Self-Help League in Indonesia, chose to be visitors rather than delegates because the conference had welcomed women from some Western countries as observers. The idea of holding such a conference had been first mooted by Margaret Cousins, an Irishwoman resident in Madras. The conference held substantive sessions on family, health, education, religion, labor conditions, and the relationship between women and government, with major contributions from May Oung of Burma, Makiko Hoshi of Japan, Mrs. Kamaluddin of Afghanistan, Shirin Fozdar of Iran, and Dr. Muthulakshmi Reddi, Dr. Lakshmibai Rajwade, and Mrs. Hamid Ali of India. Speaking on family and property, Lady Abdul Quadir of Lahore lamented that three great rights given to women by Islam—to choose their own husbands, to rescind marriage as an adult if married off as minors, and to inherit property—were being denied in practice. Ammu Swaminathan of Madras highlighted the right to property and freedom enjoyed by Malabar women as a positive example.[4]

The detailed deliberations in six sessions were followed by the formal adoption of ten resolutions at the seventh session held on January 24, 1931. On culture, the women urged the retention of "the high spiritual consciousness" that was described as "the fundamental characteristic of the people of Asia throughout the millennia." In proposing the resolution, however, Mrs. Ilangakoon clarified the need to select from outside what was right for Asia citing Tagore's interview with the *Manchester Guardian* on assimilating "the best that Europe has to offer." On education, it was resolved "to follow the precedent of Japan and institute and enforce free and compulsory primary education for every boy and girl as the fundamental necessity of progress in the various Asian countries and in Asia as a whole." A third resolution on religion advocated tolerance, love, and harmony among different communities, teaching the lives of great religious leaders in schools, and the study of comparative religion in college curricula. Perhaps the most important resolution was on the equality of status of men and women by the abolition of polygamy, equal rights over children and property, equal rights of divorce, universal adult franchise, and equal rights of nationality for married women. The All-Asian Women's Conference recorded and conveyed its opposition to the Hague Convention on Nationality because of sex-based discrimination and called on Asian women to oppose its ratification or adherence to it by any Asian country. The resolution on health called for greater spending in this vital area and research on diseases peculiar to the East. The sixth and seventh resolutions took strong stands against drinks and drugs as well as the trafficking in women and children. On labor, the conference demanded legislation on a range of issues, including maternity benefits, proper housing, and prohibition of child labor. The final two resolutions demanded the right of self-expression through full responsible government in each country and the representation of Asian womanhood at the League of Nations in Geneva to promote the cause of world peace.[5]

The preface to the report on the conference proceedings asserted that Asia was no longer willing to remain in "a state of tutelage" and was struggling to recover its earlier position as the "Giver of Light to the World." "Western ethic" had been "weighed in the balance during the last war and found wanting," and Asia had discovered the hollowness of "the supposed substance in the much-vaunted Western concepts of fellow-feeling and humanitarianism." The alternative of a women's Asia offered the vision of a different universalism and a colorful cosmopolitanism not denuded of patriotic feeling. "New conceptions of service have sprung up," declared the Asian women's manifesto of January 1931, "which are impelling every Asian country to carry patriotism beyond the narrow limits of the so-called 'National' borders, and it is more than likely that before long Asia will be united in a comity of Nations, determined to deliver the message of peace and good will to the world."[6]

Border Making and Border Crossing during the Slump

This border-crossing ambition had to negotiate the new zeal for border making triggered by the economic crisis of the Great Depression. Asianism was not just a romantic ideal: solidarities in its name and animosities undermining its lofty aspirations emerged within changing economic and political contexts. The biggest economic downturn in the worldwide system of capitalism mattered in setting limits to the possibilities of Asian connectivity. If large-scale migratory flows of labor were disrupted, even peripatetic scholars and revolutionaries of yesteryears like Benoy Kumar Sarkar and M. N. Roy became more sedentary, hemmed in by concerns about national economy and national politics. Yet the urge to break out of borders being hardened by economic constraints led to a range of societal initiatives taking the forms of women's conferences, labor congresses, and Islamic gatherings that still clung to the Asian universalist aspiration. The economic depression altered the tenor of Japanese politics and intensified nationalist conflicts in East Asia quite as much as in Europe. Japan's invasion of China in 1937 battered the idea of Asia and soured the friendship and sparked a debate between the poets Tagore and Noguchi, who had been among its most eloquent proponents. At the same time, the dispatch and experience of an Indian medical mission to China in 1938 underscored the resilience of Asian exchanges and mutual support mechanisms despite political fractures.

The 1930s slump was truly a global phenomenon. A massive downturn in the industrial economies and the New York stock market crash of October 1929 intersected with a huge crisis of agrarian production and prices. Asia experienced the economics of the Great Depression in the form of a collapse in the prices of agricultural commodities and a crunch in the flows of credit. Eur-America erected trade and immigration barriers to protect their own economies facing severe unemployment and froze foreign lending. The value of Asia's exports fell precipitously as prices tumbled of cotton and jute from India, tea from Ceylon, pearls from the Persian Gulf, silk and rice from Japan, sugar from Indonesia and the Philippines, rubber and tin from Malaya, and rice from Burma, Thailand, and Vietnam. As Asia's export horizons darkened, the finance capital that nourished the credit system vital for primary production of agricultural commodities was abruptly withdrawn. Lending and borrowing in its monetary form came to a virtual standstill in much of agrarian Asia.

"And although we cannot yet say what will happen, we can assay in some degree what has happened," John Sydenham Furnivall observed in 1939, "and we can see already that 1930 marks the close of a period. For the crisis of 1929 brought to a head the changes due to the War in the economic relations between Europe and Asia, with their necessary reactions on social and political relations; it marks the close of the period of sixty years, beginning with the opening of the Suez Canal, and, although less definitely, the close of the four hundred years from the first landing of Vasco da Gama in Calicut."[7] If the reference to a reversal of the last four centuries of history was somewhat hyperbolic, Furnivall was correct in noting a rupture with the trends of the previous sixty years. The Great Depression altered not just Europe-Asia economic relations but also tore apart a finely balanced network of Asian connections forged since the mid-nineteenth century.

Since the power of capital lay in its ability to choose its spheres of operation, European capitalists had mainly invested in the new mines and plantations of Asia. Migrant laborers from densely populated agrarian zones in India, China, and parts of Southeast Asia worked in these mines and plantations. The world depression either reversed or arrested these demographic flows. Migration had always been circular in nature, but for six decades until 1929, arrivals had typically exceeded returns. For the first three years of the slump, Indian laborers in colonial Malaya went back to their homeland in larger numbers than those who came in search of work or to join their families. Chinese workers thrown out of work tried to return as well to their own troubled country.[8] Indian and Chinese intermediary capitalists who buttressed the middle tier of the global architecture of capitalism stopped their financing and moneylending operations. The drying up of rural credit in its monetary form was a widespread phenomenon across Asia.

In September 1931, the British pound sterling was taken off the gold standard and the Indian rupee tied to it at a fixed exchange rate of 1 shilling and 6 pence. With the pound and the rupee effectively devalued against gold and the rupee artificially pegged to the pound at a high exchange rate, a dramatic outflow of gold took place from India. Gold flowed out of the hoards in the Indian countryside as a desperate attempt to tackle a generalized liquidity crisis. Gorgeous gold ornaments were stacked up in the currency office in Delhi before being dispatched to London. By the middle of the depression decade, reports from districts suggested that the gold that accumulated in rural India over decades had been virtually exhausted.[9]

The fate of Indian gold and Chinese silver saw both differences and similarities in the course of the 1930s. Between 1929 and 1931, the value of exports underwent a dramatic decline in much of agrarian Asia including gold-based India but not in silver-based China (and Iran). The devaluation of China's silver-based currency helped keep up the value of Chinese exports. The critical turning point for China came in 1933 once the United

States went off the gold standard and launched a silver purchase program driving up the international price of silver. From 1933, massive outflows of silver from China began, and the money supply contracted, causing an acute deflationary downslide of prices. Those who question the monetary explanation for the fall in prices claim that although the silver stock declined, the total money supply in China rose continuously from 1929 to 1935. They put forward an argument about the strength of financial intermediation in China in the 1930s and deny that the US silver purchase policies set off a chain of bad economic events. On this view, China in this period had a free banking system on the commodity standard and that the Chinese banks from 1929 to the currency reform of November 1935 issued real bills backed by reserves and government securities. But the historical evidence from agrarian China, especially the impressive data collected by the Hawai'i-based Institute of Pacific Relations, suggests that paper notes were freely being issued not just by banks but by landlords and grain dealers—indeed, almost by anyone who had access to a printing press. Banking could not be freer and the bills could not be less real. Strong financial intermediation was not a characteristic of agrarian China at this time. Money was tight in the villages, and it was extremely difficult to obtain even a small loan in cash.[10]

As in India, the buoyancy of output and intermediation in certain sectors of commerce and industry may have been at least in part based on the transfer of capital from the rural to the urban credit sector. The great outflow of silver from the hinterland to the coastal cities of China beginning in 1933 represented an unprecedented movement of financial capital out of agriculture, sparked by rising silver prices in the United States, a process not so dissimilar from the outflow of gold in India, which constituted a massive disinvestment by the agrarian sector.[11]

This is not to say that the Wang Jingwei faction in the Nanjing government did not try between 1932 and 1935 to alleviate the crisis in prices and credit in rural China. Unlike the Chiang Kai-shek (Jiang Jieshi) faction that was obsessed with the military unification of China, Wang Jingwei along with Chen Gongbo and Song Ziwen turned their attention to urgently needed economic and financial reform. Using the vehicle of a National Economic Council, they tried to fashion what was called a *minzu* economy that would enable China to achieve a process of self-strengthening in the face of external threats.[12] These efforts, however well-intentioned and able to muster a measure of technical skill, had to face formidable international headwinds from 1933 onward. The Wang-Chiang coalition unraveled by the end of 1935. Ultimately, the finance minister, H. H. Kung, was able to railroad the currency reform of November 1935 through the de facto nationalization of banks. The need for his drastic measures is an indication of the depths of the economic crisis faced by China's silver-based economy between 1933 and 1935.

Japan was hit by the depression much earlier than China with the collapse of its silk exports to America and a precipitous fall in rice prices in 1930. The return to the gold standard in Japan had happened at a most inopportune moment in January 1930. The initial resort to deflationary policies led to a large loss of gold reserves. In December 1931, the government fell, and Japan went off the gold standard. The resulting devaluation of the yen came as a boon to Japanese industries and exports. The British introduced a system of imperial preference in tariffs and trade in 1932 through the Ottawa agreement, which kept Japanese goods from flooding the Indian market and the markets of countries formally within the British Empire. However, the Japanese were able to take over vast portions of the Southeast Asian and West Asian markets, beating the British not just in price but also in the ability to cater to local taste. Writing of the Dutch East Indies, Furnivall reported how in 1932 Japan came to the forefront "in electric bulbs, sheet iron, cast-iron tubing, galvanized iron roofing, wire, wire nails, electric cables, accumulators, bicycles and spare parts, beer, fish preserves, sweets, toilet soap, caustic soda, resin, cement, superphosphates, triplex cases, wall tiles, window-glass, paper, glass-ware, earthenware, haberdashery, small iron ware, bicycle tires and carbide." By 1934, it was "practically impossible to name any category of goods in which European and American industry could compete with that of Japan." Java and the outer islands imported sarongs from Japan for the first time in 1930. According to Furnivall, "the Japanese not only supplied these at lower rates than European manufacturers, but they also attended more closely to market requirements and the popular taste; their goods were both cheaper and better." Once Japan went off gold in December 1931, the last

Dutch economic defenses wilted, and Chinese intermediary merchants switched to importing Japanese cottons.[13] In West Asia too, Japan had carried out a "successful economic penetration" of markets around the gulf displacing British goods.[14]

The economic crisis of the depression era had serious social and political consequences. Mahatma Gandhi launched the civil disobedience movement across India in the spring of 1930 by protesting against the salt tax and land revenue burden on India's peasantry suffering from a fall in agricultural prices and a shrinkage of credit. While giving an impetus to the forces of anti-colonial nationalism, the economic slump also contributed to conflicts along lines of race and religion. In Burma, the Chettiar moneylenders from south India foreclosed on usufructuary mortgages, forcing Burmese peasants to alienate vast tracts of rice-growing land in the Irrawaddy delta. In December 1930, a massive peasant rebellion broke out, led by a Burmese monk, Saya San, directed against both the British tax collector and the Indian financier. In Malaya, the British erected a barrier between the commercial and subsistence sectors by enacting a law preventing the alienation of rice-growing holdings from Malays to non-Malays.[15] E. V. Ramasamy Periyar, leader of the Self-Respect Movement among subordinated castes in Madras province, visited Penang, Ipoh, and Singapore in December 1929 and addressed Tamil rubber plantation workers at large rallies. Chinese laborers thrown out of work in the tin mines squatted on government-reserved land and supplied the first recruits of the Malayan Communist Party. Ho Chi Minh in Hong Kong exile founded the Indo-China Communist Party in 1930. Vietnamese Communists sought to place their imprimatur on the spontaneous peasant uprisings of the 1930s, including the formation of the Nghe-an and Ha-tinh Soviets in Annam and agrarian jacquerie in the Mekong delta farther south.[16]

The depression severely damaged peasant livelihoods in Java, but Dutch repression kept the lid on any serious outbreaks of resistance. Having put down the attempted Partai Komunis Indonesia revolution in 1927, the colonial power now imprisoned leaders of the Perserikatan Nasional Indonesia including Sukarno and Mohammad Hatta. The collapse in sugar and hemp prices along with a credit squeeze caused peasant discontent in the Philippines.[17] The move toward commonwealth status in 1936 as a staging post toward eventual independence received an unexpected fillip from the desire in the United States to toss Filipino products outside hastily constructed tariff walls and Filipino labor beyond the immigration barriers that had kept out other Asians.

The economic crisis of the depression decade turned out to be much longer and deeper than anyone had anticipated in the early 1930s. In West Asia, the prospecting for oil on both the Persian and Arabian sides of the gulf brought about something of an economic revival from the later 1930s. In South, Southeast, and East Asia, some of the ruptures in socioeconomic relationships were never fully repaired.[18] The bond-snapping impact of the depression on the unequal symbiosis of creditors and debtors had lasting repercussions into the period of World War II. Yet the quest for Asian solidarity continued among elites and subalterns alike during a decade that witnessed new expressions of animosity.

Asian Solidarity and Animosity in the Age of Anti-colonial Nationalism

The aspirations to imagine a women's Asia were matched in the interwar period by efforts to bring into being a workers' Asia. In this latter quest, tensions emerged from 1927 onward between the champions of Asian universalism and the votaries of communist internationalism who had until then worked in concert. The parting of their ways was triggered to a great extent by the collapse of the accommodation between the GMD and the Communists in China. In India, the more moderate leaders of the All India Trade Union Congress (AITUC) like N. M. Joshi were reluctant to take orders from Moscow and wanted to build regional solidarity of Asian labor in affiliation with the International Labor Office (ILO) in Geneva. Whereas the League of Nations was dominated by imperial and colonial officialdom, the ILO had space for the voices of trade union representatives to be heard. Asian spokesmen could complain about inadequate representation at conferences in Geneva and hope to strengthen their bargaining power at international forums by forging interregional connections. In the later 1920s, Indian and Japanese labor leaders broached the idea of convening an Asiatic Labor Congress under the auspices of the ILO if possible but independently if necessary. The Communists in both countries veered toward the Pan-Pacific Trade Union Secretariat established in Hankou in 1927. The tensions that had been simmering between the communist and noncommunist branches of the AITUC led to a split in 1929. The reformists including N. M. Joshi, R. R. Bakhale, and V. V. Giri formed the National Trade Union Federation (NTUF) and decided to take forward their plans for an Asiatic Labor Congress.[19]

Such a congress eventually convened in Colombo in May 1934 with labor leaders from Japan, India, and Ceylon in attendance. The Japanese delegation featured Tadao Kikukawa of the Japanese Trade Union Congress and Bunji Suzuki of the Confederation of Japanese Labor and longtime leader of the Japanese Seamen's Union. N. M. Joshi and Jamnadas Mehta led the Indian contingent, and A. E. Goonesinha, president of the Ceylon Trade Union Congress, was prominent among those representing the host country. Meeting under the shadow of the Great Depression, the Asiatic Labor Congress passed resolutions criticizing the Western dominance of politics and economics and in particular the shortsighted decisions to erect tariff barriers that had accentuated the slump. Political demands included freedom for colonized countries of Asia. Carolien Stolte has noted that the media coverage in India and Ceylon was well in excess of the size of the Asiatic Labor Congress and presented under the "twin *topoi*" of "Asia Awakened" and "Asia Oppressed." Newspapers like the *Bombay Chronicle,* the *Times of India,* and the *Hindu* praised the conference as a good beginning on the way to achieving labor solidarity across Asia. The *Hindu* of Madras claimed that India and Japan "may well claim to speak for Asia on large questions of policy." An editorial in the *Times of Ceylon* believed that the congress "would ultimately serve as the panacea for the evils that the Asiatic Worker is subjected to."[20]

The Asiatic Labor Congress met for a second session in Tokyo in May 1937 with just Indian and Japanese labor organizers in attendance. The aim of the gathering was declared to be the removal of "the racial inequalities and the capitalistic and imperialistic domination under which the working classes of Asia are placed." Even though Japanese trade unionists like Bunji Suzuki were opposed to Japan's aggressive China policy, the Indian secretary of the congress, R. R. Bakhale, soon discovered on a mission to find Chinese participants that any initiative from Japan was by that time viewed with great suspicion in China. A planned third session of the Asiatic Labor Congress to be hosted by India with both Japanese and Chinese participation in 1939 remained an unfulfilled dream.[21]

If the streams of Asian universalism and communist internationalism diverged in the domain of labor from 1927 onward, the intertwining of Asian and Islamic universalisms had a much longer afterlife than might have been expected following the Turkish abolition of the khilafat in 1924. "With the collapse of the Khilafat movement and the end of the Ottoman empire," Ayesha Jalal has argued, "the political connections between Muslims in India and West Asia were tested and reinforced rather than disrupted."[22] The Khilafat Committee continued to function, and Mohammad Ali Jauhar attended the first Motamar Al-Alam Al-Islami (World Islamic Conference) at Mecca in December 1926. Indian Muslims had differences in their attitude toward Ibn Saud as the custodian of the holy places and the Saudi hostility toward the tombs and shrines of the prophet and his family in Medina upset many Indian pilgrims.[23]

However, Indian Muslims were at one in questioning the legitimacy of the nation-state form that was being privileged in global affairs since 1919. Mohammad Ali approved of the anti-colonial Hizbul Watani party of Egypt because they "did not worship at the altar of nationalism."[24]

At Mohammad Ali's funeral in Jerusalem in January 1931, his elder brother Shaukat Ali and the grand mufti of Jerusalem, Haj Mohammad Amin al-Husseini, decided to convene a second World Islamic Conference. No one gave more eloquent expression to a different universalism of Muslims in South and West Asia than the great poet philosopher Muhammad Iqbal, who attended the second Motamar Al-Alam Al-Islami at Jerusalem in November 1931. Ayesha Jalal points out that Iqbal "regretted that the spirit of Islamic universalism had been misconstrued in Europe as something akin to the 'Yellow Peril'" in an interview with the *Bombay Chronicle* during his Indian Ocean voyage in September 1931. The specter of "Pan-Islamism" had been conjured up in "the fertile imagination of a lone French journalist." A travesty of Muslim sentiments in favor of unity against European aggression, "Iqbal proposed dropping 'Pan' from the phrase as 'Islamism' sufficed to convey the Muslim desire for a faith-based solidarity that was more of a social experiment than the political project Europeans imagined it to be."[25] Much the same could be said at this time about the needless prefix attached to the sentiments of Asianism.

The Jerusalem conference met during the depths of the Great Depression, which was forcing debt-ridden Palestinian peasants to sell their lands to European Zionists. Although the Palestinian predicament dominated the proceedings, the deliberations also focused on ways to achieve Muslim solidarity after the end of the khilafat. The delegates paid their homage at the grave of Mohammad Ali and said their Maghrib prayers at the Masjid-i-Aqsa. In his farewell address delivered in English on December 14, 1931, Iqbal urged Muslims to meet the twin challenges of materialism and nationalism by seeking spiritual unity across borders.[26]

Another famous Indian poet philosopher and critic of the nation-state, Rabindranath Tagore, traveled to West Asia in April and May 1932. In his book *Parashye*, he recalled his voyage to Japan in 1916 to witness the awakening on the eastern horizon of Asia. Subsequently, he had observed the fall and resurrection of Turkey. Now he embarked on a journey to find out how West Asia, particularly Iran and Iraq, were responding to the challenges of the new age. In *Parashye*, Tagore spelled out in the clearest terms his vision of Asian universalism. Tagore visited the graves of Sadi and Hafiz in Shiraz and claimed kinship with these Persian poets, whose religious sensibility taught the lesson of transcending bigotry. In Iraq, he deplored the past record and present instances of British imperialist aggression and urged his hosts to resend the message of universalism in the name of their Prophet across the Arabian Sea to India. In a poem painting composed in Baghdad, he prayed for the light of the east to bring together those who walked on "the same path of pilgrimage."[27]

For the English-reading public, Tagore wrote an article in the *Modern Review* later in the year titled "Asia's Response to the Call of the New Age." In Iraq, he had been asked by an eminent man, "What do you think of the English?" He had replied, "The best of them are among the best in humanity." His questioner had smilingly persisted, "What about the next best?" Tagore had remained silent because there was "a danger of intemperate language" had he replied instantly. "In Asia," he wrote in his article, "the greater part of our business is with this next best." As a consequence, there was no feeling of respect for Europe any longer across the length and breadth of Asia, and there was also a loss of the earlier fear. Tagore sensed an epochal moment in "the history of humanity":

> Perhaps in the drama of Europe the scene is being changed for the fifth act of the play. Signs of an awakening in Asia have slowly spread from one end of the horizon to the other. The glow of the new dawn above the eastern mountain ranges of humanity is indeed a great vision—it is a vision of freedom.[28]

Tagore's friend Charles Freer Andrews expressed a similar sentiment in an article on "Asia in Revolution" in the same issue of the journal in October 1932 based on a lecture he gave at the University of Cambridge. Andrews observed the entire continent of Asia in "the throes of a vast revolution." "The economic depression in Europe and America," he noted astutely, "has had an intimate relation to the events which are happening in India and the Far East." The theme of the rise of nationalism captured merely "a superficial aspect" of the Asian revolt. A deeper analysis revealed first, "an almost entire reaction in Asia against European domination" and second, "the uprising at last of the down-trodden peasantry of agricultural Asia against age-long tyranny and oppression."[29]

The disenchantment with the nation-state form expressed by poet philosophers like Tagore and Iqbal during their travels in West Asia in the early 1930s was echoed by political activists at the eastern end of the continent. One such figure was Rashbehari Bose in continued Japanese exile who launched a journal called *New Asia* in 1933. "Europe overcame Asia," in his view, "not through our admiration of her message of freedom . . . but through her overpowering greed and the racial pride that humiliates." In an insightful reading of this journal, Joseph McQuade uncovers "the alternative world-historical narratives" in anti-colonial thought that were offered as critique of the Eurocentrism inherent in prevailing concepts of the international since 1919. Rashbehari is seen to have "envisioned a global counter-geography to the imperialist internationalism of the British Empire and the League of Nations" and he did so "by exposing and inverting the global color line on which it rested." Rashbehari Bose found the "entire Colored world" to be "astir against the White incursions" and looked forward to the formation of a "Pan-Colored Alliance" to end "White imperium over the Colored races and regions."[30]

The emphasis on race undoubtedly created blind spots, especially in eliding Japan's aggression against Asian neighbors. Yet the ubiquity of the global color line led many to see it as the primary contradiction in early twentieth-century world history relegating everything else to the level of the secondary. The shared feeling of abjection from being at the receiving end of white racism in Asian and African colonies quite as much as in the United States created bonds among "oppressed peoples" but also a tendency to overlook forms of oppression that did not follow racial lines. In December 1936, W. E. B. Du Bois, the renowned African American intellectual and fighter for racial justice, arrived in Japan to a warm official and nonofficial reception (see figure 5.1). Through him, Du Bois believed Japan was extending to twelve million African Americans a message of "a common brotherhood, a common destiny." He gave a series of lectures in

5.1 W. E. B. Du Bois with Japanese professors, Tokyo, 1936 (Courtesy of W. E. B. Du Bois Papers, Robert S. Cox Special Collections and University Archives Research Center, UMass Amherst Libraries)

Osaka, Kobe, and Tokyo on a wide variety of subjects including Frederick Douglass and African American literature.

Upon his return to the United States, he was prepared to explain away Japan's aggression against China with some realist political analysis. "The [First] World War and the Great Depression," he argued, "made it impossible for Europe to pursue her Asiatic plans. Unless, therefore, Japan took advantage of this breathing spell and made herself dominant in China she would surrender China eventually to Europe." In his opinion, the Chinese owed "their chance for independence today to the fight of Japan against European aggression."[31]

Of Poets and Patriots

Yone Noguchi had long heard the call of the Ganga. He had learned about India from Sarojini Naidu early in the twentieth century and had been fascinated with the poetry and politics of both Ireland and India. Benoy Kumar Sarkar had identified him as a potential intellectual successor to Okakura during his visit to Japan in 1915. Noguchi had close interactions with Tagore and his entourage in 1916, 1924, and 1929 and had been repeatedly invited to India. At the urging among others of Kalidas Nag, he at long last set sail for India on October 17, 1935, arriving to a warm welcome in Calcutta on November 10, 1935. In a poem in his book *The Ganges Calls Me,* he wrote,

> Away from agony and thought at last the Bengal Bay
> Sets my head and foot attune to the low humming of rest.[32]

Noguchi's itinerary in South Asia for nearly three months during the winter of 1935–1936 was anything but restful. It included half a dozen lectures at Calcutta University and several more in Nagpur and Madras, where Sarvepalli Radhakrishnan praised the visiting philosopher. His old literary friend Sarojini Naidu welcomed him in her home at Hyderabad. Noguchi was given an audience by Mahatma Gandhi in his ashram at Sewagram. He attended the fiftieth anniversary celebrations of the Indian National Congress in Nagpur and held talks with V. S. Srinivasa Shastri. Ghanashyam

Das Birla, industrialist and financier of the Gandhian Congress, entertained him on several occasions. A connoisseur of Japanese dance, Noguchi met the dancer Uday Shankar in Bombay and enjoyed his performance. When he visited the home of Sarala Devi Chaudhurani, he found the paintings of *Kali* and *Saraswati* by Yokoyama Taikan and Shunso Hishida that her mother had purchased in 1903 still hanging on the walls.[33]

The high point of Noguchi's visit was the ceremonial reception accorded to him in the mango grove of Santiniketan on November 30, 1935. Tagore and Noguchi were garlanded and had sandalwood paste put on their foreheads as they sat next to each other. Everyone stood up when Tagore's song "Janaganamana Adhinayaka," an ode to "Bharatbhagyabidhata" (Dispenser of India's destiny), was performed in chorus. Kshitimohan Sen, who had met Noguchi in 1924, recited appropriate Vedic hymns, which Tagore then read out in English translation. Some of the lines sent out a warm welcome:

> Friend above all friends,
> Thou art the messenger poet with the vision of the beyond,
> Invite all minds round us here,
> May divine Wisdom
> Hasten to grace this festive assembly!

In his address, Tagore recalled his first visit to Japan where he received a welcome "extravagant in its lavishness." Ever since, he had been waiting for the auspicious moment when he could gratefully reciprocate the generous hospitality he had received. In the intervening years, many visitors had come to his ashram—among them students, teachers, and merchants. "At last the poet has come," Tagore said to Noguchi, "the poet who is the true messenger of the spirit of his people representing the culture, which is national, but above all universal, and of all time." Tagore offered his words as India's greetings to Noguchi and through him to his "nation, which is newborn in a new age, which is ready to claim the crown of deathless glory from the Dispenser of human Destiny."

Destiny decreed a different denouement. Ever since the Manchurian incident of 1931, there had been concerns about Japan's aggressive designs.

Purporting to be the champion of the distressed peasantry during the Great Depression, the Japanese military rose to a position of dominance within the state structure. A series of assassinations, including those of the Asianist prime minister Inukai Tsuyoshi in 1932 and two finance ministers, tilted the balance against civilian political leaders. Yet South and Southeast Asians suffering the yoke of a racialized capitalism and colonialism tended to give Japan the benefit of the doubt. Japan's invasion of mainland China following the Marco Polo bridge incident in May 1937 brought about a major shift in the positions of South Asian leaders who had admired Japan since the turn of the twentieth century.

One of the most incisive analyses of "Japan's Role in the Far East" came from Subhas Chandra Bose, who received news of the invasion while recuperating in the hill station of Dalhousie after long years of imprisonment and exile. In a private letter to a Czech friend, he had described the Japanese as "the British of the East" as early as 1934. Now in a lengthy article appearing in the *Modern Review* of October 1937, he dissected the dynamics of power relations playing out in East Asia. Bose analyzed the economic and strategic motivations behind Japanese imperialism and the choice it had made to expand on the Asian mainland rather than in a southerly direction toward the Philippines and Australia. The Japanese government had ignored Ishimaru's book *Japan Must Fight England* and turned toward its immediate East Asian neighbors in search of markets and materials. Bose showed the ways in which border incidents were stage-managed "as a pretext for Japanese aggression" and "militarism had come to the aid of capitalism." He noted that world opinion was on China's side and prayed "God grant that she may succeed." He remembered how Japan's "reawakening at the dawn of the present century sent a thrill throughout our Continent" and "shattered the white man's prestige in the Far East" and "put all the Western imperialist powers on the defensive—not only in the military but also in the economic sphere." However, he deplored Japan's recourse to imperialism to secure its goals and its humiliation of an Asian neighbor. "China must still live—for her own sake," he wrote, "and for humanity." He closed with a warning to India to eschew the path of imperialism in its own search for national self-fulfillment.[34]

In November 1937, the Chinese Communist general Chu Teh (Zhu De) wrote to the Congress president, Jawaharlal Nehru, seeking India's support for China's resistance. As Nehru's successor to the presidency, Subhas Chandra Bose took up the Chinese cause in earnest during 1938. At his call, All-India China Day was observed throughout India on June 12, 1938. He made another appeal on June 28 for a fundraising campaign between July 7 and 9 to finance an Indian medical mission to China. Speaking at a reception for Professor Tai-Chi Tao, director of people's education in China, at Calcutta's University Institute Hall on August 12, 1938, Bose underscored the "moral value" of India's mission and expressed his conviction that "the Chinese people will in the long run emerge triumphant out of this struggle." The medical mission consisted of five doctors led by Madan Mohanlal Atal with M. M. Cholkar, B. K. Basu, Debesh Mukherjee, and Dwarkanath S. Kotnis as team members. In his farewell message to the mission, Bose referred to the history of intimate and cordial relations between India and China, urging its members to link up with "another oppressed nation":

> Like the Indian missionaries of old our medical men are now going out to China as ambassadors of service, good-will and love. We are painfully conscious of the fact that our gift to China in this fateful hour of her history is but a small one. Nevertheless, behind this small gift there is the soul of the Indian people.[35]

The medical mission set sail on SS *Rajputana* from Bombay on September 1, 1938.

On that same day, Rabindranath Tagore sat down in Santiniketan to compose his reply to a letter he had received from Yone Noguchi. "Neither its temper nor its contents harmonize with the spirit of Japan," he wrote, "which I learned to admire in your writings and came to love through my personal contacts with you." Noguchi had professed that Japan's only enemy was "the Kuomingtang government, a miserable puppet of the West" whose leader Chiang Kai-shek had "sold his country to the West for nothing." Tagore, by contrast, saw the aggression as a war "on Chinese humanity, with all the deadly methods learned from the West." He had "believed in the message of Asia" but rejected Noguchi's "conception of an Asia raised on a tower of skulls." He could not countenance a "separation between an artist's function and his moral conscience" and bemoaned "the destruction of the inner spirit of chivalry of Japan." "And today I understand more than ever before," he concluded, "the meaning of the enthusiasm with which the big-hearted Japanese thinker Okakura assured me that *China is great*."[36]

Noguchi wrote once more to say that no one in Japan denied the greatness of the Chinese people and that Japan was only "correcting the mistaken idea of Chiang Kai-shek" and that Chiang's China was "far more military than Japan." Noguchi asserted that he was "never a eulogist of Japanese militarism" because he had "many differences with it." Tagore responded with "sorrow and shame, not anger" that he could "no longer point out with pride the example of a great Japan." He conceded that there were "no better standards prevalent anywhere else and that the so-called civilized peoples of the West are proving equally barbarous." He ended by wishing the Japanese people whom he loved "not success, but remorse."[37] Noguchi may have been correct in his assessment of Chiang Kai-shek, but in this exchange of poets, there seemed little doubt that Tagore had occupied the ethical higher ground.

The Call of Yan'an

On December 14, 1938, far away in Chungking, B. K. Basu was excited to read Tagore's reply to Noguchi in news reports. Basu kept a daily diary, which remains the best source for the Indian medical mission's work in China. The diary began on Sunday, August 28, 1938: "Started for Bombay by evening train, from Subhas Babu's Elgin Road [home]. Rashtrapati (President) presented me with a lunch box for use in Chinese battlefields and advised me on the various fighting tactics observed during the First World War" (see figure 5.2).

On August 30, in Bombay's Jinnah Hall, the doctors were given a fare-well reception presided over by Sarojini Naidu, who warned "some, or one of you may not return." On September 1, they "repeatedly played 'Vande Mataram' on the gramophone and mastered the tune, so that [they] could sing the song in China."[38]

On board the SS *Rajputana*, Basu encountered Ji Chaoding, who had worked at the Institute of Pacific Relations. He read Edgar Snow's *Red Star over China* and would soon be thrilled to meet the author. On their

5.2 Subhas Chandra Bose with the Indian medical mission, Calcutta, August 28, 1938 (Courtesy of Netaji Research Bureau, Calcutta)

arrival in Canton, Soong Ching-ling (Madame Sun Yat-sen) joined them in a grand welcoming procession in the streets of the city. The doctors then left for Hankou where Agnes Smedley, the American champion of Chinese Communism, liked the marching song composed by the Bengali poet Kazi Nazrul Islam. On October 22 came news of the fall of Canton to the Japanese forces. From late November through December 1938, the doctors spent "idle days in Chungking." On December 21, they had a meeting with foreign minister Wang Ching-wei (Wang Jingwei) who "assured safe transport to Yan'an." Basu was disappointed that people had to buy tickets to meet Madame Chiang Kai-shek and drew a contrast with her elder sister Madame Sun Yat-sen who had happily jostled with the crowds in Canton wharf.

The Indian doctors reached Yan'an in February 1939 to be welcomed by Mao Zedong and Wang Ming. They got to work at the Eighth Route Army Rear Hospital with Tagore's poems from *Gitanjali* for sustenance. A letter from Nehru to Atal brought news of Subhas Chandra Bose's reelection as Congress president. On March 15, 1939, the team had a memorable lunch meeting with Mao in his "cave" (see figure 5.3).

5.3 Mao Zedong with the Indian medical mission, Yan'an, March 15, 1939 (Courtesy of Dr. Kotnis Memorial Committee, West Bengal)

Mao considered the Indian medical mission to be of "tremendous histor-ical importance" and expressed his deep gratitude to the Indian National Congress. He did not think much of the efficacy of Gandhian nonvio-lence and emphasized the crucial role of "revolutionary violence." Cholkar, a staunch Gandhian from Nagpur, stoutly defended the method of nonviolent resistance. Mao Zedong inquired after M. N. Roy and referring to the 1927 events in Hankou said in an understatement that "a lot of damage was done to the great Revolution." The Indians were charmed by Mao's hospitality and his grace and wit. "He who takes more chillies," Mao declared at lunch, "is more revolutionary."[39] In addition to treating ordinary soldiers, the

Indian doctors took care of Zhou Enlai who had suffered a bad fracture of his arm.[40]

On August 22, 1939, Jawaharlal Nehru arrived in Chungking. Much to the disappointment of the medical mission, he did not come up to Yan'an. With the outbreak of the war in Europe, he sent a message that "complications" in the international situation were forcing him to hasten back to India. On October 1, Basu noted the "flying of Swastika and Hammer and Sickle side by side in Moscow during Ribbentrop's visit." Soon thereafter, Atal, Basu, and Kotnis left for the Shanxi front at the invitation of Zhu De. At a Muslim restaurant during the march to Chin Dung Nan, Basu recorded, "We met an aggressively anti-communist American journalist, Theodore White." On New Year's Day 1940, the Indians were treated to a welcome lunch by Zhu De before settling down to the hard work of caring for wounded soldiers on the Hebei front which saw fierce fighting. Cholkar and Mukherjee had already returned to India in mid-1939. Now in January 1940, Atal returned as well, leaving Basu and Kotnis to carry on the mission for the next three years.[41]

Meanwhile, in 1940, a Chinese artist, Xu Beihong, who in his youth had trained in both Japan and France, taught for several months in the abode of peace Santiniketan at Rabindranath Tagore's invitation and interacted with Abanindranath Tagore, Nandalal Bose, and Benode Behari Mukherjee. The idyllic atmosphere of Tagore's Santiniketan enchanted Xu: "The mango trees laden with clusters of fruit, the fiery silk-cotton flowers, the indefatigable, soft-voiced singing of birds, together with Tagore's refined speech and demeanor were to live forever in Beihong's memory." He painted Tagore's portrait and sketched Gandhi during the Mahatma's visit to Santiniketan in February 1940 (see figures 5.4 and 5.5).

From Santiniketan, Xu traveled up to the hill station of Darjeeling where he captured the magic of the Himalayas in ink and in oils. The mountains also inspired Xu to visualize a philosophical work—*The Foolish Old Man Who Removed the Mountains.*[42]

Dr. B. K. Basu ended the daily recording of events in his war diary on November 28, 1940, as he returned to Yan'an, leaving Kotnis in the Shanxi-Qahar-Hebei military region. Germany's attack on the Soviet Union on June 22, 1941 altered the Communist view of the war the world over. What

5.4 Rabindranath Tagore, 1940, by Xu Beihong (Reproduction courtesy of Xu Beihong Museum, Beijing)

was seen as an imperialist war was now redefined as a people's war. The entry of the United States into the war after Japan's bombing of Pearl Harbor on December 7, 1941, enhanced the prospects of success of the Chinese war of resistance. Mahatma Gandhi's call to launch the Quit India movement as the final assault on British rule in August 1942 brought to the fore the stark differences in Indian and Chinese priorities. At a meeting of Communists in China, Ali Aham (Wang Ta-tsai) of Indonesia supported the Quit India movement against imperialist Britain, but the Chinese Communists were determined to focus on the war against Japan. On December 10, 1942, a letter arrived from Zhu De in Yan'an bearing the sad news of the death of Kotnis the previous day of status epilepticus. The year before, Kotnis had

5.5 Gandhi, 1940, by Xu Beihong (Reproduction courtesy of Xu Beihong Museum, Beijing)

married a Chinese nurse instructor, Guo Qinglan, who just months ago had given birth to their son, Inhua. At his funeral, a large number of Chinese gathered to give Kotnis an emotional farewell as they sang,

> You came from the shores of the warm Indian Ocean,
> To brave the cold of North China.
> For the world of tomorrow
> You fought five autumns in China.
> Alas! At the end of a long night
> The fountain of your life ran dry.

Oh, comrade Kotnis, our beloved,
Your image will always be with us,
And your memory will live forever in our hearts.

The one who did not come back became a subject of film and lore in India and remembered with affection in China.[43]

Dr. B. K. Basu finally decided to wrap up the medical mission. An agreement between the Communists and the GMD, who had been fighting each other, enabled him to travel from Yan'an to Chungking. From there, he took an airplane to fly over the hump and landed in Calcutta in July 1943. He was immediately taken to the Great Eastern Hotel to be interrogated by British officers and their Indian underlings. "So I was back in my motherland," he wrote, "where this humiliating treatment is usual for Indians. Later I learned they were all armed because they were afraid I might be an agent of Subhas Chandra Bose, now in Singapore."[44]

Bengal at this time was being devastated by a man-made famine as grotesque as the one engulfing GMD-held Henan. New lines of solidarity and animosity defined the quest for freedom in the famine-ravaged lands of Asia during World War II.

CHAPTER 6

War, Famine, and Freedom in Asia

I N JANUARY 1944, Bibhutibhusan Bandyopadhyay began serializing his novel *Ashani Sanket* (Signal of danger) in the Bengali magazine *Matribhumi* (Motherland). Based on what he witnessed in rural Bengal during 1943, Bibhutibhusan presented a haunting account of an impending famine as rice disappeared from the open market and the moral economy of the village began to crack and crumble. The novel appeared in 1954 as a book four years after the death of its brilliant author. In 1973, Satyajit Ray made it into a film with the title *Ashani Sanket,* rendered in English as *Distant Thunder.* The movie in technicolor missed the nuances of the tragedy that unfolded in black print on the white pages of the novel. But it did bring to the attention of Western audiences a wartime calamity in colonial India that had been ignored by those who remembered only the awful Holocaust in Europe. In 1980, Mrinal Sen went out with his film crew to make *Akaler Sandhane* (In search of famine), which combined an inquiry into the great Bengal famine of 1943 with a searing look at contemporary poverty and hunger. And the greatest of the trio of outstanding filmmakers in postindependence India, Ritwik Ghatak, had a key character in his 1962 classic *Subarnarekha* (The golden thread) utter a poignant lament about an oblivious generation that had not seen the twin tragedies of famine and partition. Yet the memory of 1943 as a precursor to 1947 was not erased and inspired in its intensity the finest creative works in Bengali literature and film.

The question of memory and forgetting is a poignant one, especially in relation to such traumatic events as famine and partition. Having grown up in Calcutta listening to tragic tales about the Bengal famine, I published a comparative essay on three great wartime famines in Henan, Bengal, and Tonkin in 1990.[1] That year, the prize-winning author Liu Zhenyun from Henan had not even heard of the 1942 famine in his province when a friend broached the subject to him. Based on an excavation of his family's memories, Liu wrote a novella, *Remembering 1942* (*Wengu 1942* or *Wengu yijiusier*). Ten years later, a historian from Henan, Song Zhixin, began her research on the famine; she published a substantial, annotated compilation of primary sources in 2005 under the title *1942: The Great Henan Famine* (*1942: Henan dajihuang*). It was not until 2012, the seventieth anniversary of the famine, that a film, *Back to 1942* (*1942*), directed by Feng Xiaogang, was released, based on the novella by Liu Zhenyun published in 1993. A huge box office success in China, the film was panned by Western critics for being too melodramatic. Its importance lay, as Rana Mitter puts it, in enabling "the hitherto forgotten history of the famine to enter the Chinese public sphere."[2] Song Zhixin's book appeared that year in a revised edition with a still from the popular film on the new cover. A collective of journalists—Meng Lei, Guan Guofeng, and Guo Xiaoyang—came out with another book, *1942: Starving China* (*1942: Ji'e Zhongguo*), noting how Liu's novella and Feng's film had led to the rediscovery of the famine that had been "almost a historical blank" (*kongbai*).[3]

"My beloved granddaughter, don't look so shocked," Grandma Dieu Lan, born in 1920, says to Guava in Nguyen Phan Que Mai's 2021 English-language novel *The Mountains Sing*. "Do you understand why I've decided to tell you about our family? If our stories survive, we will not die, even when our bodies are no longer here on this earth." The stories narrated in the chapter titled "The Great Hunger: Nghe-An, 1942–1948" have grim resonances with Bibhutibhusan Bandyopadhyay's 1944 novel *Ashani Sanket* and Liu Zhenyun's 1992 novella *Remembering 1942*. "This time the war came in the form of *Nan doi nam At Dau*—the Great Famine of 1945—which killed two million of our countrymen. Rather than being a vicious tiger gobbling us down, the hunger was a python that squeezed out our energy, until there was nothing left of us except skin and bones." Among those killed was Dieu Lan's famished mother at the hands of a vicious character named the Wicked Ghost.[4]

In August 1943, Subhas Chandra Bose made broadcasts from Rangoon calling on the British and Japanese to agree to the safe passage of ships that would carry 100,000 tons of rice for the starving millions in Bengal. It was not an unthinkable proposition as the Allies and the Axis had let relief supplies through to Greece when famine had threatened in 1941. In the case of India, Winston Churchill refused to send supplies of food to break the famine, and the British raj in India tried its best to censor news about Bose's offer, which reached his people in the form of rumor.[5] Japan had swept through Southeast Asia between December 1941 and March 1942, driving the British from Burma, and reaching the gates of India with a rhetorical promise of "Asia for the Asiatics."

Narrative histories of "forgotten armies" and "forgotten wars" have of late highlighted the connected destiny of Asia during the tumultuous years of World War II and its immediate aftermath.[6] The wartime famines—remembered and forgotten in different ways—also underscore the shared existential reality of poverty across agrarian Asia as the era of Western imperial rule hurtled toward a violent end. These massive subsistence crises had huge political implications and undermined the legitimacy of the regimes that presided over these colossal, avoidable human tragedies. The war years enabled closer relationships to be forged among leaders and movements battling for Asian freedom from British, French, Dutch, and American colonial rule. Japan may have been the colonizer of Korea and an imperialist aggressor in China. However, its early military successes in Southeast Asia against all the Western powers during World War II gave an opportunity to Asian freedom fighters that they were not prepared to lose. The 1940s witnessed the final denouement of concerted Asian political action that had been attempted since World War I. Many of the outcomes that had been merely envisioned in the 1910s were finally realized during the 1940s. By focusing on Japanese motives, historians have often missed the active agency and interactions of the colonized peoples of South and Southeast Asia in the climactic phase of their struggle for freedom.

War and Famine

"That was the summer that death had become so casual and commonplace a thing that we had stopped reporting it," the American journalist Theodore White noted in China in 1942. "It wasn't really worthwhile putting on a shirt over our baking bodies to get the figures on anything less than a major famine that knocked off, say, a good two million human beings."[7] White eventually put on a shirt and visited Henan in March 1943 and recorded some of the most graphic accounts of the humanitarian disaster. "There were corpses on the road," White and Analee Jacoby wrote in a chapter titled "The Honan Famine" in their book *Thunder out of China*. "A girl no more than seventeen, slim and pretty, lay on the damp earth, her lips blue with death: her eyes were open, and the rain fell on them. People chipped at bark, pounded it by the roadside for food; vendors sold leaves at a dollar a bundle. A dog digging at a mound was exposing a human body. Ghostlike men were skimming the stagnant pools to eat the green slime of the waters."[8]

THE BENGAL FAMINE BEGAN in March 1943. "Bengal is a vast cremation ground," the newsletter *Biplabi* reported by November 7, 1943, "a meeting place for ghosts and evil spirits, a land so overrun by dogs, jackals, and vultures that it makes one wonder whether the Bengalis are really alive or have become ghosts from some distant epoch. And yet in the imaginative words of the poet, golden Bengal was once 'well-watered, fruitful, abundant with crops.' A garden of culture and civilization for over a thousand years."[9] The Tonkin famine tightened its python-like grip somewhat later. "When we entered the villages," an eye-witness account published on April 28, 1945, narrates, "we saw the peasants miserably dressed. Many of them had only a piece of mat to cover their bodies. They wandered about aimlessly in the streets like skeletons with skin, without any strength left, without any thoughts, and totally resigned to the ghosts of starvation and disease."[10]

Colonial rule in India had begun with a gigantic famine in 1770 and ended with another one in 1943. Some three million people perished in what was even in the 1940s described as a "man-made" Bengal famine.[11] "During that year [1942], and continuing into 1943, some three million people starved to death," Rana Mitter writes in *China's Good War*, "because of a combination of natural factors, including adverse weather, and human-made ones, such as the seizure of grain by the government to feed the military." In an earlier work, *Forgotten Ally*, Mitter had mentioned the "deaths of some four million people."[12] A staggering figure of 2 million "deaths from starvation" (one-fifth of the population) in Tonkin by March 1945 is the figure reported by historians of Vietnam.[13]

The Bengal famine was not caused by food availability decline in the province as a whole.[14] In Henan Province, there was a significant crop failure in 1942.[15] While acknowledging the drought, Meng Lei and his fellow investigators believed that "the primary cause" of the 3 million deaths was "a human-made disaster."[16] "The problem was not lack of food," Mitter contends, "but the lack of a system to bring the food where it was needed. There was grain in the neighbouring provinces of Shanxi and Hubei, but the authorities refused to transport it to Henan. . . . Venal officials were making a natural disaster into a man-made one as famine began to sweep across Henan."[17]

Since the early twentieth century, Bengal had imported small quantities of coarse Burmese rice and exported some of its own finer varieties. The Japanese occupation of Burma in March 1942 cut off these imports and had a disproportionate effect on rising food prices.[18] Henan also imported rice from Burma, Thailand, and Vietnam in the pre-1942 period.[19] The loss of even small quantities of these rice imports likely had an adverse impact on a volatile food market. All three wartime famines occurred within the context of the inflationary conditions of World War II. As grain prices soared, vulnerable social groups lost their exchange entitlement to food for their subsistence. The worldwide depression of the 1930s had ruptured social relations in the Asian countryside.[20] The bond-snapping character of the depression decade between creditors and peasant debtors supply the antecedent links in a chain of causation that led to the devastating famines of the 1940s.

In both India and China, massive public expenditure expansion stoked wartime inflation. While about half of the total war expenditure in India was said to be "recoverable" as sterling credits accumulated in the Bank of England, for now the war could be financed mostly by printing money.[21] In

January 1943, a local colonial official imagined that higher prices would enable the government to collect outstanding agricultural loans.[22] But, of course, it was the grain dealers and not the working peasantry who were benefiting from the high prices. Peasant laborers were in the role of buyers rather than sellers of food grains and other daily necessities.[23]

The British colonial state's culpability went far beyond the wrongheadedness of an individual bureaucrat. Feeding soldiers and workers involved in war-related production was the priority, not the rural poor who saw food disappearing beyond their purchasing capacity. The "policy of denial" of food and transport to the Japanese in the event of their landing led to local losses of livelihoods in coastal districts.[24]

Even if a famine is not caused by food availability decline but rather a decline in exchange entitlements to food among the poor, relief in the form of public distribution of food would be needed to break the grip of famine.[25] New Delhi was unable to impress on London the desperate need for external supplies. Madhusree Mukerjee has contended that the decision to starve Bengal by refusing to send food was a matter of Churchill's choice.[26] The famine, which began in March 1943, was not reported in the press or officially acknowledged in the British parliament until October 1943. As for Subhas Chandra Bose's request of safe passage for ships carrying rice across the Bay of Bengal from Burma in August 1943, the offer was not formally rejected but just nervously suppressed.[27]

In China, the expenditure on American troops expenditure could be met, according to the financial adviser Arthur Young, "only by running the printing presses harder."[28] The cost of one American soldier in China was equivalent to the cost of 500 Chinese soldiers, and this would become a source of tension and resentment between the two allies by 1944–1945.

The first newspaper reports of famine had appeared in October–November 1942. *Ta Kung Pao* (*Dagongbao*) initially noted worsening access to food in Henan and women being forced into prostitution. In February 1943, this newspaper published a report directly accusing the GMD authorities of incompetence that led Theodore White and Harrison Forman to undertake their fact-finding trip to Henan. The government had reacted to the criticism by shutting down the newspaper for three days. This set the tone for the state's attitude toward famine relief. The relief programs, according to Mitter, "lacked substance" and "Chiang's regime must be held responsible for the famine in Henan."[29] Mitter notes deep disquiet about "Song Meiling's [Madame Chiang Kai-shek's] behaviour" and that H. H. Kung, husband of Meiling's sister Ailing, was "suspected to be the most corrupt man in China."[30] Madame Chiang grandly announced on a visit to the United States in February 1943 that China wanted arms, not food.[31]

If the British colonial state and the GMD regime had a lot to answer for in India and China, respectively, the Vichy French regime backed by the Japanese was squarely responsible for the famine in Vietnam. The French had agreed in August 1942 to supply Japan with the entire "exportable surplus" of rice from the harvests of 1942–1943, or a minimum of just over 1 million tons of the best-quality white rice. In addition, throughout the war, peasants in Tonkin were made to switch from rice to oil seeds, peanuts (for hydrocarburants), cotton, and jute for military requirements.[32] As in India and China, official famine relief was virtually nonexistent.[33]

Any close study of the great wartime famines explodes culturalist misconceptions about the fatalism and docility of Indian peasants by contrast with the revolutionary aptitude of their Chinese and Vietnamese counterparts. If Bengali peasants died helplessly "in front of bulging food-shops," as they trekked to Calcutta in search of food,[34] Henanese peasants did not loot the restaurants that served those "whose purses were still full."[35] It was only when the Japanese launched their Ichigo offensive into Henan in the spring of 1944 that peasants armed with crude weapons vented their anger by disarming some 50,000 of the GMD troops.[36] In Tonkin, dying victims were witness to New Year's Day merrymaking and feasting in October 1944.[37] However, each one of the famines undermined the legitimacy of the state and the preexisting social structure with long-term political consequences.

How did the artistic milieu in Santiniketan, which had served as a hub of an Asian cultural ecumene, respond to the crises of the 1940s? Nandalal Bose, the painter who had the closest acquaintance with Japanese and Chinese art, did not depict the horrors of famine in his home province. That was left to his younger contemporaries—Somenath Hore and Ramkinkar Beij in Santiniketan and Jainul Abedin and Chittoprasad elsewhere in Bengal. There is, however, a deep sense of irony in his painting *Annapurna*, which was created in 1943, the year of the great Bengal famine. More than three decades earlier, Nandalal had painted a serene picture titled *Annapurna and Shiva*. Now, in a combination of tempera and Japanese wash, he created the haunting *Annapurna and Rudra* (later simply titled *Annapurna*). Annapurna, who is seated on a lotus, holds a bowl of rice in her hands. Before her stands Shiva, reduced to a skeleton holding a begging bowl. Nandalal's mood in the year of the famine is captured in one of his letters. "I have realized the following in a dream," he wrote. "Give up your attempts to find God; go on creating what you like; you are an artist, paint picture after picture."[38]

Rabindranath Tagore had died in August 1941 soon after composing his powerful essay "*Sabhyatar Sankat*" (Crisis in civilization) on the occasion of his eightieth birthday in May. In it, he narrated "the tragic tale" of the loss of his faith in the "claims of the European nations to civilization." "In India," he said two years before the famine, "the misfortune of being governed by a foreign race is daily brought home to us not only in the callous neglect of such minimum necessities of life as adequate provision for food, clothing, educational and medical facilities for the people but in an even unhappier form in the way the people have been divided among themselves." Another "great and ancient civilization" for whose "tragic history" the British could not shirk responsibility was China. Indians, he believed, were in no way inferior to the Japanese in intellectual capacity. The only difference was that while India lay at "the mercy of the British," Japan had been "spared the shadow of alien domination." Instead of upholding "the dignity of human relationship," the British had established "with baton in hand a reign of 'law and order,' in other words a policeman's rule." "Such a mockery of civilization," he declared, "can claim no respect from us."[39]

Tagore had once believed that "the springs of civilization would issue out of the heart of Europe." But now looking around him, he could see "the crumbling ruins of a proud civilization strewn like a vast heap of futility." Yet he stopped himself from committing "the grievous sin of losing faith in Man" and looked forward to "the opening of a new chapter in his history after the cataclysm is over and the atmosphere rendered clean with the spirit of service and sacrifice." "Perhaps," he allowed himself to hope, "that dawn will come from this horizon, from the East where the sun rises."[40]

War and Freedom

How was the land of the rising sun viewed during World War II by Asians struggling to free themselves from the incubus of Western imperial domination? Japan's spectacular military victories in Southeast Asia destroyed the mystique and aura of invincibility that had surrounded British, French, Dutch, and American rule among colonial subjects across that wide region. Until 1940, Japan had paid far less attention to Southeast Asia than to Northeast Asia. The proclamation of the Greater East Asia Co-prosperity Sphere by Konoye Fumimaro, the prime minister, and Matsuoka Yosuke, the foreign minister, in August 1940 signaled something of a shift in perspective. Even then, however, the sphere included only the Dutch East Indies and French Indochina in Southeast Asia. In these parts of Southeast Asia, Japan engaged scholars of Buddhism and Islam in their foreign policy initiatives in attempts to win the affection of the colonized. It was only on January 21, 1942 that the prime minister, Hideki Tojo, included Malaya, Burma, and the Philippines in the sphere in an address to the Diet and declared the aim of liberating all of Asia from British and American imperialist domination.[41] By the time the Greater East Asia Conference was convened in Tokyo on November 5–6, 1943, Netaji Subhas Chandra Bose, head of the Azad Hind (Free India) government proclaimed in Singapore on October 21, came as an observer.

On April 28, 1943, Bose's aide Abid Hasan had felt "something akin to a home-coming" when he and his leader transferred in a rubber boat from a German to a Japanese submarine in the Indian Ocean on their ninety-day voyage from Europe to Asia. "Immediately we had that feeling," he recalled decades later, "Netaji had that feeling." "The Germans," he explained, "were very friendly, very courteous, but we did feel that we had come back to an Asian nation."[42] The warmth of Japanese hospitality and the food spiced with Indian ingredients sourced from Penang were entirely to their liking. That did not prevent some cultural misunderstanding upon arrival in Japan when Hasan went out for a walk wearing a woman's kimono and drew bemused stares, having chosen the more colorful of the ones offered to their guests at a traditional Japanese inn.[43]

From Sabang in Sumatra where their submarine had docked, Bose and Hasan had flown to Japan in early May 1943. After meetings with poets and professors, generals and admirals, including Generals Arisue Yadoru and Hajime Sugiyama, and the foreign minister, Shigemitsu Mamoru, Bose finally had a face-to-face meeting with Hideki Tojo on June 10, 1943. Bose had rehearsed this meeting on the German submarine with Hasan role-playing for Tojo. The actual encounter went remarkably well. "The magic of Bose," Joyce Lebra writes, "enchanted Tojo immediately."[44] With Bose watching as a special guest, Tojo declared Japan's firm resolve to "do everything possible to help Indian independence" in a speech to the Diet on June 16, 1943. Speaking to sixty journalists on June 19 in Tokyo, Bose spoke about reviving ancient cultural ties between India and Japan that had been interrupted because of the British domination of India.[45] Yone Noguchi, who had known Benoy Kumar Sarkar and Rabindranath Tagore since the 1910s, now met Bose and was deeply impressed. On June 20, 1943, he composed a poem addressed to Subhas Chandra Bose expressing his hope that the younger leader will succeed where the great Mahatma Gandhi had fallen short.[46] The next day, Indians in Southeast Asia heard Bose's stirring broadcast calling on all patriotic Indians to advance to the field of battle.[47]

Accompanied by the veteran revolutionary Rashbehari Bose who had lived in Japanese exile since 1915, Subhas Chandra Bose and Abid Hasan arrived in Singapore on July 2, 1943. On July 4, Rashbehari offered Subhas as his "present" to an enthusiastic assembly of Indians in the Cathay Theater. Accepting the leadership of the Indian independence movement in Southeast and East Asia, Subhas Chandra Bose offered those who were prepared to follow him "nothing but hunger, thirst, privation, forced marches and death" until they held their victory parade at the Red Fort of Delhi. The following morning, July 5, on the expansive green in front of Singapore's municipal building with its Corinthian columns, Netaji Subhas Chandra Bose took the salute as supreme commander of the Indian National Army (INA) and gave the war cry "On to Delhi." Expatriate Indians, soldiers, and civilians alike, responded with great emotional fervor to his call for total mobilization.[48]

The Burmese leader Ba Maw first met Netaji in Singapore on July 6, 1943. He saw Bose as "a symbol of the long and passionate Indian revolution that had at last found its way into the wider Asian revolution which could change Asia." At their meetings in the second week of July, they "talked of great

6.1 Netaji Subhas Chandra Bose with Ba Maw and other Burmese leaders, Rangoon, August 1943 (Courtesy of Netaji Research Bureau, Calcutta)

many things, but mostly of the war and how we could use it for the liberation of our own people." This sentiment of how to take advantage of the discomfiture of the old imperial powers of the West at the hands of a new imperial power in Asia animated the strategies of many anti-colonial leaders and movements during World War II. Ba Maw personally invited Bose to witness the independence celebrations of Burma on August 1, 1943. Bose accepted and arrived in Rangoon on July 29, remembering the two and a half years he had spent as a prisoner of the British in Mandalay during the mid-1920s (figure 6.1).[49]

As significant as Japan's ambivalent relationship with various Asian independence movements were the conscious efforts made by Asian freedom fighters to forge solidarity among themselves. In 1938, the Dobama Asiyaone (We Burmans Association), led by the radical young intelligentsia known as Thakins, had established connections with the Indian National Congress of which Bose was then the president. After the outbreak of World War II, the Thakins set up the Burma Freedom Bloc in an echo of Bose's

Forward Bloc in the Indian National Congress. Ba Maw was its president and Aung San served as general secretary. In March 1940, Aung San and other Thakin delegates had two meetings with Subhas Chandra Bose in Ramgarh where an anti-compromise conference was being held in parallel with the official Congress session. Plans to coordinate the anti-imperialist movements were interrupted by the imprisonment of Indian and Burmese leaders in mid-1940. Aung San evaded arrest and left Burma in August 1940 and eventually reached Japan. Subhas Chandra Bose made a dramatic escape from India in January 1941 toward Europe and had to take a circuitous route back to Asia in 1943.[50]

In addition to negotiating with those occupying the top echelons of the Japanese government, Asian anti-imperialists experienced both high-minded idealism and high-handed arrogance of middle-tier Japanese military officers in Southeast Asia. The Burmese acknowledged the helpful role played by Suzuki Keiji in the formation of the Burma Independence Army spearheaded by the thirty comrades including Aung San, who received Japanese military training and fought against the British in early 1942. A similar role was played by Fujiwara Iwaichi in winning over Indian soldiers, who had served the British, to the cause of the INA.[51] Several others showed none of the tact or sensitivity displayed by Suzuki and Fujiwara in respecting the aspirations of Burmese and Indian freedom fighters. Not just relations with the Japanese but also Indo-Burmese relations strained during the depression era required delicate handling once Netaji Subhas Chandra Bose took charge of the Indian independence movement in Southeast Asia.

Having galvanized Indian expatriate communities in Malaya, Thailand, and Burma between July and October, Bose proclaimed the formation of the Azad Hind (Free India) government in Singapore on October 21, 1943. The Burmese foreign minister, U Nu, issued an official statement that day describing the Indian government to be "deserving of the unstinted support of every nation that believes in fairness and justice as the foundation of the New World Order."[52] A week earlier, on October 14, 1943, José Laurel had established an independent government in the Philippines. Once the Japanese government at a cabinet meeting on October 23, 1943 granted recognition to the Free India government, the stage was set for the Greater

East Asia Conference to be held in Tokyo on November 5–6, 1943. Japan chose the convenient and ultimately self-defeating path of working through the pliant Vichy regime in French Indochina. By the time Japan sought to promote Vietnamese independence in March 1945, the mantle of nationalism had passed to the Viet Minh led by Ho Chi Minh. In Indonesia, the Japanese had released Sukarno and Mohammad Hatta in 1942 from their long years in Dutch imprisonment. While handing the reins of civilian administration to Indonesian nationalists and providing them with military training, Japan withheld the formal granting of independence to the Dutch colony until it was too late in 1945.

For the leaders of the Asian countries invited to the conference, Tojo and Shigemitsu put on the charm offensive in the late autumn of 1943 as chrysanthemum flowers bloomed in Tokyo. They were all accommodated as guests in the homes of distinguished Japanese citizens to give the gathering a familial character. Gazing at the Shingawa gulf from the home of the central bank governor Shibusawa Shakuro in Shiba, Bose reflected on the achievements of Meiji Japan and its 1905 victory, much as Benoy Kumar Sarkar had done in 1915. On November 3, he visited the Meiji shrine to pay his respects on the anniversary of the adoption of the Meiji constitution.[53]

Before the conference began, Bose made sure paintings and poetry that had helped forge bonds between India and Japan since the turn of the twentieth century would figure prominently on his itinerary. He visited the Ueno Museum of Art with Anand Mohan Sahay and Abid Hasan (see figure 6.2).

Having learned that his war cry *"Chalo Delhi"* had inspired the composition of a Japanese song by Yone Noguchi for NHK titled "Marching to Delhi," he asked for and received an English translation. The first verse of this song poem in four verses visualized a freedom feast in the land of famine:

"Delhi, Delhi, to Delhi!"
The war-cry replies to a storm of cannon-balls,
And praises the might of powder and smoke.
Leap over the terror that trenches command,
And entrust your bones to a hill of the mother-land!
In a blazing sand your palm grasps,

6.2 Netaji Subhas Chandra Bose at the Ueno Art Museum with Abid Hasan and Anand Mohan Sahay, Tokyo, November 1943 (Courtesy of Netaji Research Bureau, Calcutta)

> You will find all the rewards that Death bestows,
> And the hunger you suffered from the hundreds of years
> Can't be filled till an Independence-feast is spread.[54]

On November 5, 1943, the Assembly of the Greater East Asiatic Nations (Daitoa kaigi) formally convened in the Japanese Diet and elected Hideki Tojo as chairman. For someone who had been relatively uninterested in India until June 1943, he strongly denounced "Britain's oppression of India" that was growing "in severity with every passing day." He deplored the "indescribable hardships and tribulations" to which the Indian people were being subjected, culminating in "the famine of unprecedented magnitude":

> All patriots of India are imprisoned, while the innocent masses are starving. This is a world tragedy—a calamity of all mankind. The

peoples of Greater East Asia could never let it go unattended. Happily, Mr. Subhas Chandra Bose responded to the call of the hour and with him rose the Indian patriots both within and without their country.[55]

Ba Maw felt closer to Bose and Laurel than the other Asian leaders who had gathered "for all three of us were, if I may put it that way, a mixture of East and West, although our roots remained most deeply lodged in our own native earth; we were the products of a long and radical meeting between the East and the West in our countries."[56] Bose and Ba Maw had been educated at Cambridge while Laurel had a law degree from Yale. Laurel saw "Mother Asia" as a cradle of civilization and believed that the dialectic between the Orient and the Occident produced a higher universalism. "United together one and all into a compact and solid organization," he declaimed in his speech at the conference, "there can no longer be any power that can stop or delay the acquisition by the one billion Orientals of the free and untrammeled right and opportunity of shaping their own destiny." Prince Wan Waithayakon of Thailand also did not see the new Asian spirit as wholly antagonistic to Europe and quoted the old Latin wisdom: From the West, law, from the East, light.[57]

On the morning of November 6, 1943, the assembly formally adopted a joint declaration. It is often seen as a compromise between the advocacy of the "equality of all Asian nations" by the foreign ministry led by Shigemitsu including a promise of withdrawal of Japanese troops from occupied territories and the army ministry's narrower goal of seeking Asian cooperation during the war. "The United States of America and the British Empire have in seeking their own prosperity," the declaration stated, "oppressed other nations and peoples." Asia resolved to "enjoy prosperity in common." The declaration went on to enunciate five principles that would underpin international relations after Asians had succeeded in "liberating their region from the yoke of British-American domination": first, mutual cooperation based on justice; second, respect for one another's sovereignty; third, enhancement of culture by developing the creative faculties of each race; fourth, economic development on the basis of reciprocity; and fifth, cultivation of friendly relations with all countries of the world and work for the abolition of racial discriminations.[58] Ba Maw claimed that Tokyo was a precursor to Bandung:

> This great Assembly was the first visual manifestation of the new spirit stirring in Asia, the spirit of Bandung as it was called twelve years later when it was re-incarnated at the Bandung Conference of the Afro-Asian Nations. That spirit had its first birth at the Tokyo Assembly in 1943. Even the Assembly's joint declaration consisting of the five basic principles of a new order in Asia foreshadowed the Pancha Shila or Five Principles, of the Bandung nations.[59]

Even after the adoption of the joint resolution, there was still some important unfinished business to be attended to at the conference.

Ba Maw rose to move a new motion before the assembly stating that there could be no liberation of Asia without the liberation of India. It was adopted unanimously, and the conference expressed "fully sympathy and support to the Indian struggle for independence." Subhas Chandra Bose, who had been observing the proceedings, now rose to speak. "The force of his delivery," the Japanese record noted, "compelled every member of the conference to pay attention to every phrase of his speech."[60] A Cambridge-educated interpreter, Masayoshi Kakitsubo, who had visited India as a diplomat in the mid-1930s, was given the task of translating Bose's speech. Decades later, he remembered being moved to tears as he rendered Bose's English speech into Japanese.[61] Surveying the long history of international conferences, Bose recalled his own futile attempts to get a hearing for the cause of Indian independence before the League of Nations. It was the Indian inability to distinguish between false and real universalism, Bose argued, that had led India to succumb to European power. But India had learned through misery and humiliation that true internationalism was rooted in nationalism. The first step toward "the creation of an international society" was to set up "regional federations." He expressed his determination to fight till the bitter end "no matter what the suffering and sacrifice involved may prove to be," certain of India's "ultimate victory." "I do not know," he said, "how many of us who are going to participate in the coming battle will survive to see India free. But whether we survive or not, whether we individually live to see India free or not, we are confident that India shall be free. We are confident that Anglo-American imperialism shall be wiped out of India and the menace that hangs over the whole of East Asia will be removed once and for all."[62]

Tojo responded by announcing the de jure transfer of the Andaman and Nicobar Islands to the Free India government as a first step in Japan's support of India's "long cherished ambition to achieve independence." The Asian leaders took their message beyond the conference halls to the wider public in a mass rally held in Hibiya Park. Subhas Chandra Bose was given an audience by Tenno Heika (emperor of Japan) in the Phoenix Hall of the Imperial Palace on November 10, 1943. Subhas called on Rashbehari Bose at his home, and together they attended a luncheon in his honor given by Mitsuru Toyama on November 15. He gave the veteran Asianist Okawa Shumei something of a shock by remarking casually that if Germany was defeated, he should "carry on the fight till the last even by joining the Reds." Okawa guessed that Bose had made a realistic assessment of Japan's deteriorating strategic position in the war.[63] Yet even during the tumult of World War II, there had been a "telescoped Dong Du project" of Asian students traveling east to Japan. José Laurel made a powerful impression on the Filipino pensionados studying in Tokyo. One of them, Leocadio de Asis, noted in his diary how Laurel's speech at the Greater East Asia Conference had impressed Vietnamese students, especially his espousal of the cause of "the still oppressed peoples of India, Indo-China, Java, Sumatra, and Malaya."[64] Subhas Chandra Bose visited the forty-five young Indian cadets at the Tokyo Military Academy and "like a mother he showered his heart-felt affection on them." By the time Bose said goodbye to the Shibusawa family, leaving with them his presents including a ceremonial samurai sword, he had clearly endeared himself to his Japanese hosts and left a lasting impression on them.[65]

Asian Relations toward War's End

The trickiest challenge facing leaders of South and Southeast Asia was the fraught relationship between Japan and China. Here, they had to adopt nothing short of a tightrope-walk act. The Chinese representative at the Greater East Asia Conference was none other than Wang Jingwei, who had been persuaded by Japan in 1940 to leave Chungking and take charge of the government in Nanjing. Margherita Zanasi has sensitively analyzed the reasons underlying Wang's and Chen Gongbo's decision to collaborate with Japan and traced the twists and turns in their long intellectual journey. They were keenly aware of China's military and economic weaknesses in the face of Japanese aggression, especially before the entry of the United States into the war in December 1941 fundamentally altered long-term prospects.[66] On his way back from Tokyo, Wang stopped in Fukuoka with Count Teraoka of Japan and there decided to invite Subhas Chandra Bose to Nanjing. "Though he sat through the conference practically saying nothing and expressed himself only towards the end," Wang noted, "his [Bose's] robust physique, his regal looks, exuberant energy, his spiritual convictions, and the content of his speech all go to show that he is undoubtedly a revolutionary person." Bose accepted Wang's invitation and arrived in Nanjing on November 18, 1943, proceeding immediately to pay his homage at the mausoleum of Sun Yat-sen.[67]

On the night of November 20, 1943, Subhas Chandra Bose gave a forty-minute radio address to the Chungking government and the Chinese people. It contained a lengthy autobiographical account of the ways in which he studied the ideas of Sun Yat-sen and the history of China's republican revolution. He paid glowing tributes to Sun as "a friend of India, a firm supporter of Indian independence and a strong opponent of British Imperialism." He stressed that Sun Yat-sen was committed to "the liberation of Asia and in Asian unity." "Following in the footsteps of three great men—C.R. Das, a great Indian leader, Sun Yat Sen and Okakura of Japan," he declared, "I am seized and inspired by the idea of Pan-Asian Federation." Asia needed to pursue the twin values of liberation and unity, he argued. The building blocks of Asian liberation and unity were the unity of China and the freedom of India, which in turn would "make the liberation of the oppressed peoples of West Asia possible."[68]

On November 21, Bose traveled from Nanjing to Shanghai and galvanized support for his INA among the Indian community there. He issued a second appeal to Chungking urging Chiang Kai-shek (Jiang Jieshi) not to fight against India's army of liberation. He recalled how as president of the Indian National Congress in 1938, he had sent an Indian medical mission to China and insisted that "the Indian people really sympathize with China and the

Chinese people." "Every Indian should be true to the cause of India," he insisted, "and likewise every Chinese should be true to the cause of China." How to reconcile these patriotic allegiances with the larger aim of Asian unity was the severe challenge that wartime Asian leaders faced. Chiang Kai-shek had been rebuffed by Gandhi in 1942 when he had visited India on the eve of the Mahatma's Quit India movement as an advocate of Britain and the United States. Bose reckoned in November 1943 that China would soon achieve unity "under one leader" and that by "an honorable peace," Japan would "withdraw her troops from China." He cited Mahatma Gandhi's statement in 1942 that "if India were free he would have gone on a mission to bring peace between China and Japan."[69] Bose asked his aide Abid Hasan to stay on in China for a while to negotiate an understanding with the Chungking government but to no avail.[70]

From China, Bose flew on November 22, 1943 to the Philippines, whose leaders had blazed the trail to Japan since the days of José Rizal. "One beautiful day in November 1943," an eyewitness recounted, "Bose went to Luneta Park on Manila beach to present a wreath at the famous statue of Jose Rizal." He "gazed silently at the statue of Rizal for several long, tense minutes" as the flag of Azad Hind adorned with the charka "fluttered in the morning breeze and the flowers presented by Bose at the feet of the big statue made the whole scene extremely colorful."[71]

Another uncompromising figure in the anti-colonial resistance against the United States, Artemio Ricarte, had spent long decades in Japanese exile since 1915 before returning to his homeland during World War II. Benigno Ramos, the leader of the depression-era Sakdalista movement, had also spent a few years in Japan. He was jailed in the Philippines on his return in 1938 and was released from prison by the Japanese in April 1942. While Manuel Quezon and Sergio Osmena formed a government in exile in Washington, DC, José Laurel headed the Japanese-recognized government in wartime Philippines. Laurel welcomed Subhas Chandra Bose in Manila as the "leader of 350 million Indians in their effort, which is legitimate and divine, to free themselves from the British rule."[72] Laurel's Christian ethics did not stand in the way of his espousal of an Asian universalism.

In early January 1944, Subhas Chandra Bose moved forward the head-quarters of his Free India government from Singapore to Rangoon in preparation for taking the war of independence onto Indian soil. Hostilities against British forces began on the Arakan front in February, and with "On to Delhi" as their slogan, the INA crossed the Indo-Burma frontier on March 18, 1944, toward Imphal and Kohima. High hopes of capturing Imphal in April 1944 were dashed as American air support came to the aid of besieged British ground forces. The INA and their Japanese allies were forced to retreat beginning July 1944 even though the INA continued to fight rearguard battles against the British advance into Burma until April 1945.[73]

Indo-Burmese relations during 1944–1945 provided an acid test of Asian anti-colonial unity caught in the vortex of the final phase of the war between Britain and Japan. Subhas Chandra Bose had offered a *nazar*, a gift to the new Burmese government, on September 21, 1943 when his INA held a parade outside the tomb of the last Mughal emperor, Bahadur Shah Zafar, vowing to march to Delhi. From January 1944 to April 1945, Burma remained the principal base of operations of the Indian independence movement. Bose stationed himself in Maymyo during the height of the battle for Imphal. The Azad Hind Bank, established in early April 1944, was ready with Indian currency to be used in the liberated areas by Indian administrators. Ba Maw, whose government welcomed Bose to Rangoon in January 1944, recalled that "the bonds between the two peoples became firmer and the racial tensions which had once existed under the British practically disappeared." This was no small achievement, given that the Free India government was on a sounder financial footing than its Burmese counterpart. "Netaji and I met often," Ba Maw wrote, "discussed our common problems, and did our utmost to help each other."[74]

Relations with Japan diverged for the Indian and Burmese independence movements from late 1944 onward. In the early autumn of 1944, "information trickled down unofficially from Japan that the Japanese Government was desirous of conferring a title—Order of the Rising Sun of the first merit— on Subhas Bose. His reply to this shocked the Japanese authorities not a little." Prem Kumar Sahgal, Bose's military secretary, remembered that the Japanese emissary to whom he conveyed his leader's refusal suggested that they both commit hara-kiri! Sahgal politely declined the suicide pact along with the decoration for his leader. The Japanese foreign office tells us that

Bose said "when the independence of India became a reality he would be glad to receive it [the award] along with his followers. For the time being he would like to set it aside." "Would not this incident and the other one in case of Shibusawa's presents, recorded before," the Japanese account comments, "reveal the very essence of his character?"[75]

Netaji Subhas Chandra Bose traveled to Tokyo on his third and final visit on October 29, 1944 with his aides Muhammad Zaman Kiani, A. C. Chatterjee, and Habibur Rahman and spent a month in Japan.[76] The situation was quite different in November 1944 from what it had been exactly a year ago at the time of the Greater East Asia Conference with aerial bombardment of Japan's capital now a regular occurrence. Bose held talks with the new prime minister, Kuniaki Koiso, foreign minister, Mamoru Shigemitsu, and was received by Emperor Hirohito on November 6, 1944. "Even if Japan is defeated," he told his followers, "we shall fight for India's independence till the end."[77] He lectured at Hibiya Hall and delivered a major wide-ranging address to the faculty and students at Tokyo Imperial University. He argued that a regional order had to be the foundation of a world order. The League of Nations had failed because of the selfish and shortsighted policies of the sponsor nations, particularly Britain and France. If such selfishness and shortsightedness could be abjured in Asia and the sponsor nation could "work on a moral basis," the experiment to build a new international order may well succeed. He saw the challenge to "rise to a high level of morality" to be the task not just for the leaders and politicians but rather "the youths and the students."[78] He made it a point to visit the Indian students he had sent to Tokyo and visited the ailing elder statesman Rashbehari Bose, who would die in January 1945. He sent a message to the Soviet Union through Jacob Malik, their ambassador in Tokyo. In broadcasts to his "American friends," he regretted that the United States did not help India and that in waging a war for freedom, they were not helping Japan: "We are helping ourselves," he declared, "we are helping Asia." Having got the Japanese to send an ambassador, Teruo Hachiya, to his Free India government, he commenced his return journey to Southeast Asia on November 29, 1944.[79] On January 10, 1945, Netaji was back at the war front in Burma.

Among the plans Bose and Ba Maw discussed with Aung San, who apparently "liked the idea enormously," was joint resistance by the Indians and Burmese against the British after the Japanese withdrawal with the arms left behind by Japan.[80] That plan did not come to fruition once Aung San and the Anti-Fascist People's Freedom League decided in March 1945 to turn their guns against the Japanese in temporary alliance with the advancing British forces under William Slim. The Indians and Burmese agreed not to fight against each other and that understanding held.[81] On April 24, 1945, Netaji along with men and women of the INA began an epic retreat on foot from Burma to Thailand, leaving some personnel to maintain order in Rangoon. The movement sought to regroup in Thailand, Malaya, and Singapore until the atom bombs on Hiroshima and Nagasaki in August 1945 brought the war in Asia to an abrupt end.

It was just a matter of a few months before Netaji and the INA turned their military defeat in Southeast Asia into a spectacular political victory in India. British hubris contributed in no small measure to this turnaround. On November 5, 1945, a trial by court-martial began of three INA officers— Prem Kumar Sahgal, Shah Nawaz Khan, and Gurbaksh Singh Dhillon—at Delhi's historic Red Fort. A groundswell of popular support emerged for the Hindu, Muslim, and Sikh soldiers who faced the weighty charge of waging war against the king-emperor. Accounts of the heroic fight for freedom filled the pages of the Indian press. The masterful lead defense lawyer, Bhulabhai Desai, argued that the INA had waged war under a duly constituted government and in accordance with international law. If a subject people could not take up arms to throw off a foreign yoke, he contended that there would be nothing but "perpetual slavery."[82] On December 31, 1945, the Red Fort three were sentenced to deportation for life just as the last Mughal emperor, Bahadur Shah Zafar, had been in 1858. Three days later, on January 3, 1946, the British commander in chief, Claude Auchinleck, was forced to release them to a tumultuous welcome from the Indian public. Among the dozen witnesses presented by the defense were five Japanese diplomats and generals. "I cannot forget the cheering crowds of Indians that night," a defense witness, Major General Tadashi Katakura, recalled, "when the INA officers were vindicated and released."[83]

One of the witnesses that the defense team had wanted to call was Mamoru Shigemitsu, the wartime Japanese foreign minister. But Shigemitsu was in prison and in the process of being arraigned as a class A war criminal by the International Military Tribunal in the Far East in the Tokyo trials that commenced in April 1946. Among the eleven judges at that tribunal was an Indian and a Bengali—Radhabinod Pal—from the Calcutta High Court. Pal delivered a dissenting opinion absolving all the defendants of all charges. He did not deny that the Japanese had committed many atrocities during the war, but those were covered under the class B and C indictments. He pointedly commented on the exclusion of the horrors of Western colonialism in Asia and the dropping of the atom bombs on Hiroshima and Nagasaki by the United States from the purview of war crimes.[84] Pal's dissent won him the lasting gratitude of Japan and, notwithstanding attempts by the Japanese far right to misinterpret and misappropriate him, made him one of the iconic figures alongside Rabindranath Tagore and Subhas Chandra Bose who cemented a powerful bond between India and Japan.

At the climax of the war in August 1945, the British and Japanese forces faced each other on the banks of the Sittang River. Both sides had capable interpreters so that negotiations at this delicate moment of the Japanese surrender were not lost in translation. The Japanese interpreter Saito had been present at many of the tense talks between Subhas Chandra Bose and Japanese generals in Burma. The British interpreter had trained in Japanese at the School of Oriental and African Studies at the University of London and went on to write a riveting account of the end and the aftermath of World War II in Asia. "In the long perspective," Louis Allen concluded, "difficult and bitter as it may be for Europeans to recognize this, the liberation of millions of people in Asia from their colonial past is Japan's lasting achievement."[85]

Asian Relations on Freedom's Eve

Early one morning in July 1946, a seaplane took off from the river Hooghly near the temple town of Dakshineswar in the outskirts of Calcutta. On board was the Indian leader Sarat Chandra Bose, elder brother of Subhas, accompanied by his son Sisir Kumar Bose and a family friend Manubhai Bhimani. Upon landing on the river Irrawaddy outside Rangoon, they were received by veterans of the Azad Hind movement.[86] The British government in Burma were prosecuting some INA officers despite the fiasco the British in India

6.3 Sarat Chandra Bose and Aung San, Rangoon, July 1946 (Photograph by Sisir Kumar Bose. Courtesy of Netaji Research Bureau, Calcutta)

had created for themselves during the Red Fort trials in India. Sarat Bose was a famed lawyer, and one of his prime tasks was to help in defending the INA personnel. More important was his mission to establish close ties with Burmese leaders during this crucial phase in the quest for Asian freedom.

Ba Maw was at that time a prisoner in Japan. His wife, Daw Kinmama, invited the Boses to dinner at home where they met her son-in-law Bo Yan Naing, one of the "thirty comrades," and U Maung, who had served as Burma's ambassador to Tokyo during the war. Aung San ceremonially received Sarat Bose at his party headquarters where they discussed among other subjects the problem of ethnic minorities in Burma (figure 6.3).

Sisir Bose sought out the young student leaders including Aung San's private secretary, Aung Than, who as military attaché at Burma's embassy in Japan had tossed a letter from Netaji Subhas Chandra Bose into the Soviet ambassador's car in November 1944.[87] A public reception at Rangoon's city hall followed the confabulations between Sarat Bose and Aung San on July 24, 1946. In his welcoming address, Aung San spoke glowingly of people who would be treated as patriots in a free India and a free Burma, being put on trial "for the satisfaction of bureaucratic pride and retributive justice." He described in deeply personal terms the relationship between the Indian and Burmese independence movements:

> I knew Netaji, even before I met him for the first time in Calcutta in 1940, by reading various accounts of his life of sacrifice and struggle and last of all, his own book *The Indian Struggle* which was in those days banned in India and Burma. I knew Netaji, as I came into close and frequent contact with him during this recent World War. I knew him and I knew his burning love for his country and his people, and his unflinching determination to fight for the freedom of his country. I knew him also as a sincere friend of Burma and Burmese people. Between him and myself, there was complete mutual trust; and although time was against both of us so that we could not come to the stage of joint action for the common objective of the freedom of our respective nations, we did have an understanding in those days that, in any event, and whatever happened, the INA and the BNA should never fight each other. And I am glad to tell you today that both sides did observe the understanding scrupulously on the whole.

If that was the record of the recent past, there was also a vision for the present and the future. "We stand for an Asiatic Federation in a not very, very remote future," Aung San declared. "We stand for immediate mutual understanding and joint action, wherever and whenever possible, from now on for our mutual interests and for the freedom of India, Burma and indeed all Asia." In his reply, Sarat Bose evoked the dream of an Asiatic federation articulated by Sun Yat-sen and Deshbandhu C. R. Das and agreed that it must be kept in view for the future.[88]

When Jawaharlal Nehru had stopped in Rangoon on his way back from Malaya in March 1946, Aung San had suggested to him the need to convene a gathering to promote Asian solidarity. A year later, on March 23, 1947, an Asian Relations Conference was inaugurated in Delhi by Nehru on the grounds of the historic Purana Qila built by Sher Shah Suri in the sixteenth century. Even though India was playing host, Nehru acknowledged that "the idea of such a Conference arose simultaneously in many minds and in many countries of Asia." It was organized by the Indian Council of World Affairs and was meant to be "unofficial and cultural." "Right behind the presidential *gadi* [seat] was mounted a huge map of Asia," a description of the venue noted, "the continent's name lettered on top of it in neon lights." The map would cause some controversy, but the letters shone bright. Conscious of the historic moment, Nehru spoke of "standing on this watershed which divides two epochs of human history." During the time "this mighty continent became just a field for the rival imperialisms of Europe," Asian countries had become isolated from one another. Now Asia was "again finding itself" and had "suddenly become important again in world affairs." "An Indian, wherever he may go in Asia," Nehru insisted, "feels a sense of kinship with the land he visits and the people he meets." It was only on the bedrock of Asian cooperation could the ideal of "One World" be realized.[89]

Nehru's eloquence was soon surpassed by the poet politician chosen to preside over the conference. Sarojini Naidu had missed presiding over the All-Asian Women's Conference in 1931 since she was jailed for taking part in Gandhi's civil disobedience movement. Sixteen years on, as soon as she rose to address her "Comrades and Kindreds of Asia" who had come to take "an indestructible pledge of the unity of Asia," the audience erupted in applause. "And what will Asia do with her renaissance?" she asked. "Will she arm herself for battles to conquer, to annex and exploit, or rather, will she forge new weapons and refashion her armory in accordance with ancient ideals, as soldiers of peace and missionaries of love?" Sarojini Naidu knew that this gathering of Asians had raised suspicions in the minds of leaders of the West. How "great a compliment" that is, she commented wryly, "to one poor woman who signs a humble invitation—that she should symbolize red to centuries of Western civilization!" She swept aside commonplace notions about natural boundaries or linguistic barriers standing in the way of Asian unity. In her grand perspective, "mountain passes and riverways" could not divide "the heart of Asia." Nor had "a lack of vocabulary, a lack of dictionary knowledge of words, ever prevented the true understanding between hearts." She made a compelling case for "the great diversity of Asian culture" having "cemented the unity of the Asian people." "Who wants a monotonous culture?" she declaimed. "Who wants a uniform culture?

Who wants a colorless culture?"[90] It was a colorful cosmopolitanism that would bring Asians together. Asia's ability to transcend religious difference was argued subtly. "The Western streams of culture that came with the message of the Prophet," in Sarojini Naidu's view, "the great democratic ideal became in time an inalienable part of our national culture." She articulated a clear-eyed, if idealistic, vision for the future: "Asia shall not be a country of enemies. Asia shall be a country of fellowship of the world." For skeptics who reckoned the aspiration vaulted too high beyond the realm of possibility, she had an answer: "The birds have said, 'why do you cry for the moon?' We do not cry for the moon. We pluck it from the skies and wear it upon the diadem of Asia's freedom."[91]

Such lilting poetry would soon have to contend with the leaden prose of the formation of nation-states in postcolonial Asia. "It is unfortunately a melancholy fact of history," S. W. R. D. Bandaranaike of Ceylon said striking a cautionary note, "that when the petrifying effect of foreign rule disappears, just as noble impulses are released, so too at times baser motives of selfishness and internal conflict and weakness rise to the surface." He nevertheless expressed the hope that the conference would mark "the beginning of something much greater—a federation of free and equal Asian countries."[92] Aung San, who could not attend in person, sent a message evoking "a new consciousness of the oneness of Asia" and emphasizing "the supreme necessity on the part of all the countries of Asia to stand together in weal and woe." He prayed that "the cornerstone to the edifice of an all-Asian unity and solidarity" would be laid at the conference.[93] "Widespread fighting" in Vietnam prevented Ho Chi Minh from coming, but he wished India success in realizing its twin aims of "independence and unity."[94] The large Indonesian delegation was happy to participate in their first international conference "unaccompanied by alien advisors."[95] "One country, Japan," Nehru noted in a tone of regret, "is not represented here—and that for reasons which are beyond Japanese control or ours."[96] Twenty-eight countries in all stretching from Egypt in the west to the Philippines in the east attended the Asian Relations Conference. In addition to countries on the verge of shaking off the Western yoke were several central Asian republics of the Soviet Union.

The presence of Tibet as a separate entity raised the ire of the Chinese delegation led by Cheng Yin-fun (Zheng Yanfen). The border between

China and Tibet drawn rather prominently on the map added insult to injury. Once Nehru agreed to alter the map, a Chinese delegate, George Yeh, painted Tibet in the same color as China.[97] This fracas was an early indication of how deeply both the Indian and Chinese nation-states in the making had imbibed Western colonial concepts of unitary sovereignty and rigid borders. Karima El-Said of the Egyptian Feminist Union felt constrained to issue a rejoinder to the Jewish delegation from Palestine in defense of Arab rights and against aggressive European Zionism. The Vietnamese delegation regarded the representatives of Cochinchina, Cambodia, and Laos mere puppets of their French colonial masters. Mai The Chau of Vietnam said with an air of impatience that there had been "enough words about Asian unity. Now let us act."[98]

The substantive discussions at the conference were conducted by five different groups on a variety of themes. The first group discussing "National Movements for Freedom" quickly realized the futility of pretending that the conference was apolitical. Politics pervaded their deliberations. A delegate from Ceylon expressed disquiet about the role of the two big brothers—India and China. A Burmese delegate hoped that "when India emerged as a free country, she would not allow her army to be used for suppressing the freedom movement of any country." The deployment of British Indian troops in Indonesia to aid the Dutch was a cause for much resentment. Nehru had to explain that Indian troops had been withdrawn from Indonesia by November 1946. He also professed sympathy for Vietnam's freedom struggle. But how could India declare war against France? he asked plaintively. A Vietnamese delegate acknowledged, whether graciously or grudgingly, that "the fact that Gurkha troops fought against them did not mean that the present Indian Government was against their freedom movement." "The cry of 'Asia for the Asiatics' raised by Japan for its own motives," the report of group A recognized, "gave further incentive to freedom movements in some of the southeast Asian countries." John A. Thivy, a delegate from Malaya and an INA veteran, supported the idea of a "neutrality bloc" in the emerging Cold War.[99]

The second group turned its attention to "Racial Problems and Inter-Asian Migration"—a knotty issue that needed to be addressed on "an all-Asian basis." Burma, sandwiched between India and China, feared the prospect of British imperialism being replaced by either Indian or Chinese imperialism. The "fear of being swarmed by either Indians or Chinese" had a strong economic ingredient—the past record of migrant intermediary capitalists expropriating land during the Depression and repatriating profits back to their homeland. Delegates from Ceylon and Malaya shared many of the Burmese concerns. A delegate from Ceylon insisted on each country's prerogative to determine its own immigration policy while instituting legal protections of nondiscrimination against long-settled migrant minorities.[100] On the eve of the formation of postcolonial nation-states in Asia, a consensus emerged at the conference against the principle of dual nationality or, at any rate, a preference for one nationality for a person at any one time. But seeing like a state was a project that had to contend with complex social realities.

A third group addressed the theme of "Economic Development and Social Services" with admirable thoroughness. It became clear that Asian countries had a lot to learn from one another as they planned "the transition from a colonial to a national economy." Many variations in detail notwithstanding, agricultural reconstruction and industrial development were seen to constitute the "keynote" of this transformation. Labor problems, both agricultural and industrial, were analyzed threadbare in a comparative vein. The Indian labor leader N. M. Joshi recalled the Asian labor conferences in Colombo and Tokyo before the war and looked forward to the regional meeting of labor organizations under the auspices of the International Labor Office in October 1947.[101]

"Cultural problems" were the challenge taken up by a fourth working group. The "question of values" was addressed with a sophistication that was sorely missing four decades later when "Asian values" were invoked to buttress state authoritarianism and social conservatism. There was no easy valorization in the late 1940s of the community at the expense of the individual. Faced with a diversity of Asian cultural norms, a delegate from Malaya, Brahmachari Kailasam, thoughtfully promoted "a synthetic and not merely eclectic viewpoint." The deliberations were accompanied by cultural exhibitions. An inter-Asian art exhibition featured 200 paintings by Abanindranath Tagore, Nandalal Bose, Asit Haldar, Sardar Ukil, Jamini Roy, and A. R. Chughtai. Japan may have been absent at the conference, but a Japanese brush drawing—*Fish* by Kakemonos—proved to be a major attraction for delegates and visitors alike. A scientific exhibition was appropriately presented under the rubric of "culture." A display of major archaeological finds and artifacts underscored the deep connections across the Asian continent.[102]

The fifth and final theme—"Status of Women and Women's Movements"—was ably dealt with under the guidance of Safiyeh Firoz of Iran, Paz Policarpio Mendez of the Philippines, H. Soebandryo of Indonesia, and Kamaladevi Chattopadhyay of India. Women's contributions to anticolonial movements were celebrated without compromising specific demands for gender equity so often brushed aside at nationalism's triumphal moment of arrival. The women committed themselves to the twin objectives of "service to the country" and "removal of all inequalities." A revival of the All-Asian Women's Conference of 1931 was proposed to tackle the challenges of the new era.[103]

Nearly 20,000 delegates and guests gathered at the Purana Qila for the closing plenary session on the evening of April 2, 1947 for "a true celebration of Asian fellow-feeling." Sutan Shariar, the prime minister of Indonesia, felt that "the Asian sentiment" had to be "preserved as a holy flame" if "One Asia" was to be expanded into "One World."[104] It was left to none other than Mahatma Gandhi to provide a sobering climax to the proceedings. He had already dropped in the day before and lamented the shameful inability of Indians to keep the peace among themselves (figure 6.4).

At the concluding session, he began by recalling the utter abjection of colonial rule. "We were all coolies," he said. "I was an insignificant coolie lawyer." He told the foreign guests that they had not seen the real India by coming to Delhi. For that experience, they would have to go to India's villages that had been turned into "dung heaps" in modern times.[105] What really pained him, however, was the recent history of religious strife in India. He had just spent several months dousing the flames of violence in Bengal and Bihar and applying his healing touch. During his absence from Delhi, the Congress High Command led by Jawaharlal Nehru and Vallabhbhai Patel had passed a resolution on March 8, 1947, calling for the partition of Punjab, which also had become engulfed in violence. Louis Mountbatten had arrived in India on March 22, 1947 as the last viceroy with plenipotentiary

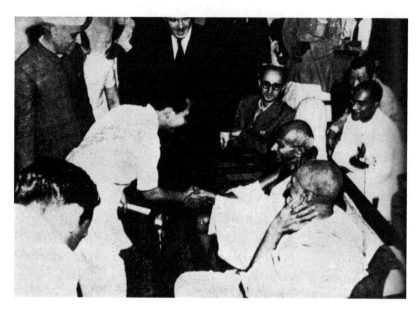

6.4 Mahatma Gandhi at the Asian Relations Conference, April 1947 (Reproduced from D. G. Tendulkar, *Mahatma: Life of Mohandas Karamchand Gandhi, 1945–1947,* vol. 7, Bombay: Vithalbhai K. Jhaveri and D. G. Tendulkar, 1954)

powers to accomplish the British withdrawal from India as quickly as possible with least possible harm to imperial interests. Gandhi described himself as Mountbatten and Nehru's prisoner in Delhi as violence of religiously defined majorities against minorities careered out of control.[106] "Do not carry the memory of that carnage beyond the confines of India," he begged the foreign visitors. It was as if it had nothing to do with the true spirit of Asia. In an assertion of innate faith, he proclaimed, "Asia has to conquer the West!" "The message of Asia is not to be learnt through European spectacles," he argued, "not by imitating the vices of the West, its gunpowder and atom bomb." He ended with a stirring call to "deliver the world and not just Asia from wickedness and sin."[107]

Nehru picked up Gandhi's cue about "the message of Asia" and mused that "some kind of common bond unites us." He surely had the cartographic controversy between India and China on his mind when he claimed that "Asia is not merely something on a map." As he saw it, the center of events was shifting from Europe toward Asia and America.[108] It fell once more to the indomitable Sarojini Naidu to conclude the conference on an uplifting note. She envisioned "a federation of free peoples" as "the gold of Asian consciousness." The heart of Asia, she was convinced, was "indivisible and one." Earlier in the day, the leader of the Chinese delegation had issued an invitation to the second Asian Relations Conference to be held in two years' time in China. "I thought of what the Prophet of Islam had said so beautifully," Sarojini Naidu remarked: "Go even as far as China to seek knowledge." "Fellow Asians," she urged, "together march forward to the Dawn."[109]

Two years later, China was in the throes of its Communist revolution. The second Asian Relations Conference was never held. The Asian Relations Organization that delegates had somewhat reluctantly resolved to establish at Nehru's instance was also stillborn. But that did not mean the idea of Asia was dead. Writing a year after the conference in the inaugural issue of the journal *United Asia*, George Catlin, the renowned British political thinker, recalled "the magnificent oratory of Mrs. Naidu." "What prospect is there," he asked, "that this high hope will be realized, and that Asia will remain united?" What would the "renascence of Asia" come to mean?[110]

CHAPTER 7

Asian Solidarity and Animosity in the Postcolonial Era

O N JULY 26, 1953, at eight in the evening, the curtains lifted for a cultural performance by a visiting Indian delegation in Peking's Hoping (Peace) Hall. The Indians began by singing in chorus "Bande Mataram," the famous ode to their motherland. The patriotic prelude was followed by an overture to their hosts as Debabrata Biswas of Bengal and Surinder Kaur of Punjab sang in duet "Hindi-Chini Bhai Bhai" composed by Harindra Nath Chattopadhyay in celebration of the brotherhood of Indians and Chinese. Among the large audience was the top leadership of the People's Republic of China with Chairman Mao Zedong in his trademark blue coat sitting unobtrusively in the fourth row. The penultimate item in the twenty-course feast of Indian music and dance was a Bengali song poem written by Sukanta Bhattacharjee, a talented radical poet who had died young. As Debabrata Biswas rendered the immortal lines of this inspiring song—"Bidroha aaj, Bidroha charidike" (rebellion today, rebellion everywhere), the young Chinese stage manager synchronized flashes of red light that enveloped the hall. The prime minister, Zhou Enlai, hosted a grand banquet following the concert that had concluded with a Kathakali dance. "Aren't you the one who performed the revolutionary songs?" Zhou Enlai asked Biswas with a warm smile and a warmer handshake, as he trooped into the banquet hall with his fellow artists. "Wonderful, wonderful—you must perform these songs wherever you go," Zhou urged the Indian singer.[1]

Biswas, best known as a brilliant exponent of Tagore's songs, had arrived in China on July 16, 1953 as part of a twenty-nine-member cultural delegation of the Indian Peace Committee that contained twenty-five renowned musicians and dancers. He had felt a thrill as he crossed from British-occupied Hong Kong to Communist China. The Chinese had arranged a small army of young interpreters and a special train for their Indian guests. A three-day rail journey brought the Indian delegates from Canton to Peking where they received a tumultuous midnight welcome at the station before being lodged at the Peace Hotel. The event on July 26 was the second of three public performances the Indians gave in the Chinese capital. In addition to touring historical sites, the Indian itinerary included a trip to a village. Biswas was suitably impressed by the newfound dignity of Chinese peasants in contrast to the appalling misery of their Indian counterparts. Mao was hailed by everyone as the great liberator from the oppressive regime of Chiang Kai-shek and the harbinger of a new democracy. A visit to the campus of Peking University reminded Biswas of Tagore's Visva-bharati in Santiniketan.[2]

Biswas had expressed a wish to meet the famous painter Qi Baishi for whom Tagore had great admiration and had met in 1924. His Chinese hosts obliged by bringing the ninety-three-year-old artist from his village to a disciple's home in Peking. Accompanied by the dancer Chandralekha, Debabrata Biswas set off for a memorable meeting with Qi Baishi, who was delighted to learn that he had not only come from Tagore's land but sang Tagore's songs. Having seen numerous pictures of tractors in the new China, Biswas broached the subject of socialist realism in art. Is China going to obliterate its great tradition in the fine arts, he asked, and be satisfied with depicting war and machinery? Qi Baishi laughed and acknowledged the utility of realism as a mode of instruction for peasants and laborers. He himself still took inspiration from nature. Asking his student to prepare some color for him, he picked up a bamboo brush and produced for his Indian guests an exquisite painting of a lobster. Biswas returned from the encounter pondering over the concept of socialist realism in art and gifted the lobster to Chandralekha who was effusive in its praise.[3]

From Peking, the Indian delegation proceeded to Tientsin where they visited the impressive central musical conservatory. There, Biswas persuaded the sitar maestro Vilayat Khan to join him in presenting Tagore's popular song "Tomar holo shuru, amaar holo sara" that promised a beginning at every end. Vilayat's prelude and interlude in the *iman* raga took Biswas's vocal presentation to new heights. Biswas commented that the fierce individualism of Indian classical musicians had been leavened by China's example of collective creativity. The next stop was Nanking where tributes were paid to Sun Yat-sen at his mausoleum and to martyrs of the Chinese Communist movement.[4] The train journey from Nanking to Shanghai took about six hours. There, a new element was added to the cultural performance with Damayanti Joshi dancing to Debabrata Biswas's rendering of Tagore's "Nrityero taale taale":[5]

> With the rhythm of your dance,
> O Nataraj,
> Make me free from all bonds,
> Wake me up from sleep and
> Let the rhythm of your bond-free song
> Fill my heart.[6]

Biswas titled the presentation "Liberation of Man," and as anticipated, the Chinese audience roared their appreciation with calls for an encore. Tagore (or Tagole, as he was called in China) was held in great respect by the Chinese. Biswas noted that of the two dozen Indian books translated into Chinese, as many as twenty-two were authored by Tagore.[7]

On the evening of August 15, 1953, as the Indians prepared to leave Shanghai for Hangchow, a most astounding scene unfolded on the railway platform. A bunch of Chinese young men and women asked Biswas to sing "Hindi-Chini," and soon everyone joined in. What followed was a cyclonic dance with the Chinese and Indians holding hands. The classical vocalist Master Krishnan from Bombay slipped and fell, but that did not deter him from swaying to the rhythm of the song as he squatted on the platform. The laughter with which the song ended masked an emotional farewell, which became even more poignant as the Indians departed a few days later from Canton. The visitors had been overwhelmed by the warmth of Chinese hospitality. On the flight back home, Biswas noticed tears flowing down the cheeks of Murti, the *mridanga* player from Madras, as he looked wistfully out of the plane's window and his China diary lay open on his lap.[8]

Less than a decade after the expression of this bonhomie, India and China would be fighting a border war in the Himalayas. The 1962 war has been long accepted as a telos by historians of Asian relations focusing on political, diplomatic, and military affairs, resulting in a blinkered view that misses the full range of cultural connections during the late 1940s and the 1950s. The people-to-people contacts between Asian countries in that period must be seen as creative efforts at "world making" in the era of decolonization that have not been studied adequately.[9] The newly independent states of Asia and Africa also sought to forge solidarity in a world divided between two hostile Cold War blocs. The most dramatic attempt in this direction was the gathering of leaders of twenty-nine Asian and African states in Bandung, Indonesia in April 1955. Perhaps more significant than this statist initiative were the many conferences of an unofficial or semiofficial kind that brought together citizens who had recently broken free from co-lonial subjecthood. The slide from solidarity to animosity had much to do with the inability of new citizens to effect change through the realization of anti-colonial aspirations and the tendency of managers of states to opt for postcolonial continuity in the definition of sovereignty and borders. The inheritances from colonizing Europe ultimately proved weightier than the legacies of the best in anti-colonial Asian thought.

The Euphoria of Asian Brotherhood and Sisterhood

On October 1, 1949, Sarat Chandra Bose had shot off a telegram from Calcutta to Mao Zedong felicitating him on the establishment of the People's Republic of China and calling on him to lay the foundation of an "Asian Bloc" for countering the "machinations of Western imperialists and freeing all Asiatic countries from foreign yoke." Mao replied by cable the same night at 11:50 p.m. welcoming "a broad friendship with the Indian people and all oppressed nations jointly to oppose imperialist aggression." On October 3, Sarat Bose published a signed editorial in the *Nation* titled

"Recognize People's Republic of China." It would be "impolitic" of India, he argued, to continue to recognize the government of Chiang Kai-shek who "must now find his recognition—or shall we say, condemnation—in the pages of Chinese history." Instead of "the dead past," India needed to "accord her recognition to the living reality of China" with "alacrity and enthusiasm" and "lay the foundations of Sino-Indian collaboration in the affairs of Asia."[10]

It took a little more time for Jawaharlal Nehru to shake off his attachment to Chiang Kai-shek. On December 30, 1949, India recognized the People's Republic of China, and on April 1, 1950, the sovereign Republic of India that came into being on January 26 established diplomatic relations with Peking. In spring 1951, an India China Friendship Association was formed with Tripurari Chakravarty, a historian of China at Calcutta University, as secretary. The first unofficial Indian representative to visit the People's Republic in April 1951 was none other than Dr. Madan Mohanlal Atal, who had led the medical mission in 1938. A six-week visit by a high-power Indian delegation led by Pandit Sundarlal, a Gandhian, followed in September–October 1951. A Chinese delegation led by Ting Si-lin, the junior minister of cultural affairs, returned the compliment with a five-week visit.[11]

The visit of the Indian delegation led by Sundarlal on the occasion of the second anniversary of the People's Republic left an especially rich corpus of firsthand impressions in its trail. The Chinese invitation was sent to Saifuddin Kitchlew, the president of the All India Peace Council, who selected an impressive array of fifteen intellectuals, journalists, and social workers for the visit. In addition to taking part in the dazzling pageantry on October 1, 1951 at Tiananmen Square presided over by Mao, the Indians had an opportunity to travel with delegates from Indonesia, Burma, Vietnam, and Pakistan to the major cities of China. Public interactions and banquets were interspersed with quieter private meetings. One afternoon, the Indians were invited to the home of Soong Ching-ling (Madame Sun Yat-sen), who was one of six vice-chairs of the People's Republic. The Indians were joined at this gathering by Mian Iftikharuddin of Pakistan. India's sole woman delegate, Hannah Sen, a noted educationist and president of the All India Women's Conference, presented Soong Ching-ling with a sari. Madame Sun Yat-sen expressed her warm appreciation for the poems of Rabindranath Tagore and Sarojini Naidu and the dance of Uday Shankar.[12]

Arunabh Ghosh has persuasively argued that cultural, scientific, and economic contacts between India and China were perhaps more significant and suggest a different chronology during the 1950s than a focus on political and diplomatic history.[13] Yet the cultural exchanges were not without political significance. Memoir-type accounts in English written by members of Indian cultural delegations merited a jointly written long review essay in the United States by Joan Bondurant, an Office of Strategic Services operative turned political scientist, and Margaret Fisher.[14] These works exhibited a range of opinions and impressions about China in the 1950s. Khwaja Ahmad Abbas, the left-leaning filmmaker from Bombay, and Russy K. Karanjia, the mercurial editor of *Blitz,* were impressed by China's rapid social progress and its determination to stand up to the West. Raja Hutheesingh, Nehru's brother-in-law, and Frank Moraes, a journalist with wartime experience in China, were skeptical about the measure of democracy in the people's democratic dictatorship. J. C. Kumarappa not surprisingly much preferred Gandhi to Mao. Muhammad Mujeeb, vice-chancellor of Jamia Millia Islamia, concluded that "in New China the question of academic freedom did not arise," but he admired China's "unity, solidarity and strength" and "the absence of 'internal conflicts' . . . which an Indian cannot but envy." Brajkishore Shastri, a labor leader affiliated to the Praja Socialist Party, felt an affinity for the Chinese people while deploring the dictatorial methods of the new rulers.[15]

One of the most insightful and entertaining of the early 1950s accounts of China was written by K. T. Shah, who visited China for six weeks as a labor delegate to take part in the May Day celebrations of 1952 and adopted the style of "a diarist, light and discursive, rather than labored, scientific, or obviously didactic."[16] Fisher and Bondurant described this former head of the Economics Department of Bombay University as "a controversial figure who thoroughly enjoyed the role of 'one-man opposition.'" The American commentators believed that he "had exercised considerable influence over Subhas Chandra Bose in opposing the Gandhian leadership of the Congress."[17] In fact, Bose had invited the very capable political economist to add intellectual heft to the National Planning Committee he had set up in 1938. Shah had worked closely with both Bose and Nehru during the freedom struggle. He broke with Nehru along with other socialists like the scientist Meghnad Saha when the Indian prime minister appeared to prefer postcolonial continuity to a radical departure from the colonial past. Shah was one of the most eloquent proponents of a democratic, secular, and federal India alongside a few farsighted colleagues including Hari Vishnu Kamath in the Constituent Assembly between 1946 and 1949. The constitution in the view of these conscientious dissenters retained too many states of exception inherited from colonial structures of state authority. K. T. Shah lost as an independent to a far less distinguished candidate belonging to the Indian National Congress in the first general elections in India as did B. R. Ambedkar who had come to a temporary accommodation with the Congress leadership during the constitution-making process.

Shah was chosen as the opposition candidate to run as an independent in the first presidential election in 1952 against Rajendra Prasad, the Congress nominee. Meghnad Saha, his friend and colleague from their National Planning Committee days and now a member of parliament from Bengal, had put forward his name. He did not have a chance of winning in an indirect election by parliamentarians and state legislators to the top constitutional post. But it was as a presidential candidate that he set off for China in April 1952. The original letter of invitation from the All-China Federation of Labor (ACFL) never reached him, most likely because of the surveillance by the intelligence bureau at the post office. "Though our home-made Constitution assures Freedom of Speech and Expression as among the Fundamental Rights of Citizens in India," he wrote, "there are so many limitations and restrictions, that the true soul of Freedom is overladen and obscured by the miasma of these exceptions."[18] A copy of the invitation was fortunately hand delivered to his home. So it was that K. T. Shah went to China as de facto leader of an unofficial trade union delegation to attend the May Day festivities at the same time as the official cultural delegation led by Nehru's sister Vijayalakshmi Pandit. One of his fellow delegates was his colleague in the Constituent Assembly, Shibban Lal Saxena, who despite his "excellent record of service and sacrifice in the days of active struggle" had been "defeated at the polls by a common-and-garden variety of Congressman."[19]

On the eve of May Day, Shah encountered Liu Shaoqi, president of ACFL and a vice-chairman of the People's Republic, who came across as "extremely well-informed, well-mannered and soft spoken." "In his quiet voice and intellectual face," Shah commented, "it is impossible to find a trace of the usual picture of a fierce Bolshevik which the capitalist world is taught to conjure up." From a peasant background and through work in labor organizations, Liu Shaoqi had emerged as "the high priest of the theoretical Communism in China." The high priest the following morning was, of course, Mao Zedong. The song "The East Is Red" with the lyrics "The East is aglow, the sun is rising, China has brought forth a Mao Tse-tung" competed in popularity with the national anthem. Giving a vivid description of the May Day celebrations, Shah noted the conspicuous absence of any display of China's armed might at this mass gathering. "Taken as a whole," he observed, "the parade was a magnificent, inspiring spectacle. It combined Goebbels' artistry with Gandhiji's sincerity." But he had no doubt that "the masses had many causes for genuine satisfaction, besides the mere hysteria of the moment."[20]

Pressed by a woman journalist for specifics on how to strengthen the bond between China and India, K. T. Shah responded with half a dozen suggestions. These included introduction of regular airmail services, a daily news section in the broadcasting corporations of both countries, a general trade treaty for the free flow of goods and services, teaching the languages and literature of the two countries in each other's universities, exchanges of teachers, and holding regular conferences among experts on subjects of mutual interest. In sharing these ideas with Vijayalakshmi Pandit, Shah noted the Chinese were tied to the Soviet Union for help and shared ideology but not averse to "achieving Asian solidarity with the working class leading." A call on the prime minister Zhou Enlai, who had "an honorable record of suffering and achievement," and the offering of gifts of goodwill along with his wife seemed "in tune with the ages-old tradition of the two countries, and yet not out of harmony with the new order." In Shah's view, early post-1949 China appeared to be doing better than early post-1947 India on the question of federalism. "While the Common Programme in China postulates 'democratic centralism,' and yet provides for such a considerable autonomy for local governing bodies," he observed, "we in India talk of real democracy, and yet so effectively centralize the real power, authority and resources of government as to make of provincial autonomy, or municipal and village self-government a tragic farce."[21]

A visit to Mukden gave Shah an opportunity to assess the drive toward industrialization in China's northeast in the wake of the Japanese and Russian inheritance. A tour of Nanking provided insights into the organization of the Chinese Communist Party. A survey of the Huai River project in the Yangtze valley was an occasion to reflect on agrarian reform in the new China. Hangchow and Shanghai were the venues to assess the progress made by Chinese trade unions. The political economist was not uninterested in the question of culture. In Shanghai, he was treated to a superbly acted stage performance of *The White-Haired Girl*. "They say this has been made into a picture," he wrote, "but I was glad I saw the real performance by a mistress of her art, rather than a pale reflection in a mechanical reproduction." He was equally convinced of the vastly improved economic and political status of women in Communist China.[22]

On his return to India, K. T. Shah briefed prime minister Jawaharlal Nehru on his tour of China and the suggestions he had made to enhance friendship between the two countries. "Naturally, he listened without any comment," Shah noted, "but I felt I had discharged a duty of every citizen of a free country in my position should take upon himself." Mahatma Gandhi before his death had personally advised him always to do so, whether his suggestions were accepted or not. During the train journey home from Delhi to Bombay, Shah reviewed his "impressions of the new life and regime in China." "It may be that we saw only what we were meant to see," he conceded, "and heard what we were intended to hear. But they could not arrange to sift and check the material we gathered, nor dictate the conclusions we might arrive at on a balance of the evidence collected." In summing up, Shah concluded that the new regime "commands the sincere allegiance of an overwhelming proportion of the people of China," and the government "worked to make democracy real and of daily experience for the masses." He was also of the opinion that China was "no tool of any other power."[23]

Watching the May Day extravaganza, Shah had wondered, "Why this expenditure of all that money and energy?" The answer he gave was that "China wants—needs—the sympathy and friendship of the working class of the world. . . . They want peace to enable them—and the rest of their class— to achieve their own prosperity."[24] Just as Shah was being received at Bombay central station on June 5, 1952 by enthusiasts eager to learn about his experiences in the "new Old World," D. D. Kosambi, a brilliant Indian historian and polymath, was attending a meeting of the preparatory committee in Beijing of an Asia-Pacific Peace Conference that was to be convened October 2–10, 1952.[25] The ocean added to the continent enabled Asian peace activists to embrace labor organizers from Latin America and Canada as well as African Americans fighting for racial equality in the United States. On September 12, 1952, W. E. B. Du Bois sent his "warmest congratulations" to the conference organizers on behalf of "16 million American Negroes." "I have seen Asia but once, in 1936, when I visited China and Japan," he explained, "and realized the leadership of the people of Asia in numbers, in hard work, and in antiquity of culture over all the peoples of the world." His own people whom he described as "the untouchables of this land" held out "their hands to Asia, applauding the People's Republic of China, the independence of India and Pakistan, and the struggle in Burma and Indo-China to achieve a new freedom and democracy."[26]

A mural copy of Diego Rivera's *The Nightmare of War, and the Dream of Peace* had adorned the conference hall in Beijing on June 6, 1952, the final day of the preparatory meeting for the October gathering. It was not just the raging Korean War but also British repression in the Malayan emergency and French aggression against the Democratic Republic of Vietnam that constituted the nightmare for the Asian organizers. Peace for Asian activists had a much broader compass than the European concern with nuclear disarmament. The conference itself, as Rachel Leow has perceptively argued, played a crucial role in the "emotional making" of an internationalism that stretched from Asia to Africa and Latin America.[27] Close to fifty countries sent more than 470 delegates and observers to the conference, the delegations from South and Southeast Asia far outnumbering those from Northeast Asia. For a meeting organized under the auspices of the World Peace Council, the representation of the Soviet Union was miniscule.

Women and workers were present in large numbers, not diplomats and politicians. They were accommodated in the newly built Peace Hotel designed by the architect Yang Yanbao. The conference witnessed plenty of drama both within and outside the conference premises as the United Nations (UN) came under fire for its partisan role in the Korean conflict and colonized Southeast Asia, not to mention its lack of recognition of the People's Republic.[28]

The conference proceedings, as Anita Willcox noted in her diary and sketches, were played out on a highly strung affective register. Perhaps the most poignant theatrical scene enacted on the Beijing stage was the reconciliation between India and Pakistan. During the preparatory meeting, the Pakistan delegation had lamented the absence of the Kashmir problem from the agenda of a conference focusing on the conflicts in Korea, Malaya, and Vietnam. The Kashmir issue and "the resultant fireworks" might "weaken Asian solidarity," Lionel Lamb, the British consul in Peking, reported hopefully to London, and divert attention from the theme of "foreign imperialistic aggression in South East Asia." Much to his disappointment, what transpired was "an emotional and sensational scene of Indian-Pakistan rapprochement." The leader of the Indian delegation and veteran freedom fighter Saifuddin Kitchlew presented a Kashmiri lacquer box to his Pakistani counterpart, Pir Manki Sharif, who in turn put a gold cap on his Punjabi brother Kitchlew's head. Kitchlew and Sharif garlanded Guo Moruo, who had brought them together. Louis Wheaton, an African American labor leader, read out a joint India-Pakistan declaration on Kashmir squarely placing the blame for the dispute on Anglo-American machinations and the ineptitude of the UN. Delegates stood on their chairs and wildly cheered the signing of the declaration. The members of the two delegations hugged and kissed, and the Indian and Pakistani women showered each other with flower petals.[29]

Besides such effusive publicly expressed bonhomie, there were quieter opportunities for Asians to learn from one another. The artist Maqbool Fida Husain was one of the sixty Indian delegates at the Asia-Pacific Peace Conference. Husain was honored to meet Qi Baishi, the master of ink painting, whom he held in the highest respect and described as the Matisse of Asia. Disdainful of socialist realism imitated from the Soviet Union, he saw no reason for Chinese artists to abandon their own rich cultural inheritance. The other Chinese artist to make a powerful impression on Husain was Xu Beihong, who in 1940 had spent several months in Tagore's Santiniketan and interacted with Bengal's leading painters. It was in India that Xu's depiction of horses took on a new life as he rode them all the way to Kashmir. A dozen years later at Xu's studio, Husain was mesmerized by a gigantic canvas of a thousand horses, each of which was imbued with grace and power. Xu's example inspired Husain to lend new vigor to his own horses.[30] Artistic genius had vaulted across the Himalayas.

China was by no means the only venue of these Asian interactions in the early Cold War era. Those whose political sensibilities were dyed in pale pink rather than flaming scarlet sought out other destinations to get together. From January 6 to 15, 1953, the First Asian Socialist Conference convened in the city hall of Rangoon, which Su Lin Lewis aptly describes as "a transnational hub for like-minded socialists from Indonesia, India, Burma, and Japan to engage in the work of socialist internationalism with an Asian inflection."[31] West Asia all the way to Lebanon was well repre-sented and an expansive definition of Asia enabled the participation of Egypt and other North African countries. India sent the largest contingent of seventy-seven delegates followed by Indonesia with twenty-six repre-sentatives. A key Indian organizer and ideologue of this effort was Ram Manohar Lohia, a leader of the 1942 Quit India movement, who broke with the Nehruvian Congress in 1948 to form a socialist party. He was a critic of "communal politics" and what he called "hanger-on politics" and urged Asian socialists to embrace "the politics of steering clear of the two big powerful combinations, the American combination and the Russian combi-nation, not of following a middle course between the two but of initiating and struggling for positive policies of freedom, social reconstruction, pro-gress and the pursuit of happiness."[32] Lohia advocated the establishment of a "Third Camp" as a bloc of countries and a "Third Force" as a popular movement since 1950 in the context of the Cold War divide. Indonesia was represented by Sutan Sjahrir, Sukarno's political rival, who had attended the 1947 Asian Relations Conference in Delhi. They were warmly wel-comed in Burma by the prime minister, U Nu, and socialist leaders U Ba Swe and U Kyaw Nyein. While the Burma Workers and Peasants Party had sent a delegation to the Asia-Pacific Peace Conference in Beijing, the Burma Socialist Party chose to play host to like-minded noncommunist leftists in Rangoon. The resolutions adopted in Rangoon emphasized a commitment to freedom of still-colonized countries, democratic socialism in those that had won independence, nondiscrimination along lines of caste or creed, and most important, equal rights for women. By the time the 1956 Second Asian Socialist Conference was held in Bombay, the Suez crisis precipitated by Britain and France as well as the Soviet invasion of Hungary that year seemed to have vindicated the socialists' anti-colonial stance and equidistance from the two power blocs.

What were the ingredients that cemented a sense of Asian solidarity? K. T. Shah had described the Indian ambassador to China as "a scholar by inclination and a writer with research pretensions" who had "become a diplomat by experience, with interests far wider than the sphere of his immediate duties."[33] In 1953 appeared the scholar diplomat Kavalam Madhava Panikkar's reflections on this large question in his book *Asia and Western Dominance*. The subtitle that 1498–1945 constituted "the Vasco da Gama epoch of Asian history" gave a misleading impression about the argument of the book. The notion of half a millennium of European dominance has remained a common error among those unwilling to take note of the different phases of the Western presence in Asia. Panikkar was closer to the mark when he wrote that "the common experience of a hundred years has created a political background. All the Asian countries have had to go through the same suffering, fight the same battles, meet the same enemy." Beyond the common political experience, Panikkar made a case for shared cultures of the common people of Asia. He credited the Bolshevik revolution with having radicalized anti-colonial movements, which acquired "moral strength by the mere existence of a Revolutionary Asia." At the same time, he recognized the pioneering role played by Japan at the turn of the twentieth century in stirring an Asian consciousness with the book by "the great Japanese artist Okakura Kakuzo" and the recovery of Asian peoples "from the 'first intoxication of the West' as Yone Noguchi called it." A "change of attitude" to arrogant claims of European intellectual and moral superiority was indicated, according to Panikkar, by "books like the *Futurism of Young Asia* by the Indian socialist, Benoy Kumar Sarkar."[34]

A British empire in decline and an American empire on the rise were not prepared to allow Asia to contrive its own destiny exactly as it pleased. Despite the overarching Cold War divide between the American and Soviet blocs, there was a significant element of British-American rivalry, as Ayesha Jalal has shown, in preferred policies toward a decolonizing Asia. So far as West Asia was concerned, the British wanted the defense of the oil-rich Gulf to center around a string of British bases. Their vision of a Middle East Defense Organization, put forth since 1951, was contradicted by the US secretary of state John Foster Dulles's concept of a "northern tier" of countries in West Asia to ring fence the Soviet Union. The American approach of bringing together pro-Western governments in Turkey, Iraq, Iran, and Pakistan into a treaty organization won out and led eventually to the forging of the Baghdad Pact of 1955.[35] In eastern Asia, the United States crafted the South East Asia Treaty Organization, which two countries of the region, the Philippines and Thailand, joined in 1954 along with Pakistan whose eastern wing lay on the cusp of South and Southeast Asia. It was in the context of these Anglo-American strategic moves and the popular movements in favor of Asian solidarity that the Bandung Conference was organized in April 1955.

The Bandung Moment and Era

"Bandung," Christopher Lee claims, "contained both the residual romance of revolution, as well as the *realpolitik* of a new world order in the making."[36] For scholars engrossed in high politics and interstate diplomacy, the road to Bandung was paved by the 1949 conference on Indonesia and the meetings in Colombo and Bogor in 1954.[37] The new interest in the role of non-state actors in Asian and global history has led to the excavation of a very different genealogy leading to Bandung and its aftermath. Eleven days before the Bandung Conference, thousands of people thronged the venue in Delhi of a nongovernmental Conference of Asian Countries on the Relaxation of International Tension, which Carolien Stolte has recently recovered from historical oblivion.[38] Nongovernmental it may have been, but nonpolitical it was not, seeking sustenance from popular peace movements and with forty-three Indian members of parliament serving on its preparatory committee. The prime mover was Rameshwari Nehru, a leading figure in the women's movement, who was married to a cousin of the Indian prime minister. Prominent women poets and writers—Kyoko Nagase of Japan, Theja Gunawardane of Ceylon, and Tran Khanh Van of Vietnam—helped set the tone of the conference. India-China friendship was a major theme, as was evident when the Chinese delegates, especially Guo Moruo, were given a rousing reception. Maulana Bhashani came with a message of Asian peace from Pakistan. Jawaharlal Nehru did not appear in public at this conference so as not to upstage Indonesia, but he received some of the delegates in private. Blurring the boundary between the unofficial and the official, good wishes were sent from Delhi for the success of the conference in Bandung. "I pray to the creator, the most gracious Allah," Bhashani declaimed, "for the success of the Conference and for the sacred unity of oppressed Asians."[39]

The Bandung Conference was blessed by the grace of Allah, or it may have ended in tragedy even before it began. On April 11, 1955, the airplane *Kashmir Princess* owned by Air India crashed on its way from Hong Kong to Jakarta. It was most likely brought down by a time bomb planted by a GMD agent. The Chinese premier Zhou Enlai was meant to be on that flight but was fortunately delayed and did not get on it. He came later via Rangoon. The participation of the People's Republic was crucial to the success of this conference of Asian and African countries.

The idea of such a conference was broached by the Indonesian prime minister, Ali Sastroamidjojo, at a meeting in Colombo of the heads of governments of India, Pakistan, Indonesia, Burma, and Ceylon on April 28–30, 1954. Some of the key organizational details were worked out at a subsequent meeting in Bogor on December 28–29, 1954. At Bogor, Jawaharlal Nehru shot down Indonesia's suggestion to invite representatives of independence movements because "that would mean an interference in internal affairs."[40] With British colonial rule continuing across the Strait of Malacca in Malaya and most of Africa struggling for freedom, this was a troubling decision by a leader of India's independence movement that lent the Bandung moment a strong statist bias. Christopher Lee writes of the spirit of Bandung pregnant with the "the feeling of political possibility." Yet the emergence of "the gate-keeper state" at nationalism's moment of arrival made certain that the "contradictions of Bandung" limited the range of "the possibilities."[41]

Representatives of twenty-nine countries—twenty-three Asian and six African—gathered in Bandung, Indonesia from April 18 to 24, 1955, with two of the soon-to-be-independent African countries taking observer status.[42] Richard Wright, the African American novelist, overestimated the significance of both race and religion at Bandung in his popular book *The Color Curtain*.[43] Carlos Romulo was closer to the mark when he remarked that the "color line" was not drawn by the sponsor states and that its "appearance" was "the result of a historic coincidence" flowing from "a common abhorrence of imperialism." There, the commonality ended. The radical mythology surrounding Bandung ignores the diversity of opinion among the organizers and participants on the question of neutrality versus alignment in the context of the Cold War. Notwithstanding these differences, the Bandung Conference was "a historical pageant, symbolizing the coming of age of Asia and Africa."[44] The Indonesian government went to great lengths in staging the conference and the stars from China, India, and Egypt acted their roles with admiring crowds outside the conference venue playing their parts as well.[45] But it was not all theater. The deliberations at Bandung nurtured the elements of Asian solidarity now being extended to embrace Africa, while containing the seeds of animosity between Asia's two most populous countries.

Sukarno, the charismatic president of Indonesia, inaugurated the conference on April 18, 1955 with a stirring address as he welcomed his guests to "the first intercontinental conference of colored people in the history of mankind." Running through his speech was an exuberant celebration of difference:

> We are of many different nations, we are of many different social backgrounds and cultural patterns. Our ways of life are different. Our national characters, or colors or motifs—call it what you will—are different. Our racial stock is different, and even the color of our skin is different. But what does that matter?

What mattered at this "conference of brotherhood" was the "unity in desire" that transcended diversity. It was not a meeting based on exclusivity on lines of religion, race, or ideology but rather "a body of enlightened tolerant opinion" that sought to "impress on the world that all men and countries have their place under the sun." The Asian and African countries were united by "a common detestation of colonialism in whatever form it appears." Sukarno was not prepared to accept that colonialism was dead—it was "a skillful and determined enemy" that appeared in "many guises." The battle against colonialism had been a long one. He recalled that April 18 was the anniversary of Paul Revere's famous midnight ride through the New England countryside at the onset of the American War of Independence, "the first successful anti-colonial war in history." He quoted Henry Wadsworth Longfellow's famous lines:

> A cry of defiance and not of fear,
> A voice in the darkness, a knock at the door,
> And a word that shall echo for evermore.

"Yes, it shall echo for evermore," Sukarno asserted. "The Light of Understanding has again been lit," he said of a rejuvenated Asia and Africa, "the Pillar of Cooperation again erected." In conclusion with the utterance of "Bismillah" (God speed), he set the Bandung Conference off to an auspicious start.[46]

Nehru's gambit to get the leaders of delegations to abandon their opening speeches did not work. Most wanted to have their say, even if that involved airing their ideological differences. Somewhat surprisingly, the most eloquent articulation of the limits of nationalism in the Bandung era came from Carlos Romulo of the Philippines, which had joined a US-sponsored treaty organization:

> Nation no longer suffices. Western European man today is paying the terrible price for preserving too long the narrow and inadequate instrument of the nation state. We of Asia and Africa emerging into this world as new nation states in an epoch when nationalism, as such, can solve only the least of our problems and leaves us powerless to meet the more serious ones. We have to try to avoid repeating all of Europe's historic errors. We have to have the imagination and courage to put

ourselves in the forefront of the attempt to create a 20th-century world based on the true interdependence of peoples.

If this sounded like a Tagorean critique of nationalism, Romulo went on to quote from one of Tagore's celebrated poems. History, he contended, had "already passed from the nation . . . to the region, the continent, the world. It is a world as envisioned by Rabindranath Tagore, 'not divided into fragments by narrow domestic walls.'"[47]

The opening speeches revealed that for the assembled Asian and African countries, there were colonialisms and colonialisms. Egypt's Gamal Abdel Nasser brought up the Palestinian question alongside denunciations of European colonialism in North Africa and white racism in South Africa. He drew support from most of the Arab delegations. Iran and Iraq expressed concern about Soviet colonialism in central Asia and Eastern Europe—a theme also alluded to by Turkey, Pakistan, and the Philippines. Prince Norodom Sihanouk of Cambodia obliquely raised the issue of Chinese Communist subversion in neighboring countries of Southeast Asia. Prince Wan Waithayakon of Thailand, a veteran of the 1943 Tokyo conference, made explicit what Sihanouk had left implicit when he made direct mention of the Thai politician Pridi Banomyong's subversive activities with Chinese help from across the border in Yunnan.[48]

Zhou Enlai took notes as these addresses were being delivered and asked to make a supplementary speech in response. "The Chinese Delegation has come here to seek unity and not to quarrel," he said with remarkable restraint. He saw no difficulty in Asian and African countries with different ideologies and social systems being able to engage in friendly cooperation. He claimed China respected the freedom of religious belief and that he had a pious imam as a member of his delegation. On the matter of subversive activities, he pointed out that the Chinese revolution was "certainly not imported from without" and quoted a Chinese proverb: "Do not do unto others what you yourself do not desire." Zhou blended public conciliation with a private charm offensive. Meetings with Wan Waithayakon and Norodom Sihanouk in his bungalow disarmed the sharp edge of their criticism. While at Bandung, Zhou negotiated an agreement with Indonesia on the vexed dual nationality question of overseas Chinese.[49] The anti-communist Romulo of the Philippines found Zhou to be "affable of manner, moderate of speech" by contrast with Nehru's "pedantry." In the American scholar George McTurnan Kahin's sober and balanced assessment of Bandung, Zhou Enlai was described as "reasonable, conciliatory," which won him accolades, especially when compared to the "overbearing and patronizing attitudes of Nehru and [Krishna] Menon," the Indian prime minister's irascible colleague.[50]

The focus on India and China in Bandung has rather obscured the quiet reentry of Japan onto the stage of Asian and global diplomacy. Douglas MacArthur had summarily rejected the invitation to Japan for the Asian Relations Conference in 1947. Japan's eagerness to accept the invitation from the five Asian organizers to come to Bandung "made Dulles jittery." Mamoru Shigemitsu, who had hosted the Greater East Asia Conference in 1943, had returned as foreign minister in Ichiro Hatoyama's government and wanted Japan to "hold on to its sovereign independence till the bitter end." To be sure, Japan's Ministry of Foreign Affairs held consultations with the US State Department. In March 1955, it was assumed that Shigemitsu would lead Japan's delegation to Bandung. Tokyo broached the subject of a Shigemitsu-Zhou meeting with Washington. Asia was Japan's natural habitat and Tokyo wanted "peaceful coexistence" with all countries. Shigemitsu declared his "ultimate ambition" was to find "a lasting solution to the problems of the region." He was to be assisted in Bandung by the Harvard-educated Kase Toshikazu and Ota Saburo, ambassador to Burma, who had played a key role during World War II in helping Indian freedom fighters. In the end, neither Hatoyama nor Shigemitsu went to Bandung ostensibly because the budget session of the Japanese Diet coincided with the dates of the Asian African conference. The economics minister Tatsunosuke Takasaki was chosen to lead the Japanese delegation, which included several of Shigemitsu's protégés including Tani Masayuki. Takasaki informed Shigemitsu by telegram that Japan had been welcomed warmly at Bandung where he described his country's "destiny" to be "identical with that of Asia." He emphasized the role of scholars and artists in building an Asian ecumene. At his meeting with Zhou Enlai, the Chinese leader said that he understood Japan's constraints in recognizing the People's Republic and assured Takasaki that China recognized the Hatoyama government.[51] Japan's participation in Bandung presaged and paved the way for Shigemitsu as deputy prime minister to lead Japan into the UN the following year. "The basis for peace and progress in Asia," he said to the UN General Assembly on that occasion in December 1956, "is to be found in the economic development of the countries of the region."[52]

Some of the more spirited debates between neutralists and aligners took place in the closed sessions at Bandung. Turkey's stout defense of the North Atlantic Treaty Organization and similar agreements provoked Nehru into launching a tirade against military pacts into which some of the Asian countries had been drawn. Zhou Enlai was more circumspect even if he disliked these treaty organizations. He had visited the prime minister of Pakistan, Mohammed Ali Bogra, who had told him that "although Pakistan was a party to a military treaty, Pakistan was not against China." That assurance had enabled them to achieve "a mutual understanding." Even though India, Burma, and China had put forward five principles, *Panchshila,* to undergird international affairs, Zhou saw no difficulty in adding or subtracting from them. He was quite prepared to accept seven principles as suggested by Pakistan. Since some delegates, such as Charles Malik of Lebanon, thought the phrase "peaceful coexistence" was associated with Communists, Zhou proposed accepting the language of the UN Charter— "Live together in peace." "The Chinese people," Zhou declared toward the end of his intervention, "do not want war with the United States."[53]

In his closing speech, Nehru hoped that Asia would not allow itself to be dragged and tied to "Europe's troubles, Europe's hatreds and Europe's conflicts."[54] Despite ideological differences, the leaders of Asia and Africa were able to agree on the text of a final communiqué. Romulo was right in saying that Bandung was characterized by "a rare degree of sanity and dignity" leading to "a first flowering of the spirit of this new Asia and Africa."[55] The Asian African conference spelled out a dozen ways of achieving economic cooperation. The section on cultural cooperation began with the claim that "the cultures of Asia and Africa are based on spiritual and universal foundations."[56] The atheist Zhou Enlai made no objection. The five principles were expanded to ten high-sounding values, which would enable nations to "live together in peace." The principles included the longstanding commitment to "the equality of all races" but also a concession to "the right of each nation to defend itself singly or collectively."[57] Conspicuous by its absence was any statement on women's rights and gender equity that had formed such a key element in unofficial Asian conferences in the past. The statist orientation of the Bandung Conference had meant that it was predominantly a male affair.

The legacy of "people's Bandungs," however, was not obliterated so easily. Zhou's proposal at Bandung to set up a permanent institution of an Asian African conference did not find favor with Nehru. But the unofficial conference in Delhi just before the Bandung Conference had resolved to establish the Afro-Asian People's Solidarity Organization. Bridging the distance between unofficial and official, this organization was set up in Cairo with the patronage of the Egyptian government in December 1957. Unlike Bandung, the Cairo conference invited representatives of eighteen African anti-colonial movements struggling for freedom. Gamal Abdel Nasser with his prestige at its peak after the Suez crisis of 1956 gave the inaugural address at the Afro-Asian Solidarity Conference in Cairo and Anwar Sadat led the Egyptian delegation. While adhering to the principles enunciated at Bandung, Cairo saw a much larger gathering of scholars, writers, musicians, and artists and a healthy dose of youthful exuberance. Women, including Rameshwari Nehru from India, were active in prominent roles and women's rights were back on the agenda.[58]

Despite an element of one-upmanship between Nehru and Zhou in Bandung, relations between the two Asian giants remained on an even keel for at least three more years. In the crucial areas of planning for development and the use of statistical methods in compiling and analyzing socioeconomic data, the collaboration between China and India deepened in the aftermath of Bandung. Dissatisfaction with Soviet models led to a Chinese "turn to India." On December 9, 1956, Zhou Enlai visited the Indian Statistical Institute in Calcutta and arranged with its director, Prasanta Chandra Mahalanobis, for an exchange of economists and statisticians. "And next year in Peking," the Chinese premier firmly told Mahalanobis before taking leave. The Chinese were keen to learn large-scale random sampling from India and a team of Chinese statisticians led by Wang Sihua soon arrived in Calcutta. Mahalanobis visited China with a team of colleagues for three weeks in June and July 1957. A hectic program of lectures and meetings was capped by a dinner with Zhou Enlai laying the road map for future cooperation. Even though two Chinese statisticians spent 1958 in Calcutta, internal Chinese politics took a turn that did not bode well for the future.[59] Mao Zedong's decision to take the Great Leap Forward left the prospects of India-China collaboration in the field of socioeconomic development by the wayside.

From Brotherhood to Fratricide

The year 1958 witnessed a series of military coups across Asia. On July 14, Bastille Day, the Hashemite monarchy of Iraq was overthrown in an anti-Western junior officers' uprising. On October 7, the pro-American military top brass of Pakistan aborted the fledgling democratic political process in Pakistan. The same month, the government of U Nu in Burma handed over power to the military led by Ne Win. What was meant to be a temporary measure to curb instability became permanent military dominance and a three-decade spell of military rule from 1962. The era of Rangoon as a cosmopolitan venue of Asian solidarity was over. The resort to martial rule was only a dramatic manifestation of the assertion of unitary sovereignty imported in colonial times from Europe by postcolonial Asian states obsessed with rigid borders. Asia had forgotten the art of political centers negotiating the exercise of power in the peripheries. The Java-based Indonesian state faced rebellions in the outer islands, some with an Islamic flavor, in the late 1950s—long before the military took state power into its iron hands from 1965. Ceylon with its Sinhalese majority denied political rights to the Tamils in the north. The Chinese and Indian states, despite their different political systems, took a remarkably similar posture toward center-region issues, abandoning precolonial and anti-colonial ideas of federal unity that had been influential in the early twentieth century. If the authoritarian party state in China adopted a hard stance toward the non-Han nationalities, Jawaharlal Nehru—the paragon of democracy—had no qualms about turning authoritarian in Kashmir and India's northeast. India acquiesced in China's "liberation" of Tibet in 1950, making it apparently irrelevant during the first decade of postcolonial bonhomie. The dissolution of brotherhood into fratricidal conflict had much to do with the choices made by postcolonial states on the nature of sovereignty.

During his 1915–1916 visit to China, Benoy Kumar Sarkar had been critical of the young Chinese republic's obsession with unification in preference to the older imperial accommodation of de jure imperium of *hwangti* with de facto independence of provinces. Sarkar died on a visit to the United States in 1949, the year of the founding of the People's Republic. Mao Zedong had moved a considerable distance from his espousal of a sovereign republic of Hunan in the early 1920s to the assertion of the centralized power of an authoritarian party state in the late 1950s. An uprising in what was described as the autonomous region of Tibet in early 1959 elicited severe repression by the coercive apparatus of the Chinese party state. The Dalai Lama, who had met his father figure Mao and attempted to come to an accommodation with Beijing until the mid-1950s, fled to India with a small entourage in March 1959 and received asylum there.

As early as 1950, India's ambassador to China, K. M. Panikkar, had allowed a slippage in his country's acknowledgment of China's "suzerainty" to "sovereignty" over Tibet. Despite disquiet in sections of the Indian establishment, India turned a blind eye to the People's Liberation Army's "liberation" of Tibet from its feudal and imperialist past that began on October 25, 1950. If Panikkar's dispatches from Beijing allowed romance to trump realism, his successor, Nedyam Raghavan, who had been finance minister in Subhas Chandra Bose's Azad Hind government in 1944–1945, was more hardheaded in his assessments of Chinese intentions. Yet the brief from New Delhi was to improve relations with China. On April 29, 1954, Raghavan and Zhang Hanfu, China's vice-minister for foreign affairs, signed an eight-year agreement on trade and intercourse between India and Tibet by which independent India renounced the extraterritorial privileges inherited from the British raj in Lhasa. The agreement was prefaced by the high-sounding *Panchshila* ideals proclaiming mutual respect and peaceful coexistence. Throughout the negotiations leading to this agreement on Tibet, the question of the border between China and India was not raised.[60]

From the late nineteenth century, the British had redefined sovereignty and frontiers in the colonies. A shift from layered to monolithic sovereignty was matched by frontiers that had been fuzzy zones being demarcated by rigid lines on maps. In a bizarre re-creation of the colonial mapmaking exercise, Jawaharlal Nehru ordered the revision and reprinting of official maps depicting the extensive Himalayan border with China in unambiguous linear fashion during the summer of 1954. It was a unilateral decision without any negotiation on the subject with China. If only government presses producing maps rather than ground realities could uphold postcolonial India's claims of territorial nationalism, the border question could be considered resolved.

The border between India and China straddled three sectors—the western, the middle, and the eastern—with major differences in perspective between the two countries in the west and the east. The contention in the west was over the arid and rugged Aksai Chin plateau abutting Xinjiang, Tibet, and Ladakh where Nehru was to say not even a blade of grass grows. The terrain in the east was very different with forbidding, thickly forested mountainsides in an area receiving some of the highest monsoon rainfall. For much of the 1950s, the borderlands of the western sector were deemed by India to be undemarcated or, at any rate, somewhat messy and confused. In the eastern sector, India took its stand on the line drawn by Henry McMahon in 1914 between the North-East Frontier Agency (NEFA) and Tibet. China rejected the legality of this border imposed by British imperialists. In any case, the representative of republican China had not accepted it and Communist China did not recognize Tibet's sovereign authority to have entered into any such agreement. While acquiescing in Tibet's incorporation into China in 1950–1951 and signing the agreement on Tibet in 1954, India did not ask China to endorse the border at the McMahon line.

It was not until August 1958 that the border question was formally taken up by India and China. In September 1957, the news of a Chinese strategic road in Aksai Chin linking Tibet and Xinjiang had become public knowledge. Although rumors about such a road-building exercise had circulated since the early 1950s, confirmation of its existence in what India considered to be part of its territory in Jammu and Kashmir brought the border issue off the back burner just as the Tibet crisis was coming to the boil. What followed in 1959 were border skirmishes and exchanges of letters between the two prime ministers revealing the extent of their disagreements. If India had yielded too easily on Tibet in 1950, its position became increasingly intransigent on the border issue a decade later. Nehru, who had accepted the element of ambiguity and uncertainty in Aksai Chin during the early 1950s, now asserted absolute certitude in the western sector as in NEFA. The vice-president Sarvepalli Radhakrishnan's son, Sarvepalli Gopal, had returned from a stint of research in the archives of London in 1959. An empirical historian of British viceregal policy, Gopal understood nothing of the nuances about sovereignty and frontiers in Indian precolonial and anti-colonial thought. He was put in charge of the historical division of India's Ministry of External Affairs, which misled Nehru not a little in taking an untenable position on India's claims in Aksai Chin.

On November 7, 1959, Zhou Enlai suggested that both sides withdraw twenty kilometers from the line of actual control to create zones of nonconfrontation. The Indian establishment saw no merit in the proposal. A final opportunity to settle the border question before the outbreak of widespread armed hostilities came in late April 1960 when Zhou Enlai came to Delhi with substantive ideas for an agreement. The Indian side led by Nehru seems to have decided even before Zhou's arrival not to negotiate in earnest. Zhou and his entourage including his foreign minister, Chen Yi, stayed in Delhi from April 19 to 25, 1960. The detailed records of the talks provide insights into the lack of political imagination of postcolonial states hemmed in by a history of colonial humiliation and even more by the colonial inheritance of concepts of unitary sovereignty and hard borders. The Chinese expressed bewilderment at the apparent Indian desire to cling to its imperialist legacy.

A close reading of the proceedings of the India-China interactions reveals that Zhou Enlai was prepared to make a pragmatic separation between theory and practice. As a British imperialist imposition, the McMahon line was in the Chinese view illegal and in theory unacceptable. However, as an opening gambit, Zhou offered the following proposition: "We stated that we do not recognize the McMahon line but that we were willing to take a realistic view with Burma and India." In fact, China reached a boundary settlement with Burma in 1960 that roughly accorded with the reviled McMahon line. A couple of days into the talks,

Zhou further elaborated on his stance: "We take the following position: a) we say that we cannot recognize the McMahon line b) but we will not cross that line since Indian troops have already reached it; and c) as regards two or three points where Indians have exceeded the McMahon line, we are willing to maintain the status quo pending negotiations." Zhou was offering to trade NEFA for Aksai Chin, where China had not only built a strategic road but was an area that was seen intrinsically connected to Xinjiang and Tibet. In NEFA China acknowledged "that what India considers its border has been reached by India's actual administration." Zhou wanted India in return to pragmatically accept that "China's administrative personnel has reached the line which it considers to be her border" in Aksai Chin.[61] Nehru scorned an offer that may well have served India's national interest in pursuit of the mirage of national pride.

What followed for six months during the latter half of 1960 was the charade of talks between the mandarins of both sides. Even the leader of the Indian team recognized that the goal was not any kind of resolution but a restatement of positions that had created an impasse.[62] In 1961, India adopted a so-called forward policy in the frontier areas of establishing military posts in zigzag fashion to counter Chinese posts and patrols.[63] The policy was the brainchild of civilian leaders in the Defense Ministry led by Krishna Menon and the Intelligence Bureau led for a decade by B. N. Mullick ensconced in the Home Ministry. "Peaceful coexistence" had now been replaced by what Mao called "armed coexistence, jigsaw pattern." India's military top brass was skeptical of the "forward" policy but went along with what had been devised by the civilian leadership. The Intelligence Bureau was more adept in the early years of independence at conducting surveillance on political opponents, including freedom fighters, than assessing the dangers on the Himalayan border. There was an assumption, utterly unsubstantiated, that the Chinese would not resort to armed retaliation in a major way.

India paid a hefty price for such wishful thinking. On July 13, 1962, the departing Chinese ambassador conveyed to Nehru that India's posture toward China was undermining Asian solidarity.[64] A flare-up on the Thagla ridge on September 8, 1962 was merely a portent of a full-scale conflagration the following month. On October 20, 1962, the People's Liberation Army launched massive attacks in the western and eastern sectors of the border.

7.1 Se-la (© Sugata Bose)

Within four days, the Chinese forces took control of the entire area up to their 1960 claim line in central and northern Ladakh as the Indian forward posts wilted before them. On October 24, Zhou Enlai proposed to Nehru that the two sides withdraw their troops twenty kilometers behind the line of actual control as it existed on November 7, 1959. Whereas the Soviet Union reckoned it was a sensible offer of a compromise, New Delhi refused. On October 25, 1962, the monastery town of Tawang in NEFA fell to the Chinese without a fight. India declared a state of emergency the next day. As the Chinese attackers swept on, the dream of Asian unity lay shattered among the boulders of the Sela (pass) (figure 7.1).

The Chinese forces began a second round of offensive operations on November 16, 1962 in both sectors. The Indian army resisted in Ladakh but retreated in NEFA. Bomdila fell to the rampaging Chinese forces on November 18, and the plains of Assam lay open to them. Swallowing his pride and setting aside his nonalignment, Nehru desperately sought American military aid. Having landed a humiliating punch, China suddenly announced a unilateral cease-fire on November 20, 1962. At the end of a monthlong border war, China kept the territory extending to its 1960 claim line in Ladakh but withdrew its forces north of the McMahon line in NEFA, which later became the Indian state of Arunachal Pradesh.

A Colombo conference of six Asian African countries hosted by Ceylon proposed that the two Asian giants resolve their differences through direct negotiations. In China's view, the role of these honest brokers was "to mediate, not arbitrate" while India insisted that China accept all the recommendations from Colombo in toto before the start of negotiations. "The Chinese Government has made the most magnanimous efforts to promote a peaceful settlement of the Sino-Indian boundary question," Zhou Enlai claimed in a letter to Nehru on April 20, 1963. He listed Chinese actions on the cease-fire and pullback, repatriation of sick and wounded soldiers, and return of captured war materiel. He described the withdrawal of Chinese frontier guards to positions far behind where they were on September 8, 1962, as "a great regard for India's dignity and self-respect."[65] Nehru, however, had gone into a deep sulk feeling betrayed by the Chinese and, at his death the following year, left a twenty-year legacy of diplomatic nonengagement between the two Asian neighbors at the highest levels of government. The nationalist rift found expression in the domain of literature and culture as well.[66]

Meanwhile, the India-China border war paved the way for improved relations between China and Pakistan. In 1959, the pro-American military dictator of Pakistan, Ayub Khan, had broached the prospect of joint defense between India and Pakistan that Nehru had not thought worthy of consideration. In the aftermath of the 1962 war, Ayub's foreign minister, Zulfiqar Ali Bhutto, moved swiftly to reach an agreement in principle with China on December 26, 1962, just as India resumed negotiations with Pakistan on Kashmir at the insistence of the Americans. In March 1963, a formal agreement was signed by Bhutto and Chen Yi settling the border between the two countries based on a swapping of territories. India was left complaining that Pakistan had given away some 2,000 square miles of Indian territory in the bargain. "You are a defeated nation, don't you see?" was Bhutto's taunt that the Indian negotiators had to endure as the Kashmir talks headed toward failure.[67]

If Bhutto spearheaded Pakistan's foreign policy effort to forge close ties with China, the more ideologically committed admirer of Mao Zedong's People's Republic was Maulana Abdul Hamid Khan Bhashani of East Pakistan. Bhashani traveled to China on a political pilgrimage in the autumn of 1963. Soon after his arrival, he fell ill. Zhou Enlai came to see him in Beijing's Union Hospital. Bhashani noticed that the nurse, who had been chatting with him when Zhou walked into his room, did not bother to get up in a show of deference to the Chinese premier. This was proof for Bhashani of not just equality but personal liberty in Communist China. What impressed him most about the Chinese was their laughter, made possible through the lifting of the deadweight of oppression. He met Puyi, the last emperor of China, whose reeducation was narrated to him as an example of the magnanimity of the regime. Mao, in Bhashani's view, was a talented poet, and he included three poems in Bengali translation for his readers, including the famous poem "Snow" translated by Bishnu Dey. The peasant leader from Bengal admired the Chinese communes and drew a dramatic contrast with his own country mired in grinding poverty. Completely oblivious of the recent gigantic famine in China, the red Maulana claimed that not a single person had suffered from hunger or died of starvation in this Communist utopia.[68]

The 1962 war had enabled the regime of Mao Zedong to retrieve a modicum of international prestige after the domestic catastrophe of the Great Leap Forward. The authoritarian party state seemed to have learned few lessons from that disaster as Mao proclaimed the Cultural Revolution in 1966. A perceptive Pakistani visitor, Hamid Jalal, could see that not all was well in China in the throes of this new tumult.[69] A left-wing fringe on India's political spectrum, by contrast, was enthused by China's chairman. This blinkered view of China hampered the prospect of a much broader Asian, and by now "third world," solidarity fomented by the Vietnamese war of resistance against the onslaught of the United States.

"Amaar nam, tomar nam, Vietnam, Vietnam" (My name, your name, Vietnam, Vietnam) was one of the slogans that rent the monsoon-laden air of Kolkata in the late 1960s. The colonial-era Harrington Street—on which stood the US consulate—was renamed Ho Chi Minh Sarani in a symbolic act of anti-imperialist solidarity in that global historical moment. Another slogan had mention of a place closer in geography—"Amaar bari, tomar bari, Naxalbari, Naxalbari"—Naxalbari is your home and mine.

Chairman Mao Zedong hailed the 1967 peasant uprising in Naxalbari as "a peal of spring thunder" of the Indian revolution; but to mix Mao's favorite metaphors, it turned out to be one that failed to "spread like a prairie fire." Why not was a puzzle that troubled me when I went in 1973 to read history as an undergraduate in Presidency College where one could still hear faint echoes of a once-reverberating cry—"Lenin, Stalin, lal salaam, Mao, Ho Chi Minh, lal salaam"—red salutes to the iconic leaders of Communist revolution. It remained one of my guiding questions as I began my doctoral research in 1978 far away in Cambridge, England. The red salutes and the Little Red Book had fallen through the trapdoor of history. But the insights in Mao's tract "On Practice" stayed with me as I delved into the theory and history of agrarian transformation in colonial and postcolonial India.

It was one thing to take a resolute stand against the brutal American war on Vietnam but quite another to imagine in Maoist China, especially in the era of the Cultural Revolution, the panacea for the global ills of inequity. The radical left in India and elsewhere in Asia remained blind to the inhumanity of the quill drivers of the Great Leap Forward and the Cultural Revolution. Such blind spots and blinkered views are not unusual in the search for better alternatives in the form of utopia. The abjection felt under Western colonial rule in Asia had led some of the most astute anti-colonial thinkers to turn a blind eye to Stalinist terror in the 1930s.

Not limited to Asian activists and thinkers, the blinkers were also worn by left-leaning scholars in the West. When in Cambridge I met the economist Joan Robinson in 1978, I was flabbergasted to find that her 1968 romance with the Cultural Revolution in China was not over.[70] It was not that anyone had full knowledge of the human toll of that misadventure quite as yet. As a schoolboy, I had witnessed how—once the widespread agrarian revolution failed to materialize—the Naxalite movement degenerated into an erratic campaign of terror in the urban jungle of Calcutta. There was an element of infantile mimicry in the proclamation "China's Chairman is our Chairman" plastered on Calcutta's walls. But that was not all there was to it. In my own study *Peasant Labor and Colonial Capital* published in 1993, I concluded that the Naxalbari uprising, limited though it was in its geographical spread, had a disproportionate impact on political psyches in India. I quoted a sympathetic scholar, Sumanta Banerjee, who likened it to the "pre-meditated throw of a pebble" designed to bring forth a series of ripples in placid waters.[71]

The impact of Naxalbari as a local expression of global Maoism was even more profound on the tenor and trajectory of South Asian historical scholarship. It triggered a productive departure from Marxist orthodoxy that held sway until then and planted the seeds of what eventually bore fruit as *Subaltern Studies.* Whatever the engagement with European theory, it is hard not to notice that Ranajit Guha's *Elementary Aspects of Peasant Insurgency in Colonial India* was informed, influenced, and even inspired by his enchantment with the Naxalite dream, whatever the pitfalls of its praxis.[72]

The end of the Maoist era in China would clear the way for the choice of a new trajectory of economic development and lay the basis for the much vaunted "rise of China" as the leading edge of the rise of Asia from the late 1970s onward. Yet these were precisely the years during which the Third Indochina War portended the apparent "meltdown of Asian internationalism." "Asian internationalism was at its zenith in early 1950," writes Christopher Goscha. "Asian internationalism was most certainly dead in early 1979." He shows how the initial conflict between the inward-looking nationalist Khmer and the internationalist Vietnamese Communist networks paved the way for the divide between China, the Association of Southeast Asian Nations (ASEAN), and Khmer Rouge on the one hand and the Vietnam-Indochina alliance on the other hand.[73] Benedict Anderson also opened his famous 1983 book *Imagined Communities* with a reference to "the recent wars between Vietnam, Cambodia and China." The Vietnamese invasion of Cambodia in December 1978 and January 1979 and the ensuing Chinese attack on Vietnam in February 1979 appeared to him to be of "world-historical importance" signaling "a fundamental transformation in the history of Marxism and Marxist movements." Recently empowered revolutionary regimes at war with each other seemed a convenient starting point to reflect on the origins of nationalism.[74] Yet the Vietnamese invasion toppled the Pol Pot regime and brought a ghastly genocide perpetrated by a doctrinaire communist regime to an end.[75] Asian universalism possessed deep enough historical roots to survive the fires of Cambodia in the late 1970s fanned by a policy of ASEAN noninterference in that human tragedy.

The year 1979 marked the beginning of a new phase in the imaginings of Asia as a political signifier and as a method of scholarly inquiry that gave interreferential Asia a fresh lease of life in the late twentieth and early twenty-first centuries. There were, of course, some attempts in the 1980s to reduce Asianism to spurious cultural essences of Asian values, but more sophisticated versions emerged as well. Broadening of the horizon of theorizing about Asia came in large measure through a creative engagement with Asianisms of the past as the basis for crafting a new future of an increasingly interconnected Asia.

Conclusion

Challenges of a Reconnected Asia

I N NOVEMBER 1977, Maitreyee Debi took Rabindranath Tagore's *Talks in China* with her as she set off from Calcutta on a trip to the People's Republic of China. If the opportunity arose, she wished to speak about the Indian poet to Chinese audiences. She was also keen to meet Xie Bing Xin, the woman who was perhaps the most innovative translator of Tagore's poetry into Chinese. Despite repeated requests to her hosts, that longed-for meeting did not materialize. Maitreyee Debi set aside her disappointment to make the most of a rare glimpse of China in the immediate aftermath of the death of Mao Zedong.[1]

The occasion for the visit by a small Indian delegation was the inauguration on December 9, 1977, of a memorial to Dwarkanath Kotnis, a member of the Indian medical mission, who had died on that date in 1942 while serving in China. The dedication ceremony in Shijiazhuang of Hebei Province in north China was an elaborate affair attended by Indian and Chinese dignitaries. The Indian ambassador, K. R. Narayanan, a future president of the Indian republic, made a good speech that was unusual, according to Maitreyee Debi, for government representatives.[2] The memory of Kotnis supplied a thin thread of connection between the two Asian neighbors estranged since 1962.

Maitreyee Debi was no uncritical admirer of Chinese communism; her attitude was at best ambivalent. She could remember Chiang Kai-shek's visit to Santiniketan with his wife and accompanied by Jawaharlal Nehru. After lunch on the veranda of Tagore's hut "Udayan," Nehru had rushed to help Madame Chiang put on her shoes. Others were also keen to perform this chivalrous act, but no one could match the speed of Nehru's dive toward Madame Chiang's feet.[3] After 1949, Maitreyee Debi had sympathized with the aims of the revolution that established the People's Republic. However, the imitation in India of the Cultural Revolution in the late 1960s struck her as nothing but madness ("*paglami*"). The murder of Gopal Sen, the vice-chancellor of Jadavpur University, and the decapitation of the statue of Ishwarchandra Vidyasagar in College Square by the Naxalites caused a feeling of revulsion in her. Throughout the 1977 visit, the Chinese were keen to emphasize that the Indians were visiting at a very auspicious moment since the tyranny of the Gang of Four was over. A Telegu poet, Shri Shri Mahakavi, who was a member of the delegation, composed a poem on the "wicked foursome" (*dushta chatushtoy*) after hearing ad nauseam about Chairman Hua Guofeng's lightning move against Mao's last wife, Jiang Qing, and her three associates. Confucius was not yet rehabilitated in post-Mao China. Maitreyee Debi's remonstrations that Marx had not been born in the time of Confucius and the ancient sage could not have known about socialism were received with some bemusement.[4]

After guided tours of an ophthalmic instruments factory, a cotton mill, and a military hospital in Shijiazhuang, the Indians were taken to other destinations in China including Beijing, Nanjing, and Shanghai. A vice-chair of the CCP, Ye Jianying, hosted a banquet for the visiting Indians in the capital. Narayanan canceled a planned trip to Canton and attended the dinner in the Great Hall of the People as the Indian ambassador had been until then denied access to such high-ups in the Communist hierarchy.[5] The remembrance of Kotnis was an icebreaker that opened the way for a visit by the Indian foreign minister, Atal Behari Vajpayee, the following year. The trip of the Indian delegation to Nanjing included the customary homage by climbing up the 490 steps to Sun Yat-sen's mausoleum. In Shanghai, Maitreyee Debi wept as she watched a moving film on Mao Zedong's funeral. She contrasted the dignity of the Chinese leader's sendoff with the disorder that had attended Tagore's and Gandhi's funeral processions in India. She also regarded Mao as a talented poet. She supplied for the benefit of her Bengali readers a translation of Mao Zedong's poem about the "orange island" of Changsha written as a tribute to his second wife, Yang Kaihui, after her execution by the GMD in 1930. As she left China in January 1978, Maitreyee Debi felt the same sense of wistfulness that Debabrata Biswas had described in 1953.[6]

In November 1979, Krishna Bose traveled with her husband, Sisir Kumar Bose, through East and Southeast Asia retracing the footprints of Netaji Subhas Chandra Bose during the struggle for freedom between 1943 and 1945. In Japan, Iwaichi Fujiwara kept telling her that he would show her how "a soldier of a defeated country" lives. Krishna found this refrain odd as the economic prosperity of the "defeated country" was by now the envy of the world. She was impressed by the strides taken by Japan in science and technology and, more generally, the reconstruction of Japan from the ruins of World War II. Having played a key role in the wartime formation of the Indian National Army, Lieutenant General Fujiwara rose to become the chief of Japan's Self-Defense Forces in the 1960s. One evening, the Boses arrived at Fujiwara's modest two-storied wood-framed home to be warmly welcomed by the general's wife, daughters, and granddaughters. A traditional Japanese dinner featuring shabu-shabu was accompanied by pure Darjeeling tea.[7]

Moving effortlessly between the early 1940s and the late 1970s, Krishna Bose blended her telling of Asian history with keen observations on contemporary Asia. As poignant as the dinner at Fujiwara's home was the lunch with Tetsuo Higuchi, daughter of Rashbehari Bose, at the Nakamuraya restaurant, which despite the change in ownership still displayed a beautiful portrait of Rashbehari's wife on its wall. The places associated with the visits of Netaji—the Imperial Hotel, Hibiya Park, Hibiya Hall, the Japanese Diet, the Meiji shrine, the Ueno Museum of Art, Tokyo University—came alive with the reminiscences and present-day concerns of the people who had worked or interacted with him. Shibusawa Shakuro's son recounted the days that Netaji had spent as a guest in their home. Masayoshi Kakitsubo narrated his experience of interpreting Netaji's speeches at the Greater East Asia Conference in 1943 and at Tokyo University in 1944. Having served as a diplomat in India during the late 1930s, Kakitsubo served as ambassador to Pakistan and deputy permanent representative of Japan at the UN in the postwar decades before being appointed by the UN secretary-general as director of the Asian Institute of Economic Development and Planning in

1970. A trip to Kyoto by taking the new bullet train named *Hikari* (Light) yielded a more somber meeting with the brother of General Tsunamasa Shidei, who had perished with Subhas Chandra Bose in the air crash in Taipei on August 18, 1945. A visit to Nara's Todaiji with its imposing statue of Buddha was a reminder of the cultural ties between India and Japan stretching back to the eighth century. Homage was paid at the Buddhist temple Renkoji in Tokyo where the mortal remains of Netaji are preserved. Earlier in 1979, NHK had broadcast a hugely popular documentary titled *Chalo Delhi* (On to Delhi) presented by a well-known director Isomura Naonori. This film including an enactment of the Red Fort trial of 1945 had rekindled interest in economically resurgent Japan in an earlier generation's involvement with India's struggle for freedom.[8]

From Japan, Krishna Bose traveled to Singapore, Kuala Lumpur, and Bangkok, major centers of Netaji's wartime activities, and also Taipei, the location of his tragic mortal end. Having landed at the glittering new Chiang Kai-shek International Airport in Taipei, the Indian visitors were more interested in the older airfield where the 1945 crash had occurred. In Singapore, the cityscape was being transformed, but the old Municipal Building with its Corinthian columns overlooking the sprawling *padang* and the Cathay Theater stood as silent witnesses of the tumultuous mobilization of Indian anticolonial sentiment during the 1940s. Even the traditional bungalow in which Subhas Chandra Bose lived and worked was still there, now home to a Chinese family. In Kuala Lumpur, the veterans of the INA gathered for a lunch meeting in a restaurant called the Bangles to relive their wartime adventures with their Indian guests. Datin Janaki Thevar Athinahappan, who as a teenager had donated her earrings and bangles and gone with the Rani of Jhansi Regiment to Burma, narrated her experience of the retreat with Netaji from Rangoon in April 1945. Americk Singh Gill had landed as a secret agent of the INA by submarine in India and recalled his escape from a prison van in Calcutta after receiving a death sentence in a secret trial by the British upon capture. Satyavati Thevar Naidu, who commanded the Singapore unit of the women's regiment after Lakshmi Swaminathan moved forward to Burma, had by now lost her sight, but tears flowed from her sightless eyes when she met the Boses at dinner. Janaki sang a patriotic song composed by Kazi Nazrul Islam that Netaji had taught the leading figures of the women's movement.[9]

The visiting Indians were bombarded with questions at a press conference by journalists of the *Malaysia New Straits Times,* the *Malay Mail,* and other newspapers. In a sign of the new times, Chen Tiu Yeng of the *Malay Mail* asked whether Asian history was being properly written. Mostly Western scholars were writing Asian history. Could they have any empathy with Asia's freedom struggle, and even if they did, was it possible for those from another culture to offer a correct interpretation? Indians in Malaysia, despite being a minority, had acquired a measure of economic prosperity and political power. A mass meeting was held one day at the headquarters of the Malay Indian Congress. An announcement by a cabinet minister, Datun Samivellu, that the new auditorium being built by the Congress would be named after Netaji drew thunderous applause from the gathering.[10] Indians in Thailand were as enthusiastic as their counterparts in Malaysia about the wartime anti-colonial movement. The Thai-Bharat Cultural Lodge provided the venue for a large meeting with veterans of the freedom struggle led by Ishwar Singh Narula, who along with Debnath Das had represented Thailand's Indian community in the Azad Hind government. Netaji last visited Bangkok on August 16–17, 1945. Krishna Bose learned with profound regret that a perfectly good plan for Bose to go underground in Thailand was rejected for a far riskier one as the war wound down to a close.[11]

By 1979, Taiwan, Singapore, and Hong Kong along with South Korea had all emerged as East Asian tigers following the flying geese model of Japan. Even Kuala Lumpur appeared impressive to Krishna Bose by comparison with her home city. It was upon reaching Bangkok that she felt closer to Calcutta. Singapore and Kuala Lumpur were shiny, clean, organized cities that exuded the signs of prosperity. By contrast, Bangkok still appeared faded and exhibited signs of poverty. There were quite a few potholes on the road from the airport to the city, and the shaking in the car provided a warm sense of familiarity.[12]

Asia in the Age of Contemporary Globalization

The four decades following the late 1940s marked the heyday of the nation-state characterized by the disruption of older forms of intra-Asian connections and the pursuit of alternative approaches to economic development.

The spectacular postwar recovery of Japan between the 1950s and 1970s provided a model for the export-led economic development paradigms of the so-called Asian tigers—South Korea, Taiwan, Singapore, and Hong Kong. Yet the example of these island nations—big, medium, and small—was not emulated by the large continental nation-states. The more populous countries of Asia—India and China in particular—followed variants of import-substituting industrialization with different degrees of success. Post-1947 India staved off the specter of colonial-era famines but remained beset by chronic malnutrition and hunger. Post-1949 China scored well in normal years in the field of basic health and education but could not prevent the largest famine of the twentieth century during the Great Leap Forward in 1959–1961. Both managed to build a heavy industrial base, but growth rates remained sluggish. Pakistan opted for the consumer goods–led textiles-first strategy for industrialization.

In 1989, Amartya Sen offered a lucid, comparative assessment of India's development experience in the first four decades since 1947. Post-1947 India did not have post-1949 China's direct and massive public action to improve living conditions. This accounted for the fifteen-year difference in average life expectancy in the two countries by the late 1980s. If India had China's lower mortality rates, "there would have been 3.8 million fewer deaths in India around the middle 1980s." As Sen put it, "every eight years or so more people in addition die[d] in India—in comparison with Chinese mortality rates—than the total number that died in the gigantic Chinese famine."[13]

By 2019, China had gone through four decades of economic reforms launched by Deng Xiaoping in 1978–1979 while India completed nearly thirty years of liberalization begun in 1991. P. V. Narasimha Rao, prime minister from 1991 to 1996, instructed his finance minister, Manmohan Singh, to dismantle what had come to be called the permits, licenses, and subsidy raj. In mid-1991, India faced an acute balance-of-payments crisis, making it necessary to seek an International Monetary Fund loan to tide over it. However, the Indian state made a virtue out of necessity by removing the many barriers to the entry, expansion, and diversification of firms by proclaiming a new industrial policy. The stifling practice of licensing the use of industrial capacity was virtually abolished. The bureaucratic logjams on the road to economic development were gradually removed. These economic reforms addressed only the first part of a two-pronged problem facing Indian economic development. The reformers pulled back from overintervention by the state in certain sectors but did not redress state negligence of social sectors, especially health and education.

The phenomenon widely described as the rise of Asia since China's engagement with the global economy since 1979 and India's reforms since 1991 exhibits some striking disparities. In 1979, the size of the economies of China and India was roughly the same. After four decades of rapid growth, China's economy was in 2019 nearly six times the size of India's economy. Even though India accelerated steadily from the 3–4 percent plodding rate of growth of the 1947–1980 period in the last forty years, China grew much faster as it quickly became the manufacturing hub of the world exporting to overseas markets. The emphasis on health care and education in the Maoist era had also enhanced the quality of labor that served as the springboard for rapid economic development in the post-1979 era.

Giovanni Arrighi contended in his book *Adam Smith in Beijing* that "when the history of the *second* half of the twentieth century will be written" in a long perspective, the odds were that "no single theme will prove to be of greater significance than the economic renaissance of East Asia." That renaissance in turn suggested that "Adam Smith's prediction of an eventual equalization of power between the conquering West and the conquered non-West might finally come true." China's economic rise led Arrighi to confidently predict in 2007 "the realization of Smith's vision of a world-market society based on greater equality among the world's civilizations more likely than it ever was in the almost two and a half centuries since the publication of *The Wealth of Nations*."[14]

It is important to ask what the dramatic acceleration of economic growth rates in Asia—not just China—meant for the global balance of power and what impact it has had internally on the pressing problems of poverty and inequality. Although millions have been lifted out of poverty, wealth inequality and income inequality between the rich and the poor have increased exponentially. Also, the rise of Asia is not a linear story but one interrupted by downturns, such as the Asian financial crisis of 1997–1998, the global economic crisis of 2008, and the pandemic-induced downturn since 2020. India was better able to ride out the 1997–1998 crisis than several countries in Southeast Asia, especially Thailand, Indonesia, and the Philippines. The economic costs had occasional unintended political benefits, however, serving as a catalyst for the fall of the Suharto-era authoritarianism and a transition to more substantive democracy in Indonesia. Despite the downturns of 1997, 2008, and 2020, with China as creditor to the United States and Asia as a whole powering ahead in manufacturing and services, the relations between Asia and the West are much different today from what they were two centuries ago. In fact, the global economic crisis adversely affected the United States and Europe much more than China and Asia and can be seen to have contributed to the redressal of the balance in favor of Asia during the 2010s.

The city of Wuhan—a conglomeration of the three towns of Wuchang, Hankou, and Hanyang located at the confluence of the Yangtze and Han Rivers—has played an outsized role in modern Asian and global history. In October 1911, an uprising in Wuchang by the followers of Sun Yat-sen heralded the fall of the Qing Empire. In 1927, Wuhan seemed to be the epicenter of an impending Asian revolution. Mao Zedong appeared in the city at the third plenum of the CCP in March of that year as the Communists tried to cement a united front with Wang Jingwei, the leader of the left-leaning wing of the GMD, against Chiang Kai-shek. Fear gripped the British concession in Hankou that dominated the economy of the region. Three months later in June, the peripatetic Indian theorist of revolution M. N. Roy showed Wang Jingwei a message from Joseph Stalin urging a Communist mobilization of the Chinese working class. The fragile alliance between Nationalists and Communists unraveled and with it any prospect of a broad-based Asian revolution.

In 2019, Asia's inexorable rise spearheaded by China seemed to be revolutionizing the global balance of economic and political power when the discovery of the SARS-CoV-2 novel virus in Wuhan at the end of the year ushered in an era of unprecedented anxiety and uncertainty. Any assessment of the impact of the global pandemic—formally declared by the World Health Organization in January 2020—on Asia's historical trajectory must be somewhat tentative. The severe lockdown of the bustling capital of Hubei Province and later in 2022 of Shanghai and Beijing as well certainly dented the confident predictions that the future was destined to be Asian. Besides, Asian countries that fell into debt to China for its infrastructural developments on the eve of the pandemic faced economic crisis, as the example of Sri Lanka's collapse in 2022 showed.

On the eve of the global pandemic, a popular book published in 2019 had captured the sense of optimism about the future. Both Asia's rise and Asian connections were expressed in these terms:

> Asians once again see themselves as the center of the world—and its future. The Asian economic zone—from the Arabian Peninsula and Turkey in the west to Japan and New Zealand in the east, and from Russia in the north to Australia in the south—now represents 50 per cent of global GDP and two-thirds of global economic growth. Of the estimated $30 trillion in middle-class consumption growth estimated between 2015 and 2030, only $1 trillion is expected to come from today's Western economies. Most of the rest will come from Asia. Asia produces and exports, as well as imports and consumes, more goods than any other region, and Asians trade and invest more with one another than they do with Europe or North America.

The author, Parag Khanna, had no doubt that looking back from 2100, it would be possible to precisely pinpoint "the date on which the cornerstone of an Asian-led world order began." It would be 2017, the month of May to be exact, when "sixty-eight countries representing two-thirds of the world's population and half of its GDP gathered in Beijing for the first Belt and Road Initiative (BRI) summit."[15] Missing from the party was India, concerned that its sovereign claims over Kashmir were being undermined by one branch of the BRI—the China-Pakistan Economic Corridor. Even though India joined the Asian Infrastructure Investment Bank launched in January 2016 as a major stakeholder, it opted out of the largest free trade bloc in the world—the Regional Comprehensive Economic Partnership—comprising the ten ASEAN countries along with China, Japan, South Korea, Australia, and New Zealand that came into force in January 2022.

India emerged at a pace second only to China as Asia recovered in the early twenty-first century the global position it had lost in the late eighteenth century. Dynamic economic growth infused a new sense of confidence. India was able to cope with the global financial crisis of 2008–2009 in a more efficient manner than most countries of the world. Yet India's performance in the areas of basic education and health care for the poor has left much to be desired in comparison with other countries of Asia, excepting Pakistan. India ran the risk, as Amartya Sen put it, of becoming half-California and half–sub-Saharan Africa. The rich in the major urban centers indulge in conspicuous consumption while the tribal peoples in India's rural and forest heartland continue to suffer acute deprivation. Moreover, as China has moved up the manufacturing chain, countries like Vietnam, Cambodia, and Bangladesh have taken its place as manufacturing centers with relatively low labor costs. India may have already missed that bus and is increasingly reliant on the buoyancy of the services sector as the agrarian sector continues to languish. If the forces of contemporary globalization have a dark underbelly, so do the flows of labor migration that constitute today's Asian interregional arena. The pandemic contributed to the slowdown in the rate of economic growth across Asia. Yet it is not this deceleration of growth but distributional issues that pose the greater challenge to emergent states of Asia.

The economic trajectory of Asia in a broad global context yields one powerful insight or conclusion. Asia has prospered not through economic autarky but by mustering the political and cultural resources to set the terms of global engagement, something that was effectively denied in the colonial era throughout all of Asia excepting Japan. In this process of denial, colonized South and Southeast Asia suffered most grievously. It is by engaging with the global economy and recovering its own agency that much of Asia is being able not just to ride the upswings of the global economy but also to reduce vulnerabilities to its more volatile downturns, such as the one that gripped the world since 2008–2009. As the United States and parts of Europe turned inward, Asia saw an opportunity to enhance intra-Asian trade and investment while keeping the lines of economic exchange open with the rest of the world. The global pandemic has injected new uncertainties about the future of global interconnections. If only Asia was to address the problems of inequity alongside achieving rapid growth in a post-pandemic world, what many predict will be an Asian century can turn out to be a truly prosperous era in the history of the continent.

In her book *Other Asias*, Gayatri Chakravorty Spivak speaks of "an effort that must be renewed again and again, with no guarantees, in the name of Asia's pluralized, where the naming names no real place." She urges us to "think of a more than merely economically diversified Pan-Asianism, a more than merely 'comparative Asianism.'"[16] Economy cannot be easily mapped on to the domain of culture. Yet the economic threshold of 1979 also marked "a dramatic increase in cultural production, ranging from visual art exhibitions to bilingual or multilingual films, to pop music, which circulated intensely within the region and aimed to define a multicultural intra-Asian culture (and consumer)." The explorer of the crafting of this Asian cultural identity, C. J. W.-L. Wee, focuses on two "significant curatorial-culturalist moments in the exhibitions of Asia." The first moment was the inaugural exhibition of the Fukuoka Art Museum unveiled in two parts—"Modern Asian Art— India, China, and Japan" in 1979 and "Festival: Contemporary Asian Art Show" in 1980. The second moment came with the Japan Foundation's thirtieth-anniversary exhibition jointly sponsored with the Tokyo City Opera Art Gallery in 2002 titled "Under Construction: New Dimensions of Asian Art." Wee describes these two cultural initiatives as the "international-regional exhibition" of 1979 and the "global-regional" exhibition of 2002, separated by the Asian financial crisis in 1997–1998 that resulted in the tawdry claims about "Asian values" to fall through the trapdoor of history.[17]

The 1979 exhibition assembled art from India, China, and Japan under the sign of Okakura Tenshin. The debt to this Japanese pioneer of the turn of the twentieth century was acknowledged by the Indian and Japanese curators and contributors to the exhibition catalog in equal measure. The Chinese essay sounded stilted by officialese and yet to free itself from the deadweight of socialist realism in art, even though new trends in artistic experimentation had already appeared in Shanghai and Beijing by the late 1970s. The next year, the exhibition became more capacious in representing the art of thirteen Asian countries—adding Bangladesh, Indonesia, Korea, Malaysia, Nepal, Pakistan, Philippines, Singapore, Sri Lanka, and Thailand. In exhibiting the works of a younger generation of Asian artists, the Fukuoka Art Museum took a significant step toward transcending the search for national essences and recognizing the interreferential character of the region's artistic creativity.[18]

The 2002 exhibition celebrating connections rather than comparisons and setting aside any search for national identity was organized under the sign of Takeuchi Yoshimi. This mid-twentieth-century theorist of "Asia as Method" had contributed more than any other contemporary intellectual to rescue Asianism from its entanglement with Japanese imperialist expansionism. Four decades before he was invoked at the exhibition, Takeuchi had urged Asian countries to "transcend the confines of nation and state to jointly address particularly urgent issues." What was needed, in his view, was "not so much an Asia defined in a historical and abstract sense but "Asia as a method" or "Asia as a function"; not for the benefit of one nation, but rather to let Asia as method enable its people to "question their own identity or acquire new identity." With nine curators from different countries led by Katakota Mami of Japan collaborating on mounting the exhibition, the collective effort drew on diverse local contexts before "remixing and reconstructing the whole." The director of the entire project, Furuichi Yasuko, stated the ambition: "Asia will be defined by Asians, instead of just being a historical concept rooted in memories, and this task is one that only we who live in the same age and space are able to do."[19] Writing half a century after Takeuchi Yoshimi, the Taiwanese scholar Chen Kuan-Hsing has creatively deployed Asia as method in the twenty-first century. New conceptions of Asia, he argues, need to be grounded in a broad range of "historical experiences" and "social practices."[20] The prospect of an overlap between Asian and Islamic universalisms in the early twenty-first century remains an intriguing possibility. Gayatri Spivak's speculation on the role of Islam in Asia is reminiscent of Benoy Kumar Sarkar's intuition on that subject a hundred years ago. "Islam is a peculiarly Asian internationality," writes Spivak, "that also embraces Africa, Europe, and latterly, the United States."[21]

The key protagonists of internationalist versions of the idea of Asia in the early twentieth century, according to the Chinese theorist Wang Hui, were Lenin, Sun Yat-sen, and Li Dazhao. In his famous essay "Democracy and Narodism in China," Lenin had regarded Russia as "undoubtedly an Asian country," not in terms of geography but on the basis of its place on the spectrum of capitalist development. Sun in his 1924 speech in Kobe had expounded on "the kingly way" in his vision of "Great Asianism," which Wang is at some pains to portray as "antithetical" to Japanese "Greater East

Asianism." He is closer to the mark in reading Li Dazhao's conception of "New Asianism" as a more direct repudiation of Japan's aggressive imperialism. For Lenin, Sun Yat-sen, and Li Dazhao, in Wang's interpretation, Asia is defined by its particular place within global capitalism. If this formulation veers a little too close to economic determinism, Wang returns toward the end of the essay to discussing "Asia's cultural potential" and "the reconstruction of the idea of Asia" as a marker of political "defiance of the colonial, interventionist, and dominating forces that have divided it." The "commonality of Asian imaginaries," we are told, "partly derives from subordinate status under European colonialism, during the Cold War, as well as in the current global order."[22]

What Wang underplays is the extent to which the socialist utopia has fallen victim to the more authoritarian strands of nation-statism. The Beijing-based critic of Japanese "Greater East Asianism" skirts around the dragon in the room—the role of a resurgent China in reimagining Asia. Well before the idea of an Indo-Pacific interregional arena acquired political traction around 2018, Prime Minister Shinzo Abe of Japan had spoken eloquently before India's parliament in 2007 about "the confluence of the two seas" and the imperative to build a "broader Asia."[23] Advocating the New Silk Road initiative—later renamed the BRI—President Xi Jinping of China declared in 2015, "The interests of Asian countries have become intertwined, and a community of common destiny has increasingly taken shape."[24] By 2022, these two rival visions of Asian and global connectivity were increasingly arrayed against each other. On the occasion of a visit to Japan by President Joe Biden in May 2022, the United States announced its commitment to an Indo-Pacific economic framework in a belated challenge to China's BRI. The American "pivot to Asia"—a declaratory promise made by President Barack Obama—has occurred in fits and starts over a decade. Even though wary of an overweening China, the rest of Asia does not share Eur-America's geopolitical priorities as the divergent responses to Russia's invasion of Ukraine in 2022 have amply shown. The message from Asia that is emerging loud and clear is that Europe's conflicts are not the most pressing global challenges.

The vital issue of what the rise of China means for the rise of Asia in the early twenty-first century is addressed by the historian Wang Gungwu in an appendix to his thought-provoking book titled *Renewal*. "The idea that a state be constituted from one nation," he writes unambiguously, "only emerged in eighteenth-century Europe." He juxtaposes to that rigid idea "the concept of *tianxia,* a vision of universality that was different from the idea of empire as exemplified in the Roman imperium." *Tianxia* signified "an enlightened realm." Modern Chinese scholars were divided on the question whether such a concept could be the foundation of a "Chinese multinational republic." One farsighted classical scholar who believed that it could was Gu Hongming whom the Indian visitor Benoy Kumar Sarkar had met in Shanghai during his search for "young Asia" in 1916. Gu Hongming's writings, Wang Gungwu noticed, had been "recently revived in China." Gu Hongming "asked the big questions about what China once stood for—not nation or empire but a moral *tiangxia* that had something to teach the world." This meditation on an intellectual of the early twentieth century led Wang Gungwu to ponder "what kind of China is now rising? Can it avoid being a nation-state that, when powerful, will emulate the national empires? Or will it be . . . a benign and peace-loving multinational state?"[25] *Renewal* was published in 2013 when the second possibility represented hope for the future. Since then, Gu Hongming's vision has been swept aside by the "Thought" of Xi Jinping. The rise of a new hegemon pursuing an ambitious project of nationalistic imperialism does not bode well for the more generous imaginaries of Asia in the twenty-first century.

The Pasts and Futures of Other Asias

Roses bloomed everywhere in Beijing as Peking University observed its 120th anniversary with a high-profile World University Presidents Symposium combined with its annual Beijing Forum. The presidents of Yale, Chicago, Tokyo, and the National University of Singapore, the vice-chancellors of Cambridge and Oxford, and the chancellor of Berkeley were present to wish Beida, as the university is affectionately called, a very happy birthday on May 4, 2018. The birthday bash opened with an impressive spectacle in a huge indoor stadium proclaiming Beida's motto of creativity, integrity, and—the slightly awkward—futurity.

Beida is a young university whose destiny has been inextricably intertwined with the turbulent history of China during the long twentieth century. It is younger than Presidency College, born in 1817, and Calcutta University, established in 1856, as well as Tokyo University set up in 1877. It is only slightly older than its neighbor, Tsinghua University, and Hong Kong University, both established in 1910–1911. Beida's faculty and students expressed pride in China's ancient civilization but seemed confident that the institution itself need not be ancient to be able to claim the future. "Universities belong to the world," the banners proclaimed, and "must be deeply rooted in the soil of the country and the nation."

A most dramatic transformation—both quantitative and qualitative—is taking place today in Chinese universities where nearly 40 million students are currently enrolled. In 2017, China launched its "Double First-Class Initiative"—the double referring to the aspiration to build world-class universities and excel in academic disciplines.[26] Not surprisingly, Beida boasts the largest number of disciplines taking part in this initiative and is the unquestioned leader among the forty-two universities that benefit from it. Its declared mission is to "contribute Chinese wisdom and the Chinese way of thinking" to global development—in other words, higher education with Chinese characteristics.

With so much state support behind the quest for academic excellence, the venue of the birthday celebrations shifted on the afternoon of May 4 to the Diaoyutai State Guest House nestled within the sprawling Qing imperial gardens. All state officials and university administrators duly quoted from the speech delivered by China's president, Xi Jinping, at the university on May 2. The president of Beida came in for some media criticism for mispronouncing an obscure Chinese character while quoting from Xi's speech.

The more substantive academic panels of the Beijing Forum took place on May 5. I chaired a session on cross-cultural conversations in global universities with scholars and academic leaders from Tokyo, Taipei, Rome, Sydney, and Hawai'i. The vice president of Tokyo University, a global historian of the nineteenth century, raised the troubling question whether the hegemony of English in academic discourse hinders genuine understanding across cultures. Alongside the forum, another big conference was under way on Karl Marx in observance of his 200th birth anniversary.

From May 7 to 12, 2018, I was honorary visiting professor at the Institute of Humanities and Social Sciences, founded in 2016, to enhance international exchanges at Beida. The institute is housed in a lovely early twentieth-century building along one of the main quads of the campus. I gave four lectures on "The Idea of Asia" that week, drawing on themes developed much more fully in this book. From the exquisite artwork on the posters that announced my lectures to the setup in my office and the lecture rooms, there was an impressive attention to detail. Each lecture had a designated faculty commentator—from Beida, Tsinghua, and Sichuan. The questions from the audience were intelligent and incisive, and the scheduled two-hour sessions tended to go on for longer.

On my gap day in my series of lectures at Beida, I took part in a Track-2 India-China Strategic Dialogue, being held a year after a tense military standoff between India and China in the Doklam valley of Bhutan. This dialogue gave me an opportunity to visit a school of a very different kind—the Central Party School of the Communist Party established in 1933 to impart political education to its cadres. Its vast campus next to the Summer Palace houses a well-curated museum. A gigantic statue of the young Mao dominates the main vista. Another sculpture of an even younger Mao with his companions has a more human touch (see figure C.1).

Beida had chosen to feature Li Dazhao, Mao's mentor, in the library of Peking University at its 120th anniversary celebrations. "The golden age is not behind us, but in front of us," this pioneering Chinese Communist had declared. "It's not in the past, but in the future." On my final evening in Beida, I sat on a bench by the lake which is the hub of campus life. As the sun went down, the iconic multistoried pagoda suddenly appeared in glorious illumination casting a golden reflection of the past in the rippling water of the lake (see figure C.2).

At Beida, I encountered another honorary visiting professor, Selcuk Esenbel, the leading historian of modern intra-Asian connections stretching from Turkey to Japan. I had visited Japan in January 2018 to speak on "The Idea of Asia" at the GRIPS Forum—a platform of Japan's National Graduate Institute for Policy Studies. During that visit, I could not help wondering whether Japan—"the birth-giver of young Asia" in Benoy Kumar Sarkar's words at the turn of the twentieth century—still held any lessons for Asia in the new millennium. Ever since the Meiji era, Japan had pursued a labor-intensive pattern of industrialization based on concerted efforts to improve

c.1 The author at the statue of the young Mao Zedong, Party School, Beijing, May 2018 (© Sugata Bose)

the quality of labor through a massive expansion of basic education and skills development. It led the way in creating rural industries and in promoting interregional trade with the rest of Asia. That Asian model of development was followed by a range of Southeast and East Asian countries and remained relevant in South Asia, which did not. In the context of contemporary challenges, Japan shares with much of South and Southeast Asia a vision of a multipolar, interconnected, and interreferential Asia. Avoiding an absolute rejection of China's BRI, Japan has set forth stringent conditions of transparency that would enable it to participate. Japan's enduring lesson for the rest of Asia can be found in its blend of the new with the old. The frenetic pace of activity in Ginza and Shinjuku is nicely balanced, I found, by the serenity of the Buddhist temples of Nishi Honganji in Kyoto and Renkoji in Tokyo. The speed of the Nozumi bullet train racing from Kyoto to Tokyo is stilled by the magical appearance of Mount Fuji on a clear winter morning. Japan continues to inspire fresh departures in South Asian art as it did just over a hundred years ago. One luminous example is *The Bridge*

C.2 The pagoda at Peking University (© Sugata Bose)

c.3 The Bridge in the Memories of Japan series (2019) by Shahid Jalal (Reproduction courtesy of Nusrat Jalal)

from Shahid Jalal's exhibition "Memories of Japan" that opened in Lahore in May 2022 (see figure C.3).

And what of the western extremity of the vast Asian continent that had caught the attention of South Asian intellectuals and political leaders alike in the aftermath of World War I? Istanbul lies on the cusp of Europe and Asia on the Bosporus. Yet a two-hour flight from Istanbul to Konya is all that it takes to land in the heart of Asia. The warmth of the reception accorded to a Hindustani and a Pakistani making that journey at the dawn of the twenty-first century by the hospitable residents of Konya suggested to me a bond that endures. A pilgrimage to the shrine of Jalaluddin Rumi reveals the resilience of the intertwining of universalisms of the Asian and Islamic assortments.

Soon after his visit to Iran and Iraq, Rabindranath Tagore published an essay in English on "Asia's Response to the Call of the New Age" in the *Modern Review* of October 1932. "What I say is that if Asia is not fully awakened," Tagore declared, "then there is no deliverance for Europe as well. The fatal arrow for Europe lies in the weakness of Asia." He could see that there was no longer any respect for Europe across the length and breadth of the Asian continent. "It is impossible for Asia today to lower her prestige before Europe," he wrote, "because, of the latter's prestige nothing remains but military browbeating." Then came a reflection and a warning:

> Once I went out to eastern Asia to welcome there the birth of the new spirit of humanity. There in the easternmost sky of Asia was fluttering the triumphant banner of Japan, encouraging new hope in the heart of Asia. I experienced joy, yet my mind was deeply disturbed.

What followed in Tagore's essay remains as relevant today as it was in 1932 even though the identity of the Asian country flaunting triumphalism has changed. The presumptive leader of Asia had "not learnt the art of civilization, which heals and unites" but had "trained her hands under Europe in the science that inflicts wounds with efficiency." "The calamity to which I refer is tragic," the poet wrote in grim prose, "not merely because of its political consequences but for its cruel destruction of human possibilities."[27] Can Asia after Europe save itself and the world from such a calamitous fate? Rising to that challenge would require a determined reimagination of a pluralized continentalism. That power of imagination lies well within the range of the best attributes of Asian universalism that can expand and not destroy the aspirations of humanity.

Notes

Introduction

1. Okakura Kakuzo, *The Ideals of the East* (London: J. Murray, 1903).

2. Okakura, *Ideals of the East,* xx, xxii, 1, 8.

3. Sugata Bose, *A Hundred Horizons: The Indian Ocean in the Age of Global Empire* (Cambridge, MA: Harvard University Press, 2006), 267–270. I made my claim about a different universalism as part of a larger contention about interpreting modern history as an interplay of multiple and competing universalisms rather than a clash of civilizations.

4. Martha Nussbaum, "Patriotism and Cosmopolitanism," in *For Love of Country: Debating the Limits of Patriotism,* ed. Joshua Cohen, 4–17 (Boston: Beacon Press, 1996).

5. Hilary Putnam, "Must We Choose between Patriotism and Universal Reason?" in *For Love of Country,* ed. Joshua Cohen, 91–97 (Boston: Beacon Press, 1996).

6. My concept of colorful cosmopolitanism is meant to evoke a kind of cosmopolitanism that springs from vernacular roots and is compatible with the best traditions of anti-colonial nationalism. There is nothing "partial" about colorful cosmopolitanism, contrary to Appiah's imposition of this limitation on rooted cosmopolitanism. See Anthony Appiah, *Cosmopolitanism in a World of Strangers* (New York: W. W. Norton, 2006).

7. Martin Lewis and Karen Wigen, *The Myth of Continents: A Critique of Metageography* (Berkeley: University of California Press, 1997), 189.

8. Prasenjit Duara, "Asia Redux: Conceptualizing a Region for Our Times," *Journal of Asian Studies* 69, no. 4 (2010): 963–983, 963.

9. Ranajit Guha, *Dominance without Hegemony: History and Power in Colonial India* (Cambridge, MA: Harvard University Press, 1998).

10. Sanjay Subrahmanyam, "One Asia, or Many? Reflections from Connected History," *Modern Asian Studies* 50, no. 1 (2016): 5–43. After taking swipes at a range of

historians of Asia, including Prasenjit Duara, K. N. Chaudhuri, Eric Tagliacozzo, Helen Siu, and Peter C. Perdue, Subrahmanyam triumphantly concludes, "One Asia or many. I believe that by now the reader will have guessed my answer." In addition to Duara, "Asia Redux," see K. N. Chaudhuri, *Asia before Europe: Economy and Civilisation of the Indian Ocean from the Rise of Islam to 1750* (Cambridge: Cambridge University Press, 1990); and Eric Tagliacozzo, Helen F. Siu, and Peter C. Perdue, eds., *Asia Inside Out: Connected Places* (Cambridge, MA: Harvard University Press, 2015).

11. Okakura, *Ideals of the East,* 237.

12. "Nobel Prize Awarded to Mr. Tagore," *Harvard Crimson,* November 22, 1913.

13. Rabindranath Tagore, *Nationalism* (New York: Macmillan, 1917; repr. Westport, CT: Greenwood Press, 1973), 15.

14. Tagore, *Nationalism,* 96.

15. Tagore, *Nationalism,* 90.

16. Rabindranath Tagore, *Talks in Japan,* ed. Supriya Roy (Kolkata: Shizen, 2007), 143.

17. Tagore, *Talks in Japan,* 141.

18. Alan Milward, *The European Rescue of the Nation-State,* 2nd ed. (London: Routledge, 2000).

19. See, for example, Christian Bailey, *Between Yesterday and Tomorrow: German Visions of Europe, 1926–1950* (New York: Berghahn, 2013), 18.

20. Dipesh Chakrabarty, *Provincializing Europe: Post-Colonial Thought and Historical Difference,* with new preface (Princeton: Princeton University Press, 2007). Chakrabarty organizes his text around the tension between Marx's universal narrative on capital and Heidegger's hermeneutic discourse on community.

21. Chaudhuri, *Asia before Europe.*

22. Prasannan Parthasarathi, *Why Europe Grew Rich and Asia Did Not: Global Economic Divergence, 1600–1850* (Cambridge: Cambridge University Press, 2011). See also Kenneth Pomeranz, *The Great Divergence: China, Europe and the Making of the Modern World Economy* (Princeton, NJ: Princeton University Press, 2000).

23. Sugata Bose, "Different Universalisms, Colorful Cosmopolitanisms," in *Cosmopolitan Thought Zones: South Asia and the Global Circulation of Ideas,* ed. Sugata Bose and Kris Manjapra (London: Palgrave Macmillan, 2010), 103. While drawing on my conceptualization of colorful cosmopolitanism in this earlier essay, I have made certain refinements in terms of exposition in this Introduction.

24. Erez Manela, *The Wilsonian Moment: Self-Determination and the International Origins of Anticolonial Nationalism* (New York: Oxford University Press, 2007). For a critique, see Rebecca E. Karl, Review of Manela, *The Wilsonian Moment, American Historical Review* 113, no. 5 (2008): 1474–1476.

25. Mahatma Gandhi, *Young India, 1919–1922* (Madras: S. Ganesan, 1922), cited in Sugata Bose, "Nation, Reason and Religion: India's Independence in International

Perspective," *Economic and Political Weekly*, 33, no. 1 (August 1–8, 1998): 2090–2097; reprinted in Sugata Bose, *The Nation as Mother and Other Visions of Nationhood*, 33–60 (Gurgaon: Penguin, 2017).

26. Tim Harper, *Underground Asia: Global Revolutionaries and the Assault on Empire* (Cambridge, MA: Belknap Press of Harvard University Press, 2021), 601–603.

27. Sugata Bose, *His Majesty's Opponent: Subhas Chandra Bose and India's Struggle against Empire* (Cambridge, MA: Belknap Press of Harvard University Press, 2011), 122.

28. Aung San, "Welcome Mr Sarat Chandra Bose," speech as chairman of a public reception in the City Hall, Rangoon, July 24, 1946, in *Netaji and India's Freedom*, ed. Sisir K. Bose, 69–72 (Calcutta: Netaji Research Bureau, 1975).

29. Takeuchi Yoshimi, "Asia as Method," in *What Is Modernity? Writings of Takeuchi Yoshimi*, ed. Richard Calichman (New York: Columbia University Press, 2005), 165.

30. Kris Manjapra, "The Mirrored World" (PhD diss., Harvard University, 2006).

31. Pankaj Mishra, *From the Ruins of Empire: The Intellectuals Who Remade Asia* (New York: Farrar, Straus and Giroux, 2012), 296, 302, 306.

32. See, for example, Gayatri Chakravorty Spivak, *Other Asias* (Oxford: Blackwell, 2008); Wang Hui, trans. Matthew A. Hale, "The Politics of Imagining Asia: A Genealogical Analysis," *Inter-Asia Cultural Studies* 8, no. 1 (2007): 1–33; Duara, "Asia Redux"; Kuan-hsing Chen, *Asia as Method: Toward Deimperialization* (Durham, NC: Duke University Press, 2010); C. J. Wan-Ling Wee, "'We Asians'? Modernity, Visual Art Exhibitions, and East Asia," *Boundary 2* 37, no. 1 (2010): 91–126; Sugata Bose, *A Hundred Horizons;* Sugata Bose and Kris Manjapra, eds., *Cosmopolitan Thought Zones: South Asia and the Global Circulation of Ideas* (London: Palgrave Macmillan, 2010); Sugata Bose, *Asia in the Bengali Imagination* (Dhaka: Golden Jubilee Lecture of the Asiatic Society of Bangladesh, 2002).

33. Chen, *Asia as Method*, 212.

34. Spivak, *Other Asias*, 212, 215, 222, 225, 232, 234, 236.

35. Chen, *Asia as Method*, 212.

36. Wang Hui, *The Politics of Imagining Asia*, ed. Theodore Huters (Cambridge, MA: Harvard University Press, 2011), 59, 61; and Wang, "The Politics of Imagining Asia," 27.The translations from the original Chinese are somewhat different in the book and the article. I have chosen mostly to quote from the book version. However, the phrase "genealogical analysis" appears in the title of the article, not in the book.

37. Wang, *The Politics of Imagining Asia*, 59, 60, 62; Wang, "The Politics of Imagining Asia," 30–33.

38. Engseng Ho, "Inter-Asian Concepts for Mobile Societies," *Journal of Asian Studies* 76, no. 4 (2017): 907–928, 907–908.

39. Rabindranath Tagore, *Parashye*, in *Rabindra-Rachanabali*, vol. 26 (Calcutta: Visvabharati, 1957), 443–445.

1. The Decline and Fall of a Continent

1. Amitav Ghosh, *Sea of Poppies* (New Delhi: Penguin Viking, 2008), 11, 78–79.

2. Amitav Ghosh, *River of Smoke* (New Delhi: Penguin, 2011).

3. Sugata Bose, *A Hundred Horizons: The Indian Ocean in the Age of Global Empire* (Cambridge, MA: Harvard University Press, 2006), 112.

4. C. A. Bayly, *The Birth of the Modern World, 1780–1914* (London: Wiley-Blackwell, 2003).

5. Angus Maddison, *Contours of the World Economy, 1–2030 AD* (New York: Oxford University Press, 2007).

6. Benoy Kumar Sarkar, *The Futurism of Young Asia, and Other Essays on the Relations between the East and the West* (Berlin: Julius Springer, 1922), iii.

7. K. N. Chaudhuri, *Asia before Europe: Economy and Civilisation of the Indian Ocean from the Rise of Islam to 1750* (Cambridge: Cambridge University Press, 1990).

8. Kenneth Pomeranz, *The Great Divergence: China, Europe and the Making of the Modern World Economy* (Princeton, NJ: Princeton University Press, 2000), 9–11, 17; Prasannan Parthasarathi, *Why Europe Grew Rich and Asia Did Not: Global Economic Divergence, 1600–1850* (Cambridge: Cambridge University Press, 2011), 1–2. For a dissenting view finding earlier origins of the great divergence, see Jean-Laurent Rosenthal and R. Bin Wong, *Before and Beyond Divergence: The Politics of Economic Change in China and Europe* (Cambridge, MA: Harvard University Press, 2011), Introduction.

9. Lisa Lowe, *The Intimacies of Four Continents* (Durham, NC: Duke University Press, 2015).

10. "By 1830 enough opium was entering China so that it covered, by itself and with a little to spare," Peter Fay estimates, "the full $9 million that teas cost the Factory. . . . No longer did the foreigners bring silver to China, they took it away." Peter Fay, *The Opium War, 1840–1842,* with new preface (1975; Chapel Hill: University of North Carolina Press, 1997), 55.

11. Carl Trocki, *Opium, Empire and the Global Political Economy* (London: Routledge, 1999), 94.

12. Amar Farooqui, *Opium City: The Making of Early Victorian Bombay* (Delhi: Three Essays Collective, 2006); Gyan Prakash, *Mumbai Fables* (Princeton: Princeton University Press, 2010).

13. Rolf Bauer, *The Peasant Production of Opium in Nineteenth-Century India* (Leiden: Brill, 2019).

14. Sugata Bose, *Peasant Labor and Colonial Capital* (Cambridge: Cambridge University Press, 1993), 45–51; Ghulam A. Nadri, *The Political Economy of Indigo in India, 1580–1930: A Global Perspective* (Leiden: Brill, 2016).

15. C. A. Bayly, *Indian Society and the Making of the British Empire* (Cambridge: Cambridge University Press, 1988).

16. Kaoru Sugihara, "Labor-Intensive Industrialization in Global History: An Interpretation of East Asian Experiences," in *Labor-Intensive Industrialization in Global History,* ed. Gareth Austin and Kaoru Sugihara, 20–43 (London: Routledge, 2013), 37.

17. Sugihara, "Labor-Intensive Industrialization," 36.

18. C. J. Baker, "Economic Reorganization and the Slump in South and Southeast Asia," *Comparative Studies in Society and History* 23, no. 3 (1981): 325–349. See also Sugata Bose, *A Hundred Horizons,* ch. 3.

19. Sugihara, "Labor-Intensive Industrialization."

20. On cotton, see Sven Beckert, *Empire of Cotton: A Global History* (New York: Penguin Random House, 2014). On jute, see Tariq Omar Ali, *A Local History of Global Capital: Jute and Peasant Life in the Bengal Delta* (Princeton, NJ: Princeton University Press, 2018); and Sugata Bose, *Peasant Labor and Colonial Capital.*

21. Ghulam A. Nadri, *The Political Economy of Indigo in India, 1580–1930* (Boston: Brill, 2016).

22. Steffen Rimner, *Opium's Long Shadow: From Asian Revolt to Global Drug Control* (Cambridge, MA: Harvard University Press, 2018).

23. Trocki, *Opium, Empire and the Global Political Economy,* 160.

24. Rabindranath Tagore, "Chine Maran Byabsay," in *Bharati,* May 1881, reproduced in *Rabindra Rachanabali.* vol. 17, (Calcutta: Visvabharati, 1957), 379–384. An English version was published forty-four years later as Rabindranath Tagore, "The Death Traffic in China," *Modern Review* 37 (July 1925). The quotations are my own English renderings of the Bengali original. In it, Tagore had not used the word "traffic"; instead, he contrasted "dacoity" and "commerce." China was described in Bengali as "Asiar ekti brihattama prachin sabhyadesh." Rimner uses the later English version in his detailed analysis of Tagore's critique in Rimner, *Opium's Long Shadow,* 107–14.

25. Tagore, "Chine Maran Byabsay."

26. Rimner, *Opium's Long Shadow,* 87–93.

27. Mike Davis, *Late Victorian Holocausts* (London: Verso, 2001).

28. Seema Alavi, *Muslim Cosmopolitanism in the Age of Empire* (Cambridge, MA: Harvard University Press, 2015); Ayesha Jalal, "Muslim Universalist Aspirations: Intimacies between the Indus-Gangetic Plain and the Indian Ocean," in *Oceanic Islam: Muslim Universalism and European Imperialism,* ed. Sugata Bose and Ayesha Jalal (London: Bloomsbury, 2020).

29. Pankaj Mishra, *From the Ruins of Empire: The Intellectuals Who Remade Asia* (New York: Farrar, Straus and Giroux, 2012).

30. It was only during and after World War I that, as Ayesha Jalal has shown, al-Afghani's ideas about Islamic universalism found resonance within the ranks of Indian anti-colonialism and beyond. Ayesha Jalal, *Partisans of Allah: Jihad in South Asia* (Cambridge, MA: Harvard University Press, 2008), 179–191.

31. Urs Matthias Zachmann, "The Foundation Manifesto of the Koakai (Raising Asia Society) and the Ajia Kyokai (Asia Association), 1880–1883," in *Pan-Asianism: A Documentary History,* vol. 1, *1850–1920,* ed. Sven Saaler and Christopher W. A. Szpilman, 53–60 (Lanham, MD: Rowman and Littlefield, 2011).

32. Fukuzawa Yukichi, "On Leaving Asia (Datsu-A Ron)," *Jiji shinpo* (newspaper), March 16, 1885; Hinohara Shozo, "Nihon wa Toyokoku taru bekarzu" (Japan Must Not Be an Oriental Country), *Jiji shinpo,* November 13, 1884. For Japan's quest for "blended modernities" in the Meiji era, see Carol Gluck, "The End of Elsewhere: Writing Modernity Now," *American Historical Review* 116, no. 3 (2011): 676–687; also Carol Gluck, *Japan's Modern Myths: Ideology in the Late Meiji Period* (Princeton, NJ: Princeton University Press, 1987).

33. Urs Matthias Zachmann, "Blowing Up a Double Portrait in Black and White: The Concept of Asia in the Writings of Fukuzawa Yukichi and Okakura Tenshin," *positions: east asia cultures critique* 15, no. 2 (2007), 344–368, 361.

34. Kannika Sattraprung, *A True Hero: King Chulalongkorn of Siam's Visit to Singapore and Java in 1871* (Bangkok: Institute of Asian Studies, Chulalongkorn University, 2008); Imtip Pattajoti Suharto, *Journeys to Java by a Siamese King* (Bangkok: Ministry of Foreign Affairs, 2001); Sachidanand Sahai, *India in 1872 as Seen by the Siamese* (Delhi: B. R. Pub. Corp., 2002); Phaisan Piammettawat, *King Chulalongkorn's Journey to India, 1872* (Bangkok: River Books, 2000).

35. Eric Tagliacozzo, *Secret Trades, Porous Borders: Smuggling and States along a Southeast Asian Frontier* (New Haven, CT: Yale University Press, 2009).

36. Benedict Anderson, *Imagined Communities: Reflections on the Origins and Spread of Nationalism* (London: Verso, 1991), ch. 7.

37. Nicole CuUnjieng Aboitiz, *Asian Place, Filipino Nation: A Global Intellectual History of the Philippine Revolution, 1887–1912* (New York: Columbia University Press, 2020), 41.

38. Caroline S. Hau and Takashi Shiraishi, "Daydreaming about Rizal and Tetcho on Asianism as Network and Fantasy," *Philippine Studies* 57, no. 3 (2009): 329–388.

39. Rudyard Kipling, "The White Man's Burden" (1899), https://www.kiplingsociety.co.uk/poem/poems_burden.htm.

40. President William McKinley, "Remarks to Methodist Delegation" (November 21, 1899); William James, "Letter to Boston Evening Transcript" (March 1, 1899); and "Remember Pekin!" leaflet of the Republican Club of Massachusetts (n.d.), all in *The Philippines Reader,* ed. Daniel B. Schirmer and Stephen Rosskamm Shalom (Boston: South End Press, 1987), 22, 27, 32–33.

41. Craig A. Smith, *Chinese Asianism, 1894–1945* (Cambridge, MA: Harvard University Asia Center, 2021), 23–24, 37–40, 47, 49–50. See also Rebecca Karl, *Staging the World: Chinese Nationalism at the Turn of the Twentieth Century* (Durham, NC: Duke University Press, 2002).

42. CuUnjieng Aboitiz, *Asian Place, Filipino Nation,* 121–124, 134.

43. Anand Yang, "An Indian Soldier's Account of China and the World in 1900–1901," in *The Boxers, China and the World,* ed. Robert Bickers and R.G. Tiedemann, 43–64 (London: Rowman and Littlefield, 2007). James Hevia has perceptively located Chinese loot within a pedagogy of imperialism. He notes the "relationship between the act of defeating China and the constitution of colonialist subjects. . . . What more commanding image could there be for the constitution of colonizing subjectivities than the appropriation of the signs of another 'sovereign' and the assimilation of those signs to oneself?" James L. Hevia, "Loot's Fate: The Economy of Plunder and the Moral Life of Objects from the Summer Palace of the Emperor of China," *History and Anthropology* 6, no. 4 (1994), 319–345, 333.

44. C. A. Bayly, "The Boxer Uprising and India: Globalizing Myths," in *The Boxers, China and the World,* ed. Bickers and Tiedemann, 147–155.

45. Rabindranath Tagore, "Samajbhed," *Bangadarshan,* June 1901.

46. Tagore printed an English version of this poem "The Sunset of the Century" as an appendix to his 1917 book *Nationalism* (New York: Macmillan, 1917; repr. Westport, CT: Greenwood Press, 1973), 157–159. In fact, the English poem drew on four sonnets in *Naibedya,* numbers 64, 65, 66, and 67. See the translator Ashis Lahiri's note in Sugata Bose, *Bharatmata* (Kolkata: Ananda, 2019), 185–190.

2. Intimations of an Asian Universalism

1. Abanindranath Tagore, *Jorasankor Dhare* (Calcutta: Visva-Bharati, 1944), 103–104.

2. Abanindranath Tagore, *Jorasankor Dhare,* 102–103.

3. Okakura, *Ideals of the East* (London: J. Murray, 1903), 233. Kutsugen was the classical Chinese poet Qu Yuan who may have had an affinity in Taikan's vision with Okakura in their rejection of arbitrary authority.

4. Benoy Kumar Sarkar, *The Futurism of Young Asia, and Other Essays on the Relations between the East and the West* (Berlin: Julius Springer, 1922), iii.

5. Ranajit Guha, *Dominance without Hegemony: History and Power in Colonial India* (Cambridge, MA: Harvard University Press, 1997).

6. Urs Matthias Zachmann, "Blowing Up a Double Portrait in Black and White: The Concept of Asia in the Writings of Fukuzawa Yukichi and Okakura Tenshin," *positions: east asia cultures critique* 15, no. 2 (2007): 345–368.

7. Swami Vivekananda to Alasinga Perumal, Balaji, G.G. Banking Corporation, and "all my Madras friends," July 10, 1893, in *Letters of Swami Vivekananda* (Kolkata: Advaita Ashrama, 1964), 39–45.

8. Surendranath Tagore, "Some Reminiscences," *The Visva-Bharati Quarterly,* August 1936.

9. Surendranath Tagore, "Some Reminiscences."

10. Abanindranath Tagore, *Jorasankor Dhare,* 107–109.

11. Reba Som, *Margot: Sister Nivedita of Vivekananda* (Gurgaon: Penguin Viking, 2017), 109–112. Sunil Gangopadhyay took a novelist's license to portray the Okakura-Nivedita relationship in a more colorful light in his book *Pratham Alo* (Kolkata: Ananda, 2015).

12. Okakura, *Ideals of the East,* 1.

13. Sanjay Subrahmanyam, "One Asia, or Many? Reflections from Connected History," *Modern Asian Studies* 50, no. 1 (2016): 5–43. The misreading of Okakura appears on 42–43.

14. Okakura, *Ideals of the East,* 3–4.

15. Okakura, *Ideals of the East,* 5–7.

16. Okakura, *Ideals of the East,* 231–233.

17. Sister Nivedita, *Collected Works* (Calcutta: Ramakrishna Sarada Mission Sister Nivedita Girls School, 1955), 58. Her essays on art, including Abanindranath's "Bharatmata," were originally published as "The Function of Art in Shaping Nationality" and "Notes on Bharatmata" in *Modern Review,* February 1907. She praised this painting again in a review of a 1910 art exhibition in Calcutta.

18. Manmatha Nath Ghosh, *Japan-Prabash* (Calcutta: The Empire Library, 1910), 1. I am grateful to Aniket De for bringing this fascinating Bengali travelogue to my attention.

19. Ghosh, *Japan-Prabash,* 3–23.

20. Ghosh, *Japan-Prabash,* 34–67.

21. Ghosh, *Japan-Prabash,* 137–139, 147–148.

22. Timothy Harper, *Underground Asia: Global Revolutionaries and the Assault on Empire* (Cambridge, MA: Harvard University Press, 2021), 39–42.

23. On Berlin, see Kris Manjapra, *Age of Entanglement: German and Indian Intellectuals across Empire* (Cambridge, MA: Harvard University Press, 2014). On Paris, see Michael Goebel, *Anti-Imperial Metropolis: Inter-War Paris and the Seeds of Third World Nationalism* (Cambridge: Cambridge University Press, 2015).

24. Nicole CuUnjieng Aboitiz, *Asian Place, Filipino Nation: A Global Intellectual History of the Philippine Revolution, 1887–1912* (New York: Columbia University Press, 2020), 115.

25. CuUnjieng Aboitiz, *Asian Place, Filipino Nation,* 95.

26. "The Charter of the Asiatic Humanitarian Brotherhood," in Yuan P. Cai, "Zhang Taiyan and the Asiatic Humanitarian Brotherhood, 1907," in *Pan-Asianism: A Documentary History,* vol. 1, *1850–1920,* ed. Sven Saaler and Christopher W. A. Szpilman, (London: Rowman and Littlefield, 2011), 175–184.

27. Linda Colley, *The Gun, the Ship, and the Pen: Warfare, Constitutions and the Making of the Modern World* (New York: W. W. Norton, 2022), 1–2.

28. Harper, *Underground Asia,* 69–70.

29. Craig A. Smith, "Chinese Asianism in the Early Republic: Guomindang Intellectuals and the Brief Internationalist Turn," *Modern Asian Studies* 53, no. 2 (2019): 582–605, quotation from Sun's speech on 595.

30. Selcuk Esenbel, "Japan's Global Claim to Asia and the World of Islam: Transnational Nationalism and World Power, 1900–1945," *American Historical Review* 109, no. 4 (2004): 1140–1170.

31. Sri Aurobindo, *Bande Mataram: Early Political Writings* (Pondicherry: Sri Aurobindo Ashram, 1997), 721–723, 757–760, 812–817, 842–845.

32. Kakuzo Okakura, *The Book of Tea* (New York: Duffield, 1906), https://www.gutenberg.org/files/769/769-h/769-h.htm, 1, 4–5.

33. Akira Iriye, *Japan and the Wider World: From the Mid-Nineteenth Century to the Present* (New York: Longman, 1997), 19.

34. Surendranath Tagore, "Some Reminiscences."

35. Abanindranath Tagore, *Jorasankor Dhare,* 105–107.

36. Mou Banerjee, "Mr. Tagore in Emerson" (paper written for Bose seminar "Tagore and His Times," Harvard University, Fall 2011), based on research in the Harvard University Archives. Banerjee's suggestion of Okakura's facilitation is more plausible than the alternative view of Krishna Dutta and Andrew Robinson that a recommendation from G. Lowes Dickinson to Lowell had clinched the deal. Krishna Dutta and Andrew Robinson, *Rabindranath Tagore: The Myriad-Minded Man* (London: Bloomsbury, 1995), 172.

37. *Okakura Kakuzo: Collected English Writings* ed. Sunao Nakamura, 3 vols. (Tokyo: Heibonsha, 1984), 3:176, 182, 393.

38. Kris Manjapra, *Age of Entanglement,* 243. See Ananda Coomaraswamy, *Art and Swadeshi* (Madras: Ganesh, 1912).

3. In Search of Young Asia

1. Benoy Kumar Sarkar, *Nabin Asiar Janmadata Japan* (The birth giver of new Asia, Japan) (Calcutta: Grihastha, 1923), 169–171.

2. These lines are from Dwijendralal Roy's famous song "Banga amaar Janani amaar" (My Bengal, my mother). The translation is by Aurobindo Ghose who expanded

"My Bengal" to "My India." Dilip Kumar Roy, *Flames and Flowers: Dwijendralal Centenary Volume* (Calcutta: S. Gupta Bros., 1963). In another famous song, "Bharat Amaar, Bharat Amaar" (my India, my India), Dwijendralal Roy had addressed India as "Asia-r tumi tirthakshetra", the pilgrimage destination of Asia.

3. Sarkar, *Nabin Asiar Janmadata Japan,* 172–178.

4. Sarkar, *Nabin Asiar Janmadata Japan,* 178–180.

5. Aniket De, *The Boundary of Laughter: Popular Performances across Borders in South Asia* (Delhi: Oxford University Press, 2021), ch. 2.

6. Ida Sarkar, *My Life with Prof Benoy Kumar Sarkar* (Calcutta: Prabhat, 1977), 3–8; Jessica Namakkal, "Decolonizing Marriage and the Family: The Lives and Letters of Benoy, Ida and Indira Sarkar," *Journal of Women's History* 31, no. 2 (2019): 124–147.

7. Lala Lajpat Rai, *Autobiographical Writings* (New Delhi: University Publishers, 1965), 201.

8. The best interpretation of Sarkar's English works can be found in Manu Goswami, "Imaginary Futures and Colonial Internationalisms," *American Historical Review* 117, no. 5 (2012): 1461–1485. With no engagement with what Sarkar wrote about Islam and Muslims, Nile Green brackets him as a "Hindu nationalist" with V. D. Savarkar, the ideologue of "Hindutva." Nile Green, *How Asia Found Herself* (New Haven, CT: Yale University Press, 2022), 164–165, 269–271. Other insightful books focusing primarily on Sarkar's English works include Kris Manjapra, *Age of Entanglement: German and Indian Intellectuals across Empire* (Cambridge, MA: Harvard University Press, 2014), 149–155, 203–206, 248; Satadru Sen, *Benoy Kumar Sarkar: Restoring the Nation to the World* (New York: Routledge, 2015); Giuseppe Flora, *Benoy Kumar Sarkar and Italy: Culture, Politics and Economic Ideology* (New Delhi: Italian Embassy Cultural Center, 1994); and Bholanath Bandyopadhyay, *The Political Ideas of Benoy Kumar Sarkar* (Calcutta: K. P. Bagchi, 1984).

9. Sarvani Gooptu located as many as 531 articles on Asia in 37 Bengali periodicals by a wide range of authors between 1860 and 1940. See Sarvani Gooptu, *Knowing Asia, Being Asian: Cosmopolitanism and Nationalism in Bengali Periodicals, 1860–1940* (New York: Routledge, 2022).

10. Sarkar, *Nabin Asiar Janmadata Japan,* i–vi.

11. Sarkar, *Nabin Asiar Janmadata Japan,* 1, 6, 13–15, 29, 36, 43.

12. Sarkar, *Nabin Asiar Janmadata Japan,* 47–52.

13. Sarkar, *Nabin Asiar Janmadata Japan,* 74–88.

14. Sarkar, *Nabin Asiar Janmadata Japan,* 103–108, 148–156, 202–205.

15. Sarkar, *Nabin Asiar Janmadata Japan,* 224–230.

16. Sarkar, *Nabin Asiar Janmadata Japan,* 244–248.

17. Sarkar, *Nabin Asiar Janmadata Japan,* 162–167.

18. Sarkar, *Nabin Asiar Janmadata Japan,* 288, 301–323, 340, 343, 360, 366, 374, 382–386.

19. Sarkar, *Nabin Asiar Janmadata Japan,* 398.

20. Goswami, "Imaginary Futures and Colonial Internationalisms," 1480.

21. Sarkar, *Nabin Asiar Janmadata Japan,* 403–406.

22. Sarkar, *Nabin Asiar Janmadata Japan,* 407–412.

23. Sarkar, *Nabin Asiar Janmadata Japan,* 408, 412, 444, 464, 469–472, 477–481.

24. Benoy Kumar Sarkar, *Bartaman Juge Chin Samrajya* (The Chinese Empire in the present age) (Calcutta: Grihastha, 1921), i–iv, 1, 4, 6.

25. Sarkar, *Bartaman Juge Chin Samrajya,* 9, 15, 33–35, 46, 71–73.

26. Among those who had traveled to Southeast Asia and coastal China before Sarkar was Indumadhab Mallick who wrote a travelogue *Chin Bhraman* (Travel in China) (Calcutta: S. C. Mazumdar, 1906).

27. Sarkar, *Bartaman Juge Chin Samrajya,* 75–82.

28. Sarkar, *Bartaman Juge Chin Samrajya,* 90, 93–96, 99–102.

29. Sarkar, *Bartaman Juge Chin Samrajya,* 115, 120, 122–123, 128, 146–149.

30. Sarkar, *Bartaman Juge Chin Samrajya,* 171, 174–177.

31. Benoy Kumar Sarkar, *Chinese Religion through Hindu Eyes: A Study in the Tendencies of Asiatic Mentality* (Shanghai: Commercial Press, 1916; repr. Delhi: Oriental, 1975), xi–xxiii.

32. Sarkar, *Bartaman Juge Chin Samrajya,* 182–194; Sarkar, *Chinese Religion through Hindu Eyes,* 1–5, 236, 258.

33. Sarkar, *Chinese Religion through Hindu Eyes,* 276, 279, 306.

34. Sarkar, *Bartaman Juge Chin Samrajya,* 195–196.

35. Sarkar, *Bartaman Juge Chin Samrajya,* 202–203.

36. Sarkar, *Bartaman Juge Chin Samrajya,* 203–205.

37. Green, *How Asia Found Herself,* 164–165, 269–271.

38. Sarkar, *Chinese Religion through Hindu Eyes,* 234. He was referring here to Edward Gibbon and "the Indian scholar Ameer Ali's luminous *History of the Saracens.*"

39. Benoy Kumar Sarkar, "Hindu-Muslim Pact," in *Deshbandhu,* ed. Semanti Ghosh and Aniket De (Kolkata: Ananda, 2023).

40. Sarkar, *Bartaman Juge Chin Samrajya,* 220–222, 239–240.

41. Sarkar, *Bartaman Juge Chin Samrajya,* 352–376.

42. Sarkar, *Bartaman Juge Chin Samrajya,* 382–386; Benoy Kumar Sarkar, "Political Tendencies in Chinese Culture," *The Modern Review* 23, no. 1 (1920): 1–8; Benoy Kumar Sarkar, *The Futurism of Young Asia, and Other Essays on the Relations between the East and the West* (Berlin: Julius Springer, 1922), 189–200.

43. Sarkar, "Political Tendencies in Chinese Culture," 3.

44. Sarkar, *Bartaman Juge Chin Samarajya,* 418, 435–436.

45. Timothy Norman Harper, "Singapore, 1915, and the Birth of the Asian Underground," *Modern Asian Studies* 47, no. 6 (2013): 1–30.

46. Grant K. Goodman, "Japanese Sources for the Study of the Indian Independence Movement: The Example of World War I," in *Netaji and India's Freedom: Proceedings of the International Netaji Seminar 1973*, ed. Sisir K. Bose, 76–110 (Calcutta: Netaji Research Bureau, 1975). Biman Behari Majumdar, *Militant Nationalism in India, 1897–1917* (Calcutta: General Printers and Publishers, 1966); Takeshi Nakajima, *Bose of Nakamuraya: An Indian Revolutionary in Japan* (New Delhi: Promilla, 2009), 46–51.

47. Sugata Bose, *A Hundred Horizons: The Indian Ocean in the Age of Global Empire* (Cambridge, MA: Harvard University Press, 2006), 59–63.

48. Cemil Aydin, *The Politics of Anti-Westernism in Asia: Visions of World Order in Pan-Islamic and Pan-Asian Thought* (New York: Columbia University Press, 2007), 114–115.

49. Goodman, "Japanese Sources," 79–91; Nakajima, *Bose of Nakamuraya*, 99–111; Aydin, *The Politics of Anti-Westernism in Asia*, 114–115.

50. Goodman, "Japanese Sources," 94–95; Harper, *Underground Asia*, 297–304; M. N. Roy, *Memoirs* (Delhi: Ajanta, 1985), 8–17; Kris Manjapra, *M. N. Roy: Marxism and Colonial Cosmopolitanism* (New York: Routledge, 2010), chs. 1 and 2.

51. Prabhat Kumar Mukhopadhyay, *Rabindrajibani o Rabindrasahitya-prabeshak* (Calcutta: Visvabharati, 1961), 2:556.

52. Mukul Dey, "Yokoyama Taikan: As I Knew Him," [a three-page unpublished essay] Mukul Dey Archives, Santiniketan, West Bengal.

53. Mukhopadhyay, *Rabindrajibani*, 2:556–557.

54. Rabindranath Tagore, *Japan Jatri*, in *Rabindra Rachanabali*, vol. 19 (Calcutta: Visvabharati, 1956), 339.

55. Mukhopadhyay, *Rabindrajibani*, 2:556.

56. Rabindranath Tagore, *Nationalism and Home and the World*, with intro. by Sugata Bose (Gurugram: Penguin, 2021), xii, 21.

57. Mukhopadhyay, *Rabindrajibani*, 2:569.

58. Mukhopadhyay, *Rabindrajibani*, 2:567.

59. Yone Noguchi, "Tagore in Japan," *The Modern Review* 20, No. 5 (1916): 528–530.

60. Mukhopadhyay, *Rabindrajibani*, 2:559.

61. Goodman, "Japanese Sources," 91–98; Tapan K. Mukherjee, *Taraknath Das: Life and Letters of a Revolutionary in Exile* (Calcutta: National Council of Education, 1998), 91–105.

62. Mukherjee, *Taraknath Das*, 105–111.

63. Taraknath Das, "Sino-Japanese Relations and Asian Independence," *Independent Hindustan* 1, no. 1 (September 1920), 16.

64. The other Indian intellectual to do so at about the same time was Aurobindo in the pages of *Arya*. See Sugata Bose, "The Spirit and Form of an Ethical Polity: A Meditation on Aurobindo's Thought," *Modern Intellectual History* 4, no. 1 (2007): 129–

144. Reprinted in Sugata Bose, *The Nation as Mother and Other Visions of Nationhood* (Gurgaon: Penguin Viking, 2017), 85–106.

65. Sarkar, *The Futurism of Young Asia,* iv, 1, 3.

66. Sarkar, *The Futurism of Young Asia,* 8, 12, 15, 18, 22.

67. Sarkar, *The Futurism of Young Asia,* 31–32, 173–174.

4. Multiple, Competing, and Overlapping Universalisms

1. Mahatma Gandhi, *Young India, 1919–1922* (Madras: S. Ganesan, 1922), 408.

2. Gandhi, *Young India,* 145.

3. Neeti Nair, *Changing Homelands: Hindu Politics and the Partition of India* (Cambridge, MA: Harvard University Press, 2011), 100.

4. Gandhi, *Young India,* 138.

5. For a more detailed analysis of Gandhi on reason and religion in justifying his support for the Turkish Khilafat, see Sugata Bose, "Nation, Reason and Religion: India's Independence in International Perspective," *Economic and Political Weekly,* 33, no. 1 (August 1–8, 1998): 2090–2097; reprinted in Sugata Bose, *The Nation as Mother and Other Visions of Nationhood* (Gurgaon: Penguin Viking, 2017), 33–59.

6. Sana Aiyar, "Revolutionaries, Maulvis, Swamis, and Monks: Burma's Khilafat Moment," in *Oceanic Islam: Muslim Universalism and European Universalism,* ed. Sugata Bose and Ayesha Jalal, 167–176 (London: Bloomsbury, 2020).

7. Ayesha Jalal, *Self and Sovereignty: Individual and Community in South Asian Islam since 1850* (London: Routledge, 2000; Delhi: Oxford University Press, 2001), 188, 194.

8. Paul Richard, *The Dawn over Asia* (Madras: Ganesh and Company, 1920).

9. Li Dazhao, "Greater Asianism and New Asianism" (1919), in *Pan-Asianism: A Documentary History,* vol. 1, *1850–1920,* ed. Sven Saaler and Christopher W. A. Szpilman (London: Rowman and Littlefield, 2011), 1:222.

10. Angus W. McDonald Jr., "Mao Tse-tung and the Hunan Self-Government Movement, 1920: An Introduction and Five Translations," *The China Quarterly* 68 (Dec. 1976): 751–777. See also Stephen Pratt, *Provincial Patriots: The Hunanese and Modern China* (Cambridge, MA: Harvard University Press, 2007). For an insightful interpretation of the anti-colonial intellectual lineage of federalism in India, early republican China, and late Ottoman Empire, see Aniket De, "Spaces of Freedom: Imperial and Anti-colonial Lineages of Federalism" (PhD diss., Harvard University, 2024), ch. 3.

11. Wang Hui, *The Politics of Imagining Asia,* ed. Theodore Huters, trans. Matthew Hale (Cambridge, MA: Harvard University Press, 2011), 15; for an earlier version and a slightly different translation, see Wang Hui, "The Politics of Imagining Asia: A Genealogical Analysis," *Inter-Asia Cultural Studies* 8, no. 1, 2007): 1–33, 4.

12. Ayesha Jalal, *Partisans of Allah: Jihad in South Asia* (Cambridge, MA: Harvard University Press, 2008), 203–210.

13. Maia Ramnath, *Haj to Utopia: How the Ghadr Movement Charted Global Radicalism and Attempted to Overthrow the British Empire* (Berkeley: University of California Press, 2011); Timothy Norman Harper, *Underground Asia: Global Revolutionaries and the Assault on Empire* (Cambridge, MA: Harvard University Press, 2020).

14. Jalal, *Self and Sovereignty,* 232–233; Sugata Bose, *A Hundred Horizons: The Indian Ocean in the Age of Global Empire* (Cambridge, MA: Harvard University Press, 2006), 132–135.

15. Jalal, *Self and Sovereignty,* 244–245.

16. C. R. Das, *Freedom through Disobedience* (Madras: Arka Publishing House, 1922), 20, 37.

17. Prabhat Kumar Mukhopadhyay, *Rabindrajibani o Rabindrasahitya-prabeshak* (Calcutta: Visvabharati, 1990), 3:176–177.

18. Mukhopadhyay, *Rabindrajibani,* 3:178–179.

19. Mukhopadhyay, *Rabindrajibani,* 3:180–181.

20. Mukhopadhyay, *Rabindrajibani,* 3:182–183.

21. Suniti Kumar Chattopadhyay, *Rabindra-sangame Dweepmoy Bharat o Shyam-Desh* (Calcutta: Prakash Bhawan, 1964), 205; Sugata Bose, *A Hundred Horizons,* 252.

22. Liang Chi Chao, "Introduction," in Rabindranath Tagore, *Talks in China* (New Delhi: Rupa, 2002), viii.

23. Liang, "Introduction," viii–ix.

24. Wei Liming, "Historical Significance of Tagore's 1924 China Visit," in *Tagore and China,* ed. Tan Chung, Amiya Dev, Wang Bangwei, and Wei Liming (New Delhi: Sage, 2011), 17. The translation of Liang's speech is by Tan Chung. Wei Liming provides the most balanced account of Tagore's reception in China and a useful corrective to Stephen Hay's exaggerated view of the criticism the poet received in Hay, *Asian Ideas of East and West: Tagore and His Critics in Japan, China and India* (Cambridge, MA: Harvard University Press, 1970).

25. Amartya Sen, "Tagore and China," in Tan Chung et al., eds., *Tagore and China,* 3–11.

26. Tagore, *Talks in China,* 3–9, 16, 23–24, 27.

27. Tagore, *Talks in China,* 51, 55–56, 81.

28. Tagore, *Talks in China,* 107, 115.

29. Mukhopadhyay, *Rabindrajibani,* 3:194.

30. Gal Gvili, "Pan-Asian Poetics: Tagore and the Inter-Personal in May Fourth New Poetry," *Journal of Asian Studies* 77, no. 1 (February 2018): 181–203.

31. Tagore, *Talks in China,* 23.

32. Krishna Bose and Sugata Bose, "The East in Its Feminine Gender: A Historical and Literary Introduction," in Rabindranath Tagore, *Purabi: The East in Its Feminine Gender,* trans. Charu C. Chowdhuri, edited and introduced by Krishna Bose and Sugata Bose, 1–43 (London: Seagull Books, 2007).

33. Tagore, *Talks in China,* 111.

34. Nandalal Bose to Rathindranath Tagore (Rabindranath's son), May 8, 1924, in Nandalal Bose, *Vision and Creation,* trans. K. G. Subramanyan (Calcutta: Visva-Bharati, 1999), 241–245; Sugata Bose, "Universalist Aspirations in a 'National' Art: Asia in Nandalal Bose's Imagination," in *Rhythms of India: The Art of Nandalal Bose,* ed. Sonya Rhie Quintanilla (San Diego: San Diego Museum of Art, 2008), 104–111; Mukhopadhyay, *Rabindrajibani,* 195; Amitava Bhattacharya, "In Search of a Forgotten Dialogue: Chinese and Indian Artists since 1924," in Tan Chung et al., eds., *Tagore and China,* 44–58.

35. Dispatch of September 8, 1924, published in the *Christian Science Monitor,* October 3, 1924, cited in Mukhopadhyay, *Rabindrajibani,* 3:195–196, 199.

36. Mukhopadhyay, *Rabindrajibani,* 3:197–198.

37. Rabindranath Tagore, *Talks in Japan* (Kolkata: Shizen, 2007), 82–83.

38. Mukhopadhyay, *Rabindrajibani,* 3:197–198.

39. Harper, *Underground Asia,* 500–501.

40. Sun Yat-sen, "Inukai Tsuyoshi ate shokan (Letter to Inukai Tsuyoshi)," (November 16, 1923) in Saaler and Szpilman, eds., *Pan-Asianism,* 1:250–252.

41. Takeshi Nakajima, *Bose of Nakamuraya: An Indian Revolutionary in Japan* (New Delhi: Promilla, 2009), 154–158.

42. Sun Yat-sen, "Pan Asianism" (1941),] in Saaler and Szpilman, eds., *Pan-Asianism,* vol. 2, *1920–Present,* 78–80.

43. Mark Mazower, *No Enchanted Palace: The End of Empire and the Ideological Origins of the United Nations* (Princeton: Princeton University Press, 2009), 49.

44. Lothrop Stoddard, *The Rising Tide of Color against White World Supremacy* (New York: Charles Scribner's Sons, 1920), vi, 297, 301.

45. Lothrop Stoddard, *The Revolt against Civilization: The Menace of the Underman* (New York: Charles Scribner's Sons, 1922), 216–217.

46. Sun Yat-sen, "Pan Asianism" (1941), 2:80–82.

47. Sun Yat-sen, "Pan Asianism" (1941), 2:83.

48. Sun Yat-sen, "Pan Asianism" (1941), 2:83–85.

49. Wang, *The Politics of Imagining Asia,* 34; see also Wang, "The Politics of Imagining Asia," 12–14.

50. Harper, *Underground Asia,* 601–603.

51. Nakajima, *Bose of Nakamuraya,* 161–178.

52. Rabindranath Tagore to Nirmalkumari Mahalanobis, 1 Sraban, Bengali 1334, July 15, 1927, in Rabindranath Tagore, *Java Jatrir Patra* (Letters of a traveler to Java),

in *Rabindra Rachanabali*, <u>vol. 19</u> (Calcutta: Visva-Bharati, 1956), 456. This letter also contains a powerful critique of Europe's arrogance and its consequent inability to touch the heart of Asia. For a more detailed account and interpretation of this voyage as an expression of a "different universalism," see Bose, *A Hundred Horizons*, 245–260. Here, I am limiting myself to a consideration of Tagore's views on the two great Indian epics that bridged the cultures of South and Southeast Asia.

53. Tansen Sen, *India, China, and the World* (Lanham, MD: Rowman and Little-field, 2017), 307.

54. Rabindranath Tagore to Nirmalkumari Mahalanobis, August 31/September 1, 1927, in Tagore, *Java Jatrir Patra*, 474. The date August 1, 1927 for this letter given in *Rabindra Rachanabali*, vol. 19 is clearly an error. Tagore wrote this letter from the Gianyar Regency in Bali during his visit on August 31/September 1, 1927.

55. Rabindranath Tagore to Mira Debi, August 31, 1927, in *Java Jatrir Patra*, 483–489.

56. Tagore to Nirmalkumari Mahalanobis, August 31, 1927, 472–473.

57. Tagore to Nirmalkumari Mahalanobis, August 31, 1927, 473.

58. Tagore to Nirmalkumari Mahalanobis, August 31, 1927, 473–474.

59. See Rabindranath Tagore to Pratima Devi, September 14, 1927 and September 17, 1927; Tagore to Amiya Chakravarti, September 17, 1927; Rabindranath Tagore to Rathindranath Tagore, September 19, 1927; Tagore to Nirmalkumari Mahalanobis, September 20, 1927; Tagore to Pratima Devi, September 26, 1927, all in Tagore, *Java Jatrir Patra*, 501–519.

60. Rabindranath Tagore to Pratima Devi, September 17, 1927, in Tagore, *Java Jatrir Patra*, 508–511.

61. Rabindranath Tagore to Rathindranath Tagore, September 19, 1927, and Tagore to Nirmalkumari Mahalanobis, September 20, 1927, in *Java Jatrir Patra*, 513–517.

62. Mukhopadhyay, *Rabindrajibani*, 3:332.

63. Tagore, *Talks in Japan*, 161–162.

64. Tagore, *Talks in Japan*, 192.

65. Quoted in Pham Chi P, "Beyond the Indian Ocean Public Sphere," *Journal of Vietnamese Studies* 16, no. 2 (2021): 60–83, quotation on 68.

5. Asia in the Great Depression

1. *All-Asian Women's Conference Report, Lahore, January 19–25, 1931* (Bombay: Times of India Press, 1931), vii, 192.

2. The other signatories were Dr. Muthulakshmi Reddi, Deputy President of the Madras Legislative Council; Dr. Poonen Lukhose of Travancore, a leader of Syrian Christians and the first female member of a legislative council in India; Lady Abdul Quadir, a leader of Muslim society and philanthropist in Lahore; Mrs. Rustomji

Faridoonji, a leader of the Parsi community and honorary secretary of the All-India Women's Education Fund Association; Shrimati Sarala Devi Chaudurani, a noted Bengali musician and freedom-fighter; Lady Hydari of Hyderabad, former president of the Muslim Women's Conference; Rajkumari Amrit Kaur, a prominent member of the Indian Christian community of north India; Mrs. Hamid Ali, a social reformer and honorary treasurer of the All-India Women's Conference; Mrs. Rameshwari Nehru of Kashmir and Delhi, social reform secretary of the All-India Women's Conference; Shrimati Protima Devi, noted Bengali artist who happened to be the daughter-in-law of Rabindranath Tagore; Ms. Khadija Begam Ferozuddin, first woman graduate of the North West Frontier Province and noted linguist; Mrs. Padmabai Sanjiva Rao, principal of the Theosophical Women's College, Benares; and Rani Lakshmibai G. Rajwade of Bombay and Gwalior, a doctor who was a member of the 1917 deputation that first asked for women's suffrage in India. *All-Asian Women's Conference Report*, 11.

3. *All-Asian Women's Conference Report*, ix–x, 22, 31–32.

4. *All-Asian Women's Conference Report*, 9, 21, 37.

5. *All-Asian Women's Conference Report*, 146, 150, 152, 154, 156–160.

6. *All-Asian Women's Conference Report*, i.

7. J. S. Furnivall, *Netherlands India: A Study of Plural Economy* (1939; Cambridge: Cambridge University Press, 2010), 428.

8. Sugata Bose, *A Hundred Horizons: The Indian Ocean in the Age of Global Empire* (Cambridge, MA: Harvard University Press, 2006), 113–114; Sunil Amrith, *Crossing the Bay of Bengal: The Furies of Nature and the Fortunes of Migrants* (Cambridge, MA: Harvard University Press, 2013), 162, 183–184.

9. For a detailed analysis of the debt crisis and gold outflows from one Indian region, see Sugata Bose, *Agrarian Bengal: Economy, Social Structure and Politics, 1919–1947* (Cambridge: Cambridge University Press, 1986), ch. 4.

10. This discussion of the impact of the Depression on agrarian India and China draws on Sugata Bose, "Starvation amidst Plenty: The Making of Famine in Honan, Bengal and Tonkin, 1942–1945," *Modern Asian Studies* 24, no. 4 (1990): 699–727. For the debates on China's silver currency and credit, see Milton Friedman and Anna Schwarz, *A Monetary History of the United States* (Princeton: Princeton University Press, 1963), 489–491; Arthur Young, *China and the Helping Hand* (Cambridge, MA: Harvard University Press, 1963), 6; Ramon Myers, *The Chinese Economy: Past and Present* (Belmont, CA: Wadsworth, 1980), 174–177; Loren Brandt and Thomas Sargent, "Interpreting New Evidence about China and U.S. Silver Purchases," *Journal of Monetary Economics* 23, no. 1 (1989): 31–51; "Trade Capital and Paper Money in Chinese Villages," in Institute of Pacific Relations, *Agrarian China*, 157–160 (London: G. Allen and Unwin, 1939). For Iran, see Bose, *A Hundred Horizons*, 85–87.

11. Bose, "Starvation amidst Plenty."

12. Margherita Zanasi, *Saving the Nation: Economic Modernity in Republican China* (Chicago: University of Chicago Press, 2006).

13. Furnivall, *Netherlands India,* 430–433.

14. Bose, *A Hundred Horizons,* 92–93.

15. On Burma, see Michael Adas, *The Burma Delta: Economic Development and Social Change on an Asian Rice Frontier, 1852–1941* (Madison: University of Wisconsin Press, 1974); on Malaya, see Lim Teck Ghee, *Peasants and Their Agricultural Economy in Colonial Malaya, 1874–1941* (New York: Oxford University Press, 1977).

16. On the peasant rebellions in Burma and Vietnam, see James C. Scott, *The Moral Economy of the Peasant: Rebellion and Subsistence in Southeast Asia* (New Haven: Yale University Press, 1976), 114–156.

17. On peasant discontent in 1930s Philippines, see Benedict Kerkvliet, *The Huk Rebellion: A Study of Peasant Revolt in the Philippines* (Lanham, MD: Rowman and Littlefield, 2002); Norman Owen, *Prosperity without Progress: Manila Hemp and Material Life in the Colonial Philippines* (Berkeley: University of California Press, 2022); David Reese Sturtevant, *Popular Uprisings in the Philippines, 1840–1940* (Ithaca, NY: Cornell University Press, 1976).

18. These themes are treated in much greater detail in Bose, *A Hundred Horizons,* ch. 3.

19. Carolien Stolte, "Bringing Asia to the World: Indian Trade Unionism and the Long Road towards the Asiatic Labor Congress, 1919–1937," *Journal of Global History* 7, no. 2 (July 2012): 257–278; Josephine Fowler, "From East to West and West to East: Ties of Solidarity in the Pan-Pacific Revolutionary Trade Union Movement, 1923–1934," *International Labor and Working Class History* 66 (2004): 99–117.

20. Stolte, "Bringing Asia to the World," 270–274.

21. Stolte, "Bringing Asia to the World," 274–275.

22. Ayesha Jalal, "Muslim Universalist Aspirations: Intimacies between the Indus-Gangetic Plain and the Indian Ocean," in *Oceanic Islam: Muslim Universalism and European Imperialism,* ed. Sugata Bose and Ayesha Jalal, 19–56 (London: Bloomsbury, 2020), 38.

23. Jalal, "Muslim Universalist Aspirations," 39; Bose, *A Hundred Horizons,* 211–213, 218–220, 224–229.

24. Jalal, "Muslim Universalist Aspirations," 41.

25. Jalal, "Muslim Universalist Aspirations," 47.

26. Jalal, "Muslim Universalist Aspirations," 52–53.

27. For a detailed consideration of the significance of Tagore's trip to Iran and Iraq, see Bose, *A Hundred Horizons,* 260–271.

28. Rabindranath Tagore, "Asia's Response to the Call of the New Age," *The Modern Review* 52, no. 4 (October 1932): 369–373.

29. C. F. Andrews, "Asia in Revolution," *The Modern Review* 52, no. 4 (October 1932): 373–376.

30. Joseph McQuade, "The *New Asia* of Rash Behari Bose: India, Japan and the Limits of the International, 1912–1945," *Journal of World History* 27, no. 4 (2016): 641–667, quotes on 659, 662, 664, 666.

31. Seok-Won Lee, "The Paradox of Racial Liberation: W. E. B. Du Bois and Pan-Asianism in Wartime Japan, 1931–1945," *Inter-Asia Cultural Studies* 16, no. 4 (2015): 513–530, quotes on 522, 524–525.

32. Yone Noguchi, *The Ganges Calls Me* (Tokyo: Kyobunkwan, 1938).

33. Madoka Nagai Hori, "Yone Noguchi and India: Towards a Reappraisal of the International Conflict between R. Tagore and Y. Noguchi," in "Changing Perceptions of Japan in South Asia in the New Asian Era: The State of Japanese Studies in India and Other SAARC Countries," Proceedings of a Symposium at Jawaharlal Nehru University, New Delhi, November 2009 (Kyoto: Kokusai Nihon Bunka Kenkyu Senta, 2011).

34. Subhas Chandra Bose, "Japan's Role in the Far East," *The Modern Review* (October 1937), reprinted in *Netaji Collected Works,* vol. 8, *1933–1937,* ed. Sisir K. Bose and Sugata Bose, 411–429 (Calcutta: Netaji Research Bureau, 1995).

35. Subhas Chandra Bose, "Congress Medical Mission to China," in *Netaji Collected Works,* vol. 9, *Congress President, 1938–1939,* ed. Sisir K. Bose and Sugata Bose, 36–39 (Calcutta: Netaji Research Bureau, 1995).

36. Yone Noguchi to Rabindranath Tagore, July 23, 1938, and Rabindranath Tagore to Yone Noguchi, September 1, 1938, in "Oriental Panorama I: From Poet to Poet," *The Living Age,* April 1939, reproduced from the *Visva Bharati Quarterly.*

37. Noguchi to Tagore, October 2, 1938, and Tagore to Noguchi, October 1938, in "Oriental Panorama I: From Poet to Poet," *The Living Age,* April 1939.

38. B. K. Basu, *The Call of Yan'an: Story of the Indian Medical Mission to China, 1938–43* (New Delhi: All India Kotnis Memorial Committee, 1986).

39. Basu, *The Call of Yan'an,* chs. 11–14.

40. Basu, *The Call of Yan'an,* ch. 19.

41. Basu, *The Call of Yan'an,* chs. 21, 22, 23, 24, 27, and 28.

42. Lio Jingwen, *Xu Beihong: Life of a Master* (Beijing: Foreign Language Press, 1987), 148–151.

43. Basu, *The Call of Yan'an,* chs. 38 and 41. Guo Qinglan, *My Life with Kotnis* (Delhi: Embassy of the People's Republic of China, 2006), 255.

44. Basu, *The Call of Yan'an,* ch. 41.

6. War, Famine, and Freedom in Asia

1. Sugata Bose, "Starvation amidst Plenty: The Making of Famine in Bengal, Honan and Tonkin, 1942–1945," *Modern Asian Studies* 24, no. 4 (1990): 699–727. This section draws a few elements from the article, which largely stands the test of time, while taking account of research published in the last three decades.

2. Rana Mitter, *China's Good War: How World War II Is Shaping a New Nationalism* (Cambridge, MA: Belknap Press of Harvard University Press, 2020), 202–210.

3. Mitter, *China's Good War,* 206.

4. Nguyen Phan Que Mai, *The Mountains Sing* (Chapel Hill, NC: Algonquin Books, 2021).

5. Sugata Bose, *His Majesty's Opponent: Subhas Chandra Bose and India's Struggle against Empire* (Cambridge, MA: Belknap Press of Harvard University Press, 2011), 250; Madhusree Mukerjee, *Churchill's Secret War: The British Empire and the Ravaging of India during World War II* (New York: Basic Books, 2010), 175–179, 195–203.

6. Christopher Bayly and Tim Harper, *Forgotten Armies: The Fall of British Asia* (Cambridge, MA: Harvard University Press, 2006); and Bayly and Harper, *Forgotten Wars: Freedom and Revolution in Southeast Asia* (Cambridge, MA: Harvard University Press, 2010).

7. Typescript by Theodore H. White, China and Asia Correspondent Papers, 1939–1948, Box 60, Papers of Theodore H. White Papers, Collections of Harvard University Archives, Personal Collections.

8. Theodore White and Annalee Jacoby, *Thunder out of China* (New York: Sloane, 1946).

9. *Biplabi,* November 7, 1943.

10. *Viet Nam Tan Bao,* April 28, 1945, cited in Ngo Vinh Long, *Before the Revolution: The Vietnamese Peasants under the French* (Cambridge, MA: MIT Press, 1973), 132–133.

11. Amartya Sen, *Poverty and Famines: An Essay on Entitlement and Deprivation* (Oxford: Clarendon Press, 1981), 196–202; Paul Greenough, *Prosperity and Misery in Modern Bengal: The Famine of 1943–44* (New York: Oxford University Press, 1982), 299–309.

12. Mitter, *China's Good War,* 202; Rana Mitter, *Forgotten Ally: China's World War II, 1937–1945* (Boston: Houghton Mifflin Harcourt, 2013), 271.

13. Huynh Kim Khanh, *Vietnamese Communism 1925–1945* (Ithaca, NY: Cornell University Press, 1986), 301.

14. Sen, *Poverty and Famines,* 76.

15. In Bose, "Starvation amidst Plenty," I had written, "The assertion by Lloyd Eastman that the spring and summer harvests of 1942 in Honan were 25% below

normal is not supported by available statistics and could be open to question. If the official crop data of the National Agricultural Research Bureau are to be believed, there was little, if any, shortfall in aggregate crop production, especially wheat, in 1942. A University of Nanking study also showed that in 15 provinces under KMT rule the total weight of crops in 1938–42 averaged 1.5% higher than in 1931–37, wheat being 15.5% higher, sweet potatoes 20.5% higher and rice 6.1% lower. Eastman himself notes 'how government exactions exacerbated the farmers' privation' and does not see the Honan famine simply or even mainly as a food supply crisis" (702). My skepticism of Eastman's assertion was misplaced; his impressions were closer to the mark than the statistics. There clearly was food availability decline in Henan Province, but that was compounded manifold by the exactions of the GMD government. See Lloyd Eastman, *Seeds of Destruction: Nationalist China in War and Revolution, 1937–1949* (Palo Alto: Stanford University Press, 1984).

16. Quoted in Mitter, *China's Good War*, 206.

17. Mitter, *Forgotten Ally*, 267.

18. Sugata Bose, *Agrarian Bengal: Economy, Social Structure and Politics, 1919–1947* (Cambridge: Cambridge University Press, 1986), 88.

19. "Missionary Tells of China's Plight," *New York Times*, November 18, 1942.

20. On India, see Bose, *Agrarian Bengal;* and C. J. Baker, *An Indian Rural Economy: The Tamilnad Countryside, 1880–1955* (Oxford: Oxford University Press, 1984). On Vietnam, see James C. Scott, *The Moral Economy of the Peasant: Subsistence and Rebellion in Southeast Asia* (New Haven: Yale University Press, 1976). The impact of the 1930s depression on agrarian relations in China has not been the subject of comparable studies, but there is a mass of contemporary evidence in Institute of Pacific Relations, *Agrarian China: Selected Source Materials from Chinese Authors* (Shanghai: Allen and Unwin, 1938).

21. R. N. Poduval, *Finance of the Government of India since 1935* (Delhi: Premier Publishing Company, 1951), 119–120.

22. Bose, *Agrarian Bengal*, 89.

23. Bose, *Agrarian Bengal*, 90–94.

24. Bose, *Agrarian Bengal*, 95.

25. Bose, *Agrarian Bengal*, 95.

26. Mukerjee, *Churchill's Secret War.* See also Janam Mukherjee, *Hungry Bengal: War, Famine, and the End of Empire* (Oxford: Oxford University Press, 2015).

27. The offer of rice from Southeast Asia was made by Subhas Bose in radio broadcasts to India. See note by R. Tottenham, Additional Secretary, Home Department, Government of India, September 1943, in Home Political Files (National Archives of India), cited in Krishna Bose, *Charanarekha Taba* (Your footprints) (Calcutta: Ananda, 1982), 66–67.

28. Arthur Young, *Chinese Wartime Finance and Inflation in Wartime China, 1937–1945* (Cambridge, MA: Harvard University Press, 1965) 270, 299–305. See also White and Jacoby, *Thunder out of China;* and Han Suyin, *Birdless Summer* (London: Jonathan Cape, 1968) 293–295.

29. Mitter, *Forgotten Ally,* 272.

30. Mitter, *Forgotten Ally,* 277.

31. "Mme Chiang Asks Arms Not Food; Says Ammunition Is Great Need," *New York Times,* February 25, 1943.

32. Khanh, *Vietnamese Communism,* 299.

33. Khanh, *Vietnamese Communism,* 301.

34. Greenough, *Prosperity and Misery,* 266.

35. White and Jacoby, *Thunder out of China,* 171.

36. White and Jacoby, *Thunder out of China,* 177–178; James E. Sheridan, *China in Disintegration: The Republican Era in Chinese History, 1912–1949* (New York: Free Press, 1975), 262.

37. Long, *Before the Revolution,* 233–238.

38. Nandalal Bose to Kanai Samanta, February 1943, in Nandalal Bose, *Vision and Creation,* trans. K. G. Subramanyan (Calcutta: Visvabharati, 1999), 269.

39. Rabindranath Tagore, *Crisis in Civilization* (Santiniketan: Visvabharati, 1941), 7–9.

40. Tagore, *Crisis in Civilization,* 11.

41. Joyce C. Lebra, ed., *Japan's Greater East Asia Co-Prosperity Sphere in World War II: Selected Readings and Documents* (Kuala Lumpur: Oxford University Press, 1975), ix–xxi.

42. Abid Hasan, "A Soldier Remembers," transcript of an interview with Sisir Kumar Bose, Krishna Bose, et al., second installment, *The Oracle* 7, no. 1 (January 1985), 22.

43. Hasan, "A Soldier Remembers," 25.

44. Joyce Lebra, "Bose's Influence on the Formulation of Japanese Policy toward India and the INA," in *Netaji and India's Freedom: Proceedings of the International Netaji Seminar 1973,* ed. Sisir K. Bose (Calcutta: Netaji Research Bureau, 1975), 321.

45. Lebra, "Bose's Influence," 321–322; Subhas Chandra Bose, "What British Imperialism Means for India" (June 19, 1943), in *Netaji Collected Works,* vol. 12, *Chalo Delhi: Writings and Speeches, 1943–1945,* ed. Sisir K. Bose and Sugata Bose (Calcutta: Netaji Research Bureau, 2007), 17–19.

46. Yone Noguchi, "Subhaschandrer Prati, 20 June 1943," Bengali translation, in *Bir Bandana,* ed. Krishna Bose and Jyotirmoy Chattopadhyay (Calcutta: Netaji Research Bureau, 1975), 12–13.

47. Subhas Chandra Bose, "The Blood of Freedom-Loving Indians" (June 1943), in *Netaji Collected Works,* 12:26–28.

48. See Bose, *His Majesty's Opponent,* 244–248.

49. Ba Maw, *Break-through in Burma: Memoirs of a Revolution, 1939–1946* (New Haven: Yale University Press, 1968), 348–352; Bose, *His Majesty's Opponent*, 247–251. See also Ba Maw, "The Great Asian Dreamer," text of the Netaji Oration, Netaji Research Bureau, 1964, in *The Oracle* 2, no. 1 (January 1980): 8–15. Ba Maw was unable to travel from Burma to India in 1964, but the script of his lecture was later obtained through the good offices of a common Japanese friend.

50. Jan Becka, "Subhas Chandra Bose and the Burmese Freedom Movement," in *Netaji and India's Freedom: Proceedings of the International Netaji Seminar 1973,* ed. Sisir K. Bose (Calcutta: Netaji Research Bureau, 1975), 54–58.

51. Lebra, *Japan's Greater East Asia Co-Prosperity Sphere,* xviii–xix; Fujiwara Iwaichi, *F. Kikan: Japanese Army Intelligence Operations in Southeast Asia during World War II,* trans. Akashi Yoji (Hong Kong: Heinemann Asia, 1983).

52. Jan Becka, "Subhas Chandra Bose and the Burmese Freedom Movement," 59.

53. "Subhas Chandra Bose and Japan," 4th Section, Asian Bureau, Ministry of Foreign Affairs, Government of Japan, August 1956, English translation, in *Netaji and India's Freedom,* ed. Sisir K. Bose, 329–421 (Calcutta: Netaji Research Bureau, 1975), 358–359. On the global historical significance of the Meiji constitution, see Linda Colley, *The Gun, the Ship and the Pen: Warfare, Constitutions and the Making of the Modern World* (New York: W. W. Norton, 2022),. 357–400.

54. Yone Noguchi, "Marching to Delhi," in *Tankobon* (Tokyo, 2012).

55. Hideki Tojo, "The Construction of Greater East Asia and the Establishment of World Peace," quoted in Li Narangoa, "The Assembly of the Greater East Asiatic Nations, 1943," in *Pan-Asianism: A Documentary History,* vol. 2, *1920–Present,* ed. Sven Saaler and Christopher W. A. Szpilman (Lanham, MD: Rowman and Littlefield, 2011), 2:252.

56. Ba Maw, *Break-through in Burma,* 338.

57. Nicole CuUnjieng Aboitiz, *Asian Place, Filipino Nation: A Global Intellectual History of the Philippine Revolution, 1887–1912* (New York: Columbia University Press, 2020), 164–165; Ba Maw, *Break-through in Burma,* 341–342.

58. Li Narangoa, "Greater East Asiatic Nations," 2:245, 248.

59. Ba Maw, *Break-through in Burma,* 339.

60. "Subhas Chandra Bose and Japan," 362–363.

61. Krishna Bose, *Charanrekha Taba,* 26.

62. "Subhas Chandra Bose and Japan," 362–363; Subhas Chandra Bose, "Netaji at the Assembly of Greater East Asian Nations" (October–November 1943), in *Netaji Collected Works* 12:148–151; audio and video recordings in the archives of Netaji Research Bureau.

63. "Subhas Chandra Bose and Japan," 364–368; Subhas Chandra Bose, "Netaji at the Assembly" 12:152–153.

64. CuUnjieng Aboitiz, *Asian Place, Filipino Nation*, 170–173.

65. "Subhas Chandra Bose and Japan," 366.

66. Margherita Zanasi, *Saving the Nation: Economic Modernity in Republican China* (Chicago: University of Chicago Press, 2006), ch. 7.

67. "Subhas Chandra Bose and Japan," 368–369; Subhas Chandra Bose, "Netaji at the Assembly of Greater East Asian Nations," 12:153–154.

68. "Subhas Chandra Bose and Japan," 369–372.

69. "Subhas Chandra Bose and Japan," 372–373; Subhas Chandra Bose, "Appeal to Chungking" (November 21, 1943), in *Netaji Collected Works*, 12:161–162.

70. Krishna Bose, "Sainiker Smriti," in *Prasanga Subhaschandra* (Calcutta: Ananda, 1993), 11–56, 47; Krishna Bose, *Netaji: Subhas Chandra Bose's Life, Politics and Struggle* (New Delhi: Picador, 2022), 93–162, 147.

71. This description of "A Memorable Day at Statue of Philippine Martyr" was provided by the Japanese journalist C. Hagiwara who met Bose in Singapore, Bangkok, Rangoon, Maymyo, and Manila and was "impressed by his calm and rather meditative personality" and his ability to keep "a firm balance between passion and reason." UPA report in *Hindusthan Standard,* November 4, 1945.

72. CuUnjieng Aboitiz, *Asian Place, Filipino Nation*, 159–165.

73. For more detailed analyses of events of this period, see Sugata Bose, *His Majesty's Opponent,* ch. 8; Leonard A. Gordon, *Brothers against the Raj: A Biography of Indian Nationalists Sarat and Subhas Chandra Bose* (New York: Columbia University Press, 1990), 491–547; see also Peter Ward Fay, *The Forgotten Army: India's Armed Struggle for Independence, 1942–1945* (Ann Arbor: University of Michigan Press, 1995); Bayly and Harper, *Forgotten Armies.*

74. Ba Maw, *Break-through in Burma,* 352.

75. "Subhas Chandra Bose and Japan," 399. Krishna Bose, *Charanrekha Taba,* 80.

76. See Sugata Bose, *His Majesty's Opponent,* 284–287.

77. Hariprabha Takeda, *The Journey of a Bengali Woman to Japan* (Kolkata: Jadavpur University Press, 2019), 141–142.

78. Subhas Chandra Bose, "The Fundamental Problems of India" (November 1944), in *Netaji Collected Works,* 12:285–301.

79. "Subhas Chandra Bose and Japan," 402–404; Sugata Bose, *His Majesty's Opponent,* 286–287.

80. Ba Maw, *Break-through in Burma,* 370–371, 383.

81. G. S. Dhillon, "The Indo-Burman Relations during World War II," *The Oracle* 7, no. 3 (July 1985): 15–22; Peter W. Fay, "Netaji and Aung San: Constancy or Opportunism," *The Oracle* 15, no. 2 (April 1993): 12–28; Joyce C. Lebra, "Japan and Burmese Independence: The Case of the Burma Independence Army," *The Oracle* 15, no. 3 (July 1993): 10–26.

82. Moti Ram, *Two Historic Trials in Red Fort* (New Delhi: Roxy Printing Press, 1946); Bhulabhai Desai, "Address of Counsel for Defence, Red Fort Trial, December 1, 1945," *The Oracle* 15, no. 4 (October 1993): 31–55.

83. Tadashi Katakura, "I Remember My Days with Subhas Chandra Bose," *The Oracle* 1, no. 1 (January 1979): 25–27.

84. On "the inconvenient judge" Radhabinod Pal, see Partha Chatterjee, *I Am the People: Reflections on Popular Sovereignty Today* (New York: Columbia University Press, 2020), ch. 1.

85. Louis Allen, *The End of the War in Asia* (London: Hart-Davis MacGibbon, 1976), 262; see also the review by Krishna Bose, *The Oracle* 1, no. 1 (January 1979): 70–73.

86. Sisir Kumar Bose, *Subhas and Sarat: An Intimate Memoir of the Bose Brothers* (New Delhi: Aleph, 2016), 229.

87. Sisir Kumar Bose, *Subhas and Sarat,* 230–231.

88. Aung San, "Welcome Mr. Sarat Chandra Bose," and "Sarat Chandra Bose's Reply," Rangoon City Hall, July 24, 1946, in *Netaji and India's Freedom: Proceedings of the International Netaji Seminar 1973,* ed. Sisir K. Bose (Calcutta: Netaji Research Bureau, 1975), 69–75.

89. "Two Preliminary Questions" and "Opening Plenary Session: First Session," *Asian Relations: Being Report of the Proceedings and Documentation of the First Asian Relations Conference, New Delhi, March–April 1947* (New Delhi: Asian Relations Organization, 1948), 3, 15–16, 20–25 (hereafter *Asian Relations*).

90. "Presidential Address," *Asian Relations,* 27–29.

91. "Presidential Address," *Asian Relations,* 30–31.

92. "First Session: Speeches by Leaders of Delegations," *Asian Relations,* 40–41.

93. "First Session: Speeches by Leaders of Delegations," *Asian Relations,* 37–38.

94. "The Closing Plenary Session," *Asian Relations,* 245.

95. "Second Session: Speeches by Leaders of Delegations," *Asian Relations,* 48.

96. "The Opening Plenary Sessions," *Asian Relations,* 68.

97. Tansen Sen, *India, China, and the World: A Connected History* (Lanham, MD: Rowman and Littlefield, 2017), 338–345.

98. "The Opening Plenary Sessions," *Asian Relations,* 62–65.

99. "The Round Table Groups," *Asian Relations,* 73, 77–78, 80–87.

100. "The Round Table Groups," *Asian Relations,* 96–99; Sunil S. Amrith, *Crossing the Bay of Bengal: The Furies of Nature and the Fortunes of Migrants* (Cambridge, MA: Harvard University Press, 2013), 220–223.

101. "The Round Table Groups," *Asian Relations,* 154, 173.

102. "The Round Table Groups," *Asian Relations,* 203, 205, appendices.

103. "The Round Table Groups," *Asian Relations,* 208, 222–225.

104. "The Closing Plenary Session," *Asian Relations*, 234–241.

105. "The Closing Plenary Session," *Asian Relations*, 242–243.

106. On the politics of this period, see Ayesha Jalal, *The Sole Spokesman: Jinnah, the Muslim League and the Demand for Pakistan* (Cambridge: Cambridge University Press, 1985), ch. 7; on Gandhi at this crucial moment, see Sugata Bose, "Unity or Partition: Mahatma Gandhi's Last Stand, 1945–1948," in *The Nation as Mother and Other Visions of Nationhood* (Delhi: Penguin Viking, 2017), 127–148.

107. "The Closing Plenary Session," *Asian Relations*, 244–245.

108. "The Closing Plenary Session," *Asian Relations*, 247–249.

109. "The Closing Plenary Session," *Asian Relations*, 251–254.

110. George Catlin, "Asia and the World," *United Asia* 1, no. 1 (May–June 1948), 12.

7. Asian Solidarity and Animosity in the Postcolonial Era

1. Debabrata Biswas, *Antaranga Chin* (Intimate China) (Calcutta: Abaniranjan Roy, 1958; Calcutta: Kathashilpa, 1978), 21, 28–33. The menu of the twenty-course cultural feast was as follows: (1) "Bande Mataram" sung in chorus, (2) "Hindi-Chini Bhai Bhai" in duet by Surinder Kaur and Debabrata Biswas, (3) tabla by Indorkar, (4) comedy by Chandrasekharan, (5) mridangam by Murti, (6) classical vocal by Master Krishnan, (7) Vyadha dance by Gopalkrishna, (8) Tamil song by Ellappa Pillai, (9) Assamese folk song by Dilip Sharma, (10) Bharatnatyam dance by Chandralekha, (11) Sitar by Vilayat Khan, (12) Punjabi folk song by Surinder Kaur, (13) tabla by Dasappa, (14) shehnai by Golwalkar, (15) classical vocal by Hirabai Barodkar, (16) veena by Devendrappa, (17) Hindi light classical vocal by Jyotsna, (18) Kathak dance by Damayanti Joshi, (19) Bengali song by Debabrata Biswas, and (20) Kathakali dance as a collective. Other delegates included Sachin Sengupta as leader, Kalimullah Khan as secretary, and the poet Vollathol.

2. Biswas, *Antaranga Chin*, 1–2, 11, 20, 50–53, 77–79.

3. Biswas, *Antaranga Chin*, 74–76.

4. Biswas, *Antaranga Chin*, 82, 84–85.

5. Biswas, *Antaranga Chin*, 90, 97.

6. Rabindranath Tagore, *Purabi: The East in Its Feminine Gender,* ed. Krishna Bose and Sugata Bose, trans. Charu C. Chowdhuri (Calcutta: Seagull Books, 2007), 119–121.

7. Biswas, *Antaranga Chin*, 98.

8. Biswas, *Antaranga Chin*, 99–100, 103–105.

9. See Adom Getachew, *Worldmaking after Empire: The Rise and Fall of Self-Determination* (Princeton, NJ: Princeton University Press, 2020). Getachew studies the anti-colonial thought of African, African American, and Caribbean intellectuals

who questioned the nation-state idea and advocated regional federations in their "world making" project during the process of decolonization. In Asia, anti-colonial intellectuals insisted on federalism within each country as the basis for a broader Asian federation.

10. Sarat Chandra Bose, *I Warned My Countrymen,* ed. Sisir K. Bose (Calcutta: Netaji Research Bureau, 1968), 298–300.

11. Herbert Passin, "Sino-Indian Cultural Relations," *The China Quarterly* 7 (July–September 1961): 85–100; Pandit Sundarlal, ed., *China Today* (Allahabad: Hindustani Culture Society, 1952); K. M. Panikkar, *In Two Chinas: Memoirs of a Diplomat* (London: Allen and Unwin, 1955).

12. Sundarlal, *China Today,* 176.

13. Arunabh Ghosh, "Before 1962: The Case for 1950s China-India History," *Journal of Asian Studies* 76, no. 3 (2017): 697–727.

14. Margaret W. Fisher and Joan V. Bondurant, "The Impact of Communist China on Visitors from India," *Far Eastern Quarterly* 15, no. 2 (1956): 249–265.

15. Fisher and Bondurant, "The Impact of Communist China"; Sundarlal, *China Today;* Khwaja Ahmad Abbas, *China Can Make It* (Bombay: People's Publishing House, 1952); and Khwaja Ahmad Abbas, *In the Image of Mao Tse-tung* (Bombay: People's Publishing House, 1953); Russy K. Karanjia, *China Stands Up and Wolves of the Wild West* (Bombay: People's Publishing House, 1952); Raja Hutheesing, *The Great Peace: An Asian's Candid Report on Red China* (New York: Harper, 1953); Frank Moraes, *Report on Mao's China* (New York: Macmillan, 1953); J. C. Kumarappa, *People's China: What I Saw and Learnt There* (Wardha: All-India Village Industries Association, 1952); Muhammad Mujeeb, *A Glimpse of New China* (Delhi: Maktaba Jamia, n.d.); Brajkishore Shastri, *From My China Diary* (Delhi: Siddhartha Publications, 1953).

16. K. T. Shah, *The Promise That Is New China* (Bombay: Vora, 1953), preface.

17. Fisher and Bondurant, "The Impact of Communist China on Visitors from India," 254.

18. Shah, *The Promise That Is New China,* 2.

19. Shah, *The Promise That Is New China,* 30.

20. Shah, *The Promise That Is New China,* 125–126, 130–135, 140.

21. Shah, *The Promise That Is New China,* 156, 162, 165–166, 186–187.

22. Shah, *The Promise That Is New China,* 196, 211, 225, 240, 245, 257, 263, 279, 295, 318.

23. Shah, *The Promise That Is New China,* 334, 338–339.

24. Shah, *The Promise That Is New China,* 140–141.

25. D. D. Kosambi, "For Peace in Asia and the Pacific, Peace in the World," *Bulletin of the Preparatory Committee for the Peace Conference of the Asian and Pacific Regions* 6, no. 11 (1952): 1–4.

26. W. E. B. Du Bois, telegram to Peace Conference of the Asian and Pacific Regions, September 12, 1952, W. E. B. Du Bois Papers, MS 312, Special Collections and University Archives, University of Massachusetts, Amherst.

27. Rachel Leow, "A Missing Peace: The Asia-Pacific Peace Conference in Beijing, 1952 and the Emotional Making of Third World Internationalism," *Journal of World History* 30, nos. 1–2 (2019): 21–53.

28. Leow, "A Missing Peace," 24, 31–32, 39.

29. Leow, "A Missing Peace," 39–40.

30. Susan S. Bean, "East Meets East in Husain's Horses," in M. F. Husain, *Lightning* (New York: Asia Society Museum / Ahmedabad: Mapin, 2019). See also Susan S. Bean, *Midnight to the Boom: Painting in India after Independence* (Salem, MA: Peabody Essex Museum in association with Thames and Hudson, 2013), 86–91.

31. Su Lin Lewis, "Asian Socialism and the Forgotten Architects of Post-Colonial Freedom," *Journal of World History* 30, nos. 1–2 (2019): 55–88, quotation 66. See also Kyaw Zaw Win, "The 1953 Asian Socialist Conference in Rangoon: Precursor to the Bandung Conference," in *Bandung 1955: Little Histories,* ed. Derek McDougall and Antonia Finnane (Victoria: Monash University Press, 2010).

32. Rammanohar Lohia, "United Asia: The Task before Socialists," *United Asia* 1, no. 1 (May–June 1948), 21.

33. Shah, *The Promise That Is New China,* 123.

34. K. M. Panikkar, *Asia and Western Dominance: A Survey of the Vasco da Gama Epoch in Asian History, 1498–1945* (London: George Allen and Unwin, 1953), 251, 493–495.

35. Ayesha Jalal, "Towards the Baghdad Pact: South Asia and Middle East Defence in the Cold War, 1947–1955," *International History Review* 11, no. 3 (August 1989): 409–433.

36. Christopher Lee, "Introduction: Between a Moment and an Era," in *Making a World after Empire: The Bandung Moment and Its Political Afterlives* ed. Christopher Lee, 1–42 (Columbus: Ohio University Press, 2019), 3.

37. See, for example, Amitav Acharya, *East of India, South of China: Southeast Asia in Sino-Indian Encounters* (New York: Oxford University Press, 2017), 62.

38. Carolien Stolte, "The People's Bandung: Local Anti-Imperialists on an Afro-Asian Stage," *Journal of World History* 30, no. 1 (June 2019): 125–156.

39. Stolte, "The People's Bandung," 148–149.

40. Acharya, *East of India, South of China,* 70.

41. Lee, "Introduction: Between a Moment and an Era," 15, 19. The phrase "the gate-keeper state" is from Frederick Cooper, *Africa since 1940: The Past of the Present* (Cambridge: Cambridge University Press, 2002).

42. The twenty-nine countries in attendance were Afghanistan, Burma, Cambodia, Ceylon, China (People's Republic), Egypt, Ethiopia, Gold Coast, India, Indonesia,

Iran, Iraq, Japan, Jordan, Laos, Lebanon, Liberia, Libya, Nepal, Pakistan, Philippines, Saudi Arabia, Sudan, Syria, Thailand, Turkey, Vietnam (Democratic Republic of/North), Vietnam (State of/South), and Yemen.

43. Richard Wright, *The Color Curtain: A Report on the Bandung Conference* (New York: World Publishing Company, 1956).

44. Carlos Romulo, *The Meaning of Bandung* (Chapel Hill: University of North Carolina Press, 1956), 2–3, 35.

45. Naoko Shimazu, "Diplomacy as Theatre: Staging the Bandung Conference of 1955," *Modern Asian Studies* 48, no. 1 (2014): 225–252.

46. "Speech by President Sukarno of Indonesia at the Opening of the Conference," in *Asia-Africa Speaks at Bandung* (Jakarta: Ministry of Foreign Affairs, Government of Indonesia, 1955), 19–29; also, "Speech by President Soekarno at the Opening of the Asian-African Conference, April 18, 1955," in George McTurnan Kahin, *The Asian-African Conference, Bandung, Indonesia, April 1955* (Ithaca, NY: Cornell University Press, 1956), 39–51.

47. Romulo, *The Meaning of Bandung*, 68, 72.

48. *Asia-Africa Speaks at Bandung*, 49–50, 67–71, 78–86, 129–133; Kahin, *The Asian-African Conference*, 9, 12–14.

49. *Asia-Africa Speaks at Bandung*, 63–66; Kahin, *The Asian-African Conference*, 14–15; "Supplementary Speech by Premier Chou En-lai at the Asian-African Conference, April 19, 1955), in Kahin, *The Asian-African Conference*, 52–56. See also Antonia Finnane, "Zhou Enlai in Bandung: Film as History in the People's Republic of China," in *Bandung 1955: Little Histories*, ed. Derek McDougall and Antonia Finnane, 89–125 (Caulfield: Monash University Press, 2010).

50. Romulo, *The Meaning of Bandung*, 11; Kahin, *The Asian-African Conference*, 15, 36.

51. Kweku Ampiah, *The Political and Moral Imperatives of the Bandung Conference of 1955: The Reactions of the US, UK, and Japan* (Leiden: Brill, 2007), 93–94, 171–173, 181, 189–190, 230–231.

52. Deputy Prime Minister Mamoru Shigemitsu's Speech on the Occasion of Japan's Admission to the United Nations, December 18, 1956, Ministry of Foreign Affairs, Japan, https://www.mofa.go.jp/policy/un/address5612.html.

53. "Speech by Premier Chou En-lai to the Political Committee of the Asian-African Conference, April 23, 1955," and "Speech by Prime Minister Nehru before the Political Committee of the Asian-African Conference, April 22, 1955," in Kahin, *The Asian-African Conference*, 56–61, 64–72.

54. "Excerpt from the Closing Speech by Prime Minister Nehru at the Asian-African Conference, April 24, 1955," in Kahin, *The Asian-African Conference*, 73–75.

55. Romulo, *The Meaning of Bandung*, 48, 53.

56. "Final Communique of the Asian-African Conference," in Kahin, *The Asian-African Conference*, 76–80.

57. "Final Communique of the Asian-African Conference," 83–85.

58. Stolte, "The People's Bandung," 149–156. On India's diplomatic path from Bandung to the nonaligned movement, see Itty Abraham, "From Bandung to NAM: Non-alignment and Indian Foreign Policy, 1947–1956," *Commonwealth and Comparative Politics* 46, no. 2 (2008): 195–219.

59. Arunabh Ghosh, *Making It Count: Statistics and Statecraft in the Early People's Republic of China* (Princeton: Princeton University Press, 2020), 213–215, 218–219, 223–246.

60. Nirupama Rao, *The Fractured Himalaya: India, Tibet, China, 1949–1962* (Gurgaon: Penguin Viking, 2021).

61. Manjari Chatterjee Miller, *Wronged by Empire: Post-Imperial Ideology and Foreign Policy in India and China* (Palo Alto: Stanford University Press, 2013), 72–81. Miller was the first scholar to make extensive use of the transcripts of the India-China talks of April 1960 in the archives of the Nehru Memorial Museum and Library.

62. Jagat Singh Mehta, *The Tryst Betrayed: Reflections on Diplomacy and Development* (Gurgaon: Penguin Random House, 2015).

63. It was the provocation of this forward policy that Neville Maxwell emphasized in pinning the responsibility of the war on India. Neville Maxwell, *India's China War* (London: Cape, 1970).

64. Srinath Raghavan, *War and Peace in Modern India* (Ranikhet: Permanent Black, 2010), 287–288.

65. Zhou Enlai to Jawaharlal Nehru, April 20, 1963, in *The Sino-Indian Boundary Question II* (Peking: Foreign Languages Press, 1965), 13–21.

66. On the depiction of China in Hindi literature under the shadow of the 1962 war, see Adhira Mangalagiri, *States of Disconnect: The China-India Literary Relation in the Twentieth Century* (New York: Columbia University Press, 2023), ch. 4.

67. Raghavan, *War and Peace in Modern India*, 310.

68. Maulana Abdul Hamid Khan Bhashani, *Mao Tse Tung-er Deshe* (In Mao Zedong's country) (Dhaka: Punthipatra Prakashani, 1967), 8–9, 11–12, 24, 40–52, 60–66.

69. Hamid Jalal's manuscript of his impressions of China (in the possession of Ayesha Jalal).

70. Joan Robinson, *The Cultural Revolution in China* (Harmondsworth: Penguin, 1969).

71. Sugata Bose, *Peasant Labour and Colonial Capital: Rural Bengal since 1770* (Cambridge: Cambridge University Press, 1993), 176–178.

72. Ranajit Guha, *Elementary Aspects of Peasant Insurgency in Colonial India* (New Delhi: Oxford University Press, 1983; Durham, NC: Duke University Press, 1999).

73. Christopher Goscha, "Vietnam, the Third Indochina War and the Meltdown of Asian Internationalism," in *The Third Indochina War: Conflict between China, Vietnam and Cambodia, 1972–1979,* ed. Odd Arne Westad and Sophie Quinn Judge, 158–186 (New York: Routledge, 2006),158, 181.

74. Benedict Anderson, *Imagined Communities: Reflections on the Origins and Spread of Nationalism* (London: Verso, 1983), 1.

75. See Ben Kiernan and Eve M. Zucker, "Introduction"; William Kwok, "The Political Organization of Genocide"; Kosal Path, "The Khmer Republic's Mass Persecution"; and Daniel Bultmann, "Medical Experiments, Blood and Gall," all in *Political Violence in Southeast Asia since 1945: Case Studies from Six Countries,* ed. Eve Monique Zucker and Ben Kiernan (New York: Routledge, 2021). For the roots of China's policy toward Cambodia in the 1965–1966 massacres in Indonesia, see Ben Kiernan and Eve M. Zucker, "Introduction"; and the excellent chapter Geoffrey Robinson, "A Time to Kill," both in *Political Violence in Southeast Asia since 1945.*

Conclusion

1. Maitreyee Debi, *Achena Chin* (Unknown China) (Calcutta: Ananda,1978), 11, 101–102.

2. Debi, *Achena Chin,* 37–39.

3. Debi, *Achena Chin,* 3.

4. Debi, *Achena Chin,* 10, 31, 86.

5. Debi, *Achena Chin,* 24–25, 45–46, 82–85, 106–107.

6. Debi, *Achena Chin,* 116, 125–126, 130, 150–151.

7. Krishna Bose, *Charanrekha Taba* (Your footprints) (Calcutta: Ananda,1982), 75–83.

8. Bose, *Charanrekha Taba,* 22–27, 29–31, 34, 38–39, 56–57, 68, 83–84, 94–96.

9. Bose, *Charanrekha Taba,* 121–122, 127–128, 144–145, 159–161.

10. Bose, *Charanrekha Taba,* 157–158.

11. Bose, *Charanrekha Taba,* 168–173.

12. Bose, *Charanrekha Taba,* 162, 164–165.

13. Amartya Sen, "Indian Development: Lessons and Non-Lessons," *Daedalus* 118, no. 4 (1989): 369–392.

14. Giovanni Arrighi, *Adam Smith in Beijing: Lineages of the Twenty-First Century* (London: Verso, 2007), 1–2, 8.

15. Parag Khanna, *The Future Is Asian* (New York: Simon and Schuster), 1, 4.

16. Gayatri Chakravorty Spivak, *Other Asias* (Oxford: Blackwell, 2008), 235.

17. C. J. W.-L. Wee, "'We Asians'? Modernity, Visual Art Exhibitions, and East Asia," *boundary 2* 37, no. 1 (Spring 2010): 91–126.

18. Wee, "'We Asians'?"

19. Wee, "'We Asians'?" See also C. J. W.-L. Wee, *The Asian Modern: Culture, Capitalist Development, Singapore* (Hong Kong: Hong Kong University Press, 2007).

20. Chen Kuan-Hsing, *Asia as Method: Towards Deimperialization* (Durham, NC: Duke University Press, 2010).

21. Spivak, *Other Asias,* 212, 215, 222, 225, 232, 234, 236.

22. Wang Hui, *The Politics of Imagining Asia,* ed. Theodore Huters, trans. Matthew A. Hale (Cambridge, MA: Harvard University Press, 2011), 62.

23. Shinzo Abe, "Confluence of the Two Seas," speech to the Parliament of India, August 22, 2017, www.mofa.go.jp/region/asia-paci/pmvo708/speech-2.html.

24. Quoted in Nayan Chanda, "The Silk Road: Old and New," *Global Asia* 10, no. 3 (2015): 13–15, 14.

25. Wang Gungwu, *Renewal: The Chinese State and the New Global History* (Hong Kong: The Chinese University Press, 2013), 131–134, 138, 140, 147.

26. On the massive expansion of Chinese universities in a global historical perspective, see William C. Kirby, *Empires of Ideas: Creating the Modern University from Germany to America to China* (Cambridge, MA: Belknap Press of Harvard University Press, 2022).

27. Rabindranath Tagore, "Asia's Response to the Call of the New Age," *The Modern Review* 52, no. 4 (October 1932): 369–373.

Index

Note: Page numbers followed by I indicate illustrations; page numbers followed by p indicate photographs.

Conference (1931), 116–119; border and economic issues during, 119–125, 146; economic disruption during, 10–11; efforts toward workers' Asia, 125–131; Indian Medical Mission, 135–141; poets and patriots during, 131–135

Greater Asianism (Sun Yat-sen), 92, 104, 107–108, 217–218

Greater East Asia Conference (1943), 153–159

Greater East Asianism, 217–218

Green, Nile, 63, 75

Guan Guofeng, 143

Guha, Ranajit, 3, 42, 204

Gu Hongming, 71, 219

Gunawardane, Theja, 188

Guo Moruo, 99, 184, 188

Guo Xiaoyang, 143

Gupta, Herambalal, 79

Gvili, Gal, 101

Habermas, Jürgen, 16

Hachiya Teruo, 162–163

Hafiz, 128

Haldar, Asit, 170

Hamid, Abdul, 30, 53, 91

Hara Tomitaro, 81, 83

Harding, Warren, 106

Harper, Timothy N., 10, 53

Hasan, Abid, 150–151, 154, 155p, 160

Hasan Hatano Uho, 54

Hashimoto Gaho, 46, 48

Hatoyama Ichiro, 192

Hatta, Mohammad, 124, 154

Hattori Unokichi, 66

Hau, Caroline S., 34

H. H. Kung, 123, 148

Higuchi Tetsuo, 208

"Hindu-Muslim Unity" (Gandhi), 9, 88

Hinohara Shozo, 31

Hirohito, Emperor, 162

Hishida Shunso, 2, 40–41, 41l, 48, 132

Hizbul Watani party, 127

Ho, Engseng, 18

Ho Chi Minh, 91, 104, 124, 154, 168

Hong Kong, 211

Hore, Somenath, 148

Hori San, 48

Hua Guofeng, 207

Hu Hanmin, 53

Husain, Maqbool Fida, 184–185

Hu Shih, 100–101

al-Husseini, Mohammad Amin, 127

Hutheesingh, Raja, 179

Ibn Saud, 127

Ibrahim, Abdurresid, 43, 54

Ideals of the East, The (Okakura), 1, 46–48

"Idea of Asia, The" (S. Bose), 221

Iftikharuddin, Mian, 178

Imagined Communities (Anderson), 204

Imazato Juntaro, 109

indentured labor, 20, 21, 25

India: border war with China (1962), 13; British colonial rule and trade, 21, 23, 26, 27–28, 32, 88–89, 107, 155–156; civil society initiatives with China, 12; Conference of Asian Countries on the Relaxation of International Tension held in, 187–188, 194; fall of GDP, 20; famines, 142–143, 144, 145–146, 246n15; founding of sovereign Republic, 178; and globalization, 211–212, 214–215; during Great Depression, 120, 121; great rebellion (1857), 29; Himalayan border war with China (1962), 177; Hindu majoritarianism, 17–18; Jallianwala Bagh massacre (1919), 89; late-nineteenth century famines, 28;

174, 175, 177–178; Cultural Revolution, 202, 203; Great Leap Forward, 195, 202; and Himalayan border issues, 199; May Day festivities (1952), 181; meetings with Indians, 136–138; on Naxalbari revolution, 203; photographs of, 137p; as poet, 202, 207–208; statues of, 222p; as student of Li Dazhao, 92; at third plenum of CCP, 213

Martin, C. A. *See* Bhattacharya, Narendranath

Marxism, 204, 207

Matheson, James, 19

Matsuoka Yosuke, 150

Maung, U, 165

Mazzini, Giuseppe, 52

McKinley, William, 35

McMahon, Henry, 197

McQuade, Joseph, 129

Mehta, Jamnadas, 126

Mei Lanfang, 102

Mendez, Paz Policarpio, 171

Meng Lei, 143, 146

Menon, Krishna, 192, 199

Might vs. Right rule, 106–108

migrant labor, 7, 10, 25, 26, 121

Mitter, Rana, 143, 146, 147–148

Miyazaki Toten, 53

Mohammad, Mahathir, 4

Moraes, Frank, 179

Mountains Sing, The (P. Nguyen), 143

Mountbatten, Louis, 171–172

Muhammad, Prophet, 54

Mujeeb, Muhammad, 179

Mukerjee, Madhusree, 147

Mukerji, Dhan Gopal, 80

Mukherjee, Benode Behari, 138

Mukherjee, Debesh, 134

Mukherjee, Jatindranath. *See* Jatin, Bagha

Mullick, B. N., 199

Museum of Fine Arts, Boston, 55, 57

Muslim Asia. *See* Islamic universalism

Myanmar, 18

myth of continents, 3–4

Myths of the Hindus and Buddhists (Coomaraswamy and Sister Nivedita), 58

Nag, Kalidas, 95, 131

Nagase Kyoko, 188

Naidu, Sarojini, 116–117, 131, 135, 167–168, 172–173, 179

Naidu, Satyavati Thevar, 209

Narayanan, K. R., 206–207

Narula, Ishwar Singh, 210

Nasser, Gamal Abdel, 191, 194

National Council on Education, 50

National Graduate Institute for Policy Studies, GRIPS Forum (Japan), 221

Nationalism (R. Tagore), 5, 81

National Trade Union Federation (NTUF), 126

nation-state model: authoritarian forms of, 218; critiques of, 10, 127; and globalization, 210–211; H. Wang on, 16–17, 92; impacts on Asia, 12–13, 168; post-WWII, 6, 14; Romulo on, 190–191

Nehru, Jawaharlal, 182, 192; authoritarian turn of, 195; and Bandung Conference, 188, 190, 193; and Chiang Kai-shek, 178, 206–207; Himalayan border issues, 197–201; hosts Asian Relations Conference, 12, 166–169, 172–173; partition of Punjab, 171; perceived preference for postcolonial continuity, 180; travels of, 138

Southeast Asia: European balance of power in, 29, 33; intraregional trade, 26. *See also specific countries*

South East Asia Treaty Organization, 187

South Korea, 211, 214

Soviet Union. *See* Russia / Soviet Union

Spain, 33

Spencer, Herbert, 71

Spirit of Japanese Poetry, The (Noguchi), 59–60

Spirit of the Chinese People, The (Gu), 71

Spivak, Gayatri Chakravorty, 15–16, 216, 217

Sri Lanka, 18, 214

Stalin, Joseph, 203, 213

Stettheimer, Florine, 68, 69I

Stieler, Ida. *See* Sarkar, Ida

Stoddard, Lothrop, 105–106

Stolte, Carolien, 126, 187–188

Studio Party, or Soiree (Stettheimer) painting, 68–69, 69I

Subaltern Studies, 204

Subrahmanyam, Sanjay, 47

Suehiro Tetcho, 33–34

Suez crisis, 186, 194

Sugihara Kaoru, 26

Sugiyama Hajime, 151

Suharto, 213

Sukarno, 124, 154, 189–190

Sundarlal, Pandit, 178

"Sunrise over Mount Tai" (Z. Xu), 101

Sun Temple, India, 56

Sun Yat-sen, 10, 76, 103, 176, 207, 213, 217; address at Kobe Prefectural Girls' School (1924), 104–105; call for national assembly, 104; collaboration with Indian revolutionaries, 79–80, 83–84, 166; death of, 108; as founding father of Chinese republic, 53; invitation to R. Tagore, 96; photographs of, 105p;

S.C. Bose tribute to, 159; takes exile in Japan, 8, 36–37, 43, 53, 61, 104–105; on typology of civilizations, 106–107

Suzuki Bunji, 126

Suzuki Keiji, 153

swadeshi movement (1905), India, 8, 39–42, 48, 50, 63

Swaminathan, Ammu, 118

Swaminathan, Lakshmi, 209

Tagliacozzo, Eric, 33

Tagore, Abanindranath, 138, 170; artwork of, 2, 48–49, 49I; as Japanese wash technique artist, 2, 39–41, 48, 65, 99–100; and Okakura, 56; on Sister Nivedita, 46

Tagore, Dwarkanath, 27–28

Tagore, P. N. *See* Bose, Rashbehari

Tagore, Rabindranath, 45, 164, 175–176, 179, 191; as Asian universalist, 2, 13, 18; Bolpur school of, 48; on British drug trade, 27–28; critiques of Western imperialism, 21, 37–38; on future balance of power, 8–9, 11; hosts artist B. Xu at Santiniketan, 138; as international lecturer, 4–5, 13, 56–57, 59, 80, 83, 85, 95–101, 118; invitation by Sun sent to, 96; as Nobel Prize for Literature recipient, 57; paintings of by B. Xu, 139I; photographs of, 82p, 98p; on *Ramayana* and *Mahabharata*, 110–114; relations with Noguchi, 132, 134–135; on Sino-Japanese conflict, 11; travels of, 10, 62, 80, 85, 95–103, 109–115, 128; on West's bestiality, 37–38; writings of, 4–5, 56–57, 60, 61, 66, 81, 97, 101, 109–110, 114, 117, 128–129, 132, 136, 176, 206, 224–225; on WWI as war of retribution, 81–82

R. Tagore's travels to, 114–115; student exchanges in Japan, 52

Vivekananda, Swami, 1, 44

Wales, Prince of, 94

Wang Gungwu, 218–219

Wang Hui, 16–17, 92, 107–108, 217–218

Wang Jingwei, 53, 103, 108–109, 122, 136, 158–159, 213

Wang Ming, 136

Wang Sihua, 194–195

Wang Tao, 31

Wang Tongzhao, 101

Wan Waithayakon, 156, 191

war, famine, and freedom, in Asia: Asian relations on freedom's eve, 164–173; Asian relations toward war's end, 158–164; war and famine, 145–149; war and freedom, 150–158

Waseda University, 66

wealth / income inequality, 212–213

"Weary Pilgrim, A" (R. Tagore), 114

Weber, Max, 67

Web of Indian Life, The (Nivedita), 55

We Burmans Association, 152

Wee, C.J.W.-L., 216

Western imperialism: economic divergence from Asia, 20–29; and intra-Asian economics, 21; investment in Asian mines and plantations, 121; Panikkar on, 186; as rule of Might, 106; white, Christian and capitalistic identity of, 4, 15, 28, 35. *See also* anti-Westernism

Wheaton, Louis, 184

white, Christian and capitalistic identity, European, 4, 15, 28, 35

White, Mr. *See* Bhattacharya, Narendranath

White, Theodore H., 138, 145, 147

white supremacy: as global color line, 130; of Stoddard, 105–106; of W. Wilson, 91

"Why Europe Needs a Constitution" (Habermas), 16

Wigen, Karen, 3

Willcox, Anita, 184

Wilson, Woodrow, 9, 88–89, 91

women's rights, 116–119, 171, 186, 194

Woods, James Haughton, 56, 66

workers' Asia, 125–131

World Health Organization, 213–214

World Islamic Conferences, 11, 127–128

World Parliament of Religions, Chicago, 44–45

World Peace Council, 183–184

World University Presidents Symposium (2018), 219–222

World War I: interdependent political and revolutionary action during, 8, 64, 77; R. Tagore on, 81–82. *See also specific countries*

World War II: atom bombs on Hiroshima / Nagasaki, 163; effects on Asian solidarity, 11–12; famines during, 144; as people's war, 139. *See also specific countries*

Wright, Richard, 189

Wu Tingfang, 31–32, 72

Xie Bing Xin. *See* Bing Xin

Xi Jingping, 218, 219, 220

Xuan Zhang, 72

Xu Beihong, 138, 139–140I, 185

Xu Zhimo, 96, 99, 101

Yan Fu, 71

Yang, Anand, 37

Yang Yanbao, 183